A PICTORIAL HISTORY OF COSTUME

WOLFGANG BRUHN - MAX TILKE

A PICTORIAL HISTORY
OF COSTUME

A SURVEY OF COSTUME OF ALL PERIODS AND PEOPLES FROM ANTIQUITY

TO MODERN TIMES INCLUDING NATIONAL COSTUME IN

EUROPE AND NON-EUROPEAN COUNTRIES

WASMUTH

A PICTORIAL HISTORY OF COSTUME

PLAYERS PRESS, Inc.
P. O. Box 1132
Studio City CA 91614-0132

ISBN 0-88734-920-X
Library of Congress Catalog Number: 95-19731

Library of Congress Cataloging-in-Publication Data

Bruhn, Wolfgang.
    [Kostümwerk. English]
    A pictorial history of costume : a survey of costume of all
periods and peoples from antiquity to modern times including
national costume in Europe and non-European countries / Wolfgang
Bruhn, Max Tilke. -- 1st U.S. ed. by Players Press.
        p.   cm.
    English translation originally published: New York : Praeger,
1955.
    Includes index.
    ISBN 0-88734-920-X (hc : alk. paper)
    1. Costume--History--Pictorial works.   I. Tilke, Max, 1860-1942.
II. Title.
GT513.B763 1995
391'.0222--dc20   95-19731
                                                   CIP

© by Ernst Wasmuth Verlag Tübingen
Fürststraße 133, D-7400 Tübingen
Telephon 0 70 71 / 3 36 58 · Telefax 0 70 71 / 3 57 76
All rights reserved
Printed in Germany

ISBN 3-8030-5008-1

PREFACE

The excellent reception accorded Bruhn-Tilke's "Kostümwerk" when it first appeared in Germany in 1941, and the interest in it that has been manifested since, have made it desirable that an English edition should be published.

This book is the result of a life-time of study by Max Tilke who for many years collaborated in the production of Dr. Rosenberg's "Geschichte des Kostüms", and his knowledge of costume was as considerable as his love of drawing and painting. Dr. Wolfgang Bruhn, Curator of the Berlin State Library and Director of the famous Lipperheide Kostümbibliothek, collaborated as an expert advisor and editor of the captions to the plates based on Dr. Tilke's own notes.

With its 200 plates representing nearly 4000 specimens of costumes the book embraces the whole subject of the history of costume. It presents a survey of the most important garments of all times and all peoples from Antqiuity to the end of the 19th century.

The original German edition was a bulky volume with plates printed on one side of the paper only. In order to achieve a more handy volume the present edition has the plates printed on both sides of the paper. The economy thus effected has made it possible to publish at a very reasonable price inspite of the enormous increases in the cost of printing that have taken place since 1941. By printing on both sides of the paper the original sequence of the plates has had to be altered for technical reasons, but these changes are few and not of importance. The twelve plates representing cuts or patterns of costumes which appeared in the text of the original edition have been excluded from the present volume as they are incorporated in Tilke's complementary work, "Kostümschnitte und Gewandformen" (1948).

The colour plates are facsimiles from the originals coloured by Max Tilke. The monochrome plates have been produced partly from Tilke's drawings and partly from engravings and photographs in the Lipperheide Kostümbibliothek. Our sincere thanks are due to the directors of the Staatliche Kunstbibliothek for permitting the use of patterns from engravings and photographs selected by Dr. Wolfgang Bruhn.

DETAILS OF THE PLATES

ANTIQUITY

ANCIENT EGYPT. *Old Kingdom till about 2000 B.C., Middle Kingdom about 2100, New Kingdom about 1530 B.C.* 1

Top Group

1. King of the 5th Dynasty wearing a loin-cloth of pleated gold material, with a lion's tail fixed at the back. (Privilege of the king, probably of the early times when the chiefs of the African primitive race ornamented themselves with such trophies). In front of the loin-cloth a stiff triangular piece of linen, and over it the regal ornaments. The head is covered with the striped head-cloth with the sacred uraeus (cf. 10 side view). Further royal insignia: The artificial medium-sized beard and the two types of sceptre, the crook and the whip (probably originally a symbol of agriculture and stock-rearing).

2. Egyptian of rank. His high rank is shown by the ceremonial loin-cloth (partly made of golden material like the king's) and by the stick and club (commander's baton). He wears a short curled wig.

3. Egyptian woman, grinding grain with an ancient hand-mill. The tunic indicates a better class woman; the slave women usually wear hardly any clothes. The hair is tied up by bands.

4. Woman of rank dressed in a tunic; the original braces for keeping up the garment are widened here and cover the breasts, thus forming a V-neck. The material is light and diaphanous. In addition a linen mantle, coloured collar embroidered with glass beads. Wrist and ankle bracelets. Over the parted hair a wig with a decorated metal fillet or diadem.

5. Woman returning from the market in a checked tunic with wide white braces. Ornamental collar, bracelets, large black kerchief (obviously not a wig).

Centre Group

6. Official or man of rank with a stick. Simple loin-cloth in the style of the Old Kingdom. The shaven head is not covered by a cap or wig, which is necessary in the hot sun.

7. Official (Middle Kingdom) with a lengthened loin-cloth, neck decoration, wig and short beard as a sign of rank. The beard, not favoured by the Egyptians, is shaved off. But on ceremonial occasions in order to enhance the dignity of the wearer, an artificial beard is fixed by means of ribbons to the ears. The longest beard was worn by the king.

8. Egyptian of the 5th Dynasty with the linen triangle in front of the loin-cloth (cf. 1). Collar with pendant. Wig.

9. Woman of the Middle Kingdom. Patterned tunic (similar to 8). Wig, fan.

10–16. New Kingdom from 1600 B.C.

10. King of the New Kingdom acting as sacrificial priest.

Bottom Group

11. Man of rank in a shirt-like garment with two loin-cloths, collar and wig with a feather stuck into it and carrying a stick with an animal's head (originally a king's sceptre, later on carried by high officials and ordinary people).

12. Man with shirt-like garment, but only one loin-cloth visible; collar; band tied round the wig.

13. Mourner from a funeral procession.

14. Woman wearing a mantle. The greater variety in garments corresponds to that of the men. In the New Kingdom, fashion requires a tight fitting garment, exposing one shoulder, and a wide mantle, carried across the front and draped over one shoulder. Both are often quite diaphanous allowing the shape of the body to be seen.

15. Man of rank in a shirt-like garment with two sleeves and a very small loin-cloth on top. Neck ornamentation and wig.

16. Lower official or king's servant. Neck decoration, bracelets and loin-cloth with a heart-shaped piece of material in front. On the head a perfume container which slowly drips.

ANCIENT EGYPT. *Times of Rameses I. – Rameses III. 1350–1200 B.C.* 2

Top Group

1. High Official with the white ostrich feather fan, a high decoration of honour, which gradually became the emblem of rank, for instance for *King's Favourite* and other titles of honour. Princes and the highest officials or army commanders were given the feather fan. Collar (round collar), wig and bast sandals. The loin-cloth is wrapped over the long tunic.

2. Scribe; a vocation found frequently in ancient Egypt. The reed pen is stuck into the wig behind the ear. He carries the paint box with red and black under his arm, and the papyrus scroll in his hand. The boxes on the floor with protecting bags are for the rolled-up papyri.

3. Temple attendant carrying a vessel with sacrificial liquid.

4. High Priest from Heliopolis with a leopard's skin (decorated with silver stars). Priests' garments were not sewn. The hair is shorn. He wears a wig which is seldom worn by priests.

5. Sacrificial priest with incense burner. Loin-cloth, leopard skin, white band on upper part of body. Straw sandals.

6 and 10. Royal princes in war apparel, distinguished by a long plaited lock on the side of their heads. This lock, originally only worn by children, was later, in a conventionalized form, a prerogative of princes. The armour consists of leather covered with metal pieces. No. 10 has leather strips wound spirally round the body. He has also a feather fan.

7. Companion of the Prince, with his master's bow and shield, covered with skin.

8. The King with the characteristic regal girdle decoration hanging down in front (cf. Plate I, 1). The Pharaoh wears the peculiar royal helmet (cheperesh) with the uraeus; the sacred vulture who protects the king in war is embroidered on the armoured jacket as though enfolding him with its wings.

9. The King's bow-bearer dressed in a tight protective quilted garment covered with small bronze plates. On his head a quilted cap.

Bottom Group

11 and 12. Nubian archers.

13–15. Soldiers with ordinary kerchief and heart-shaped leather front piece over the loin-cloth or (14 and 15) a quilted outer tunic carrying sickle-shaped knives, clubs or battle-axe. Shields with eye-holes.

3   ANCIENT EGYPT. *New Kingdom about 1350 B.C.*

Top Group

1. The King. The hood with the uraeus falls down on both sides in two pleated strips and is gathered on his back like a plait. He wears an artificial beard as a sign of a king, a diaphanous garment over the loin-cloth (invisible), girdle decoration and sandals made of papyrus (cf. Plate I, 1).

2. The King's footman or runner wearing an outer garment interwoven with gold. He carries quiver and bow, stick or club by means of which the runners made way for the royal procession.

3. Queen of the 19th Dynasty (14th cent. B.C.) in her hand the scourge, one of the royal insignia. On her wig the sacred vulture head-dress, usually worn by queens. She is dressed in two diaphanous garments (the new fashion for noble ladies): the light tunic and the light mantle fastened on the chest. The old tunic has been discarded. Not until the end of the 20th Dynasty is a short undergarment of thicker material worn again under tunic and mantle.

4. King with a blue wig, diadem with the sacred uraeus, artificial beard, collar, girdle decorations and two sceptres or insignia: scourge and crook.

5. Princess. Around the wig an ornamental band; collar, tunic, mantle, bare footed. (According to a wooden statuette in the Louvre, Paris).

Centre Group

6. King performing the sacrificial ritual and offering a golden ointment box. The king, like all officiating priests, is scantily clad, bare-footed and does not wear anything besides the two crowns, the neck decoration, the wide royal loin-cloth and girdle decoration.

7. Blind priest playing the harp. The head is shaven, without a wig. Flowing mantle.

8. The god Mônt of Hermonthis, with a hawk's head and feather decoration, also with solar disk and sacred uraeus. He carries the handle-cross, the so-called Nile-key which was the symbol of life and the attribute of many gods. (Hermonthis is the modern Erment near Thebes). The god Horus (light and sun-god) with the hawk's head is often similarly represented, the hawk was his sacred emblem.

9. The Queen as *wife of a god*. The Egyptian gods had a harem of living noble ladies; especially the god Ammon (the chief deity at Thebes with a human or a ram's head). Usually the queen (the Pharaoh's wife) is the earthly wife of Ammon, the *wife of a god*. Her attributes are plumes, solar disk, diadem, neck ornaments, the handle-cross and lotus sceptre. According to the old rite she wears the tight fitting tunic widening from below the knees and leaving the breasts exposed, a garment worn by the women of older times. Even Cleopatra, the friend of Anthony and Caesar, was represented as *wife of a god* in this costume. The light-bronze colour of the women is depicted as yellow, the colour of the men's skin is red.

10. The god Osiris in human form. He is the god of a younger popular legend symbolizing the master of the earth who gave the Egyptians laws and taught them agriculture. Killed later on by Seth or Typhon, the god of darkness, he reigned as king of the dead in the nether world, while Horus, the son of Osiris and Isis became the god of light and lord of the living. Osiris as a king wears a gold crown similar to the one worn by Upper-Egyptian kings with feathers on its sides, a white royal beard, he carries the two regal sceptres: scourge and crook and wears a coloured mantle. The skin is represented as green in accordance with the myth.

Bottom Group

11. Woman playing the harp dressed in a long tunic with slits for the arms; flower garlands on head and neck.

12. Woman playing the tambourine, collar, embroidered chastity belt, light mantle tied by a knot on the breast.

13. Slave girls with earthenware jug and leather bag, collar and chastity belt which (like the one of No. 12) holds up the narrow leather strip between the legs.

14. Slave girl with a light cloth extending from the hips to the knees, carrying so-called lotus flowers (Nelumbinum). Hair band and garland of flowers.

15. Hired female mourner from a funeral procession.

4   ANCIENT EGYPT. *New Kingdom (Late Period)*

1. Rameses II. (1324–1258 B.C.) on his war-chariot. The king as an archer; the reins attached to the girdle; two uraeus serpents, the symbol of royal dignity, are floating over his war-helmet (cheperesh). Quivers, long daggers or straight narrow swords, are attached to his girdle and chariot. (Relief according to Lepsius).

2. King Harmahib (1374–1350 B.C.) carried by soldiers on a litter. By the side of the king walks the *fan-bearer* whose office is only honorary. The real lower *fan-bearers* walk in front and behind the soldiers. In front of the procession: captives. The king holds the crook, which is a royal insignium like the scourge and the sickle-shaped sword. (Relief according to Lepsius).

3. Priests carrying in procession the sacred barge of Ammon Re. The barge which was kept in the holy of holies of the temple is adorned with the head of the animal sacred to the god. It has side rudders and a cabin is provided with fans and manned with bronze figurines. (Relief, according to Lepsius.)

4. A quilted armoured shirt with embroidery. Illustration at the tomb of Rameses III. (Rampsinit, about 1180) the last efficient king of the declining New Kingdom.

5 and 7. Banners and standards.

6. Soldier with a large shield from the Middle Kingdom. The New Kingdom adopted a different shape of shields (Cf. Pl.2)

Bottom Group

8. Isis priestess dressed in Graeco-Roman style. (Marble statuette, Rome, Capitoline Museum).

9. Isis priestess in Egyptian style with a mantle tied in a knot over the right shoulder while the left lappet falls loosely over the arm (Bronze figure, formerly Berlin Altes Museum).

10. Woman's costume. Mantle as No. 9. (Basalt figure, Munich, Antiquarium).

11 and 12. Saïte Priests with a mantle with jagged edges (Saïte Period, 7th and 6th centuries B.C.)

13. Egyptian clad in a mantle.

14. Ptolemy Euergétes (247–221 B.C.) with crown and mantle, sceptre and handle-cross.

ASSYRIA AND NEIGHBOURING PEOPLES *(12th–7th centuries B.C.)*   5

The Kingdom of Assur on the upper Tigris about 1500; from 885 (Asurnazirpal) great power, in 729 united with Babylonia; 606 end of Assyria.

Top Group

1. High dignitary in a long fringed tunic with short sleeves. Tasselled sash, fillet, neck ornaments. Bracelets on the upper arms and wrists. A sword worn by the aristocracy even in peace time. The sheath mounted with metal.

2. Assyrian king as officiating priest with a high cap and short tunic, the ceremonial garment of the priests. Priest's sticks with knobs or fan- or brush-shaped ends. His royal rank is marked by the mantle thrown over one shoulder and the tassels attached to the girdle.

3. Simple official with boots and hose (from a later period).

4. King with a cap decorated with gold braid, ends of which hang down the back. Fringed garment and mantle thrown over one shoulder. Purple-violet colour. Bracelets on the upper arm and wrists. Ear-rings (as 1–3). In his right hand, the long royal official staff. (Asurnazirpal, 884–860 B.C., according to a relief in the British Museum, London).

5 and 6. Canopy and fan-bearers of the king, beardless with broad sashes.

7. Bow-bearers of the king with a fringed skirt (as 5 and 6).

Centre Group

8. Warrior with metal helmet, double sword-belt with a metal buckle as a protection where the bands are crossed. Sword, long spear, round shield, hose and boots.

9. Lightly armed archer, with sword and simple cap.

10. Heavily armed warrior with coat of mail made of small metal pieces.

11. Ordinary woman with fringed skirt and mantle thrown over one shoulder.

12. Man in a short tunic and sash.

13. Captive with felt cap (member of a non-Assyrian tribe).

Bottom Group

14. Tribute-bearer from Northwest Mesopotamia.

15. Citizen from Nineveh (Capital of Assyria).

16. Prince from *Muzri* (modern Kurdistan).

17. Tribute-bearers from Palestine in the reign of King Jehu.

18 and 19. The Assyrian sacrificial mantle, front and back view.

(18 King Asurnazirpal; 19 King Salmanassar III. 860–826 B.C.)
According to originals and Layard: *Discoveries in the Ruins of Nineveh and Babylon*, with use of O. Jones, *Grammar of Ornament*, for the colouring.

BABYLONIA AND ASSYRIA   6

(Babylonia, the country between the Euphrates and Tigris was divided into Southern Sumer and Northern Akkad; south of the Euphrates was Chaldea)

Top Group

1. Old Babylonian priest-king (Gudea about 2250 B.C.) in a wide woven mantle, led by a god wearing the traditional skin mantle and horned cap.

2. King Khammurabi (about 2000 B.C.) wearing a Sumerian mantle and lamb skin cap. Relief.

3. Idol of the Babylonian-Assyrian weather god Adad with metal disks hanging down from the girdle.

4. King Merodach-Baladan of Babylonia (722–710 B.C.) dressed in a white tunic, held together by a girdle. At the back the tunic is pleated and the edge is fringed. Pointed cap elongated into a kind of tube.

5. Noble Babylonian lady in a long-sleeved tunic and fringed cape. Metal rings round the neck. Reconstructed by Max Tilke after an ivory figure in the Louvre, Paris.

6. Shows the head of a similar figure with cap and fillet tying up the hair at the nape of the neck.

Centre Group

7. King Asurbanipal (668–626 B.C., called *Sardanapalus* by the Greeks) on a couch in the garden of his harem. His head is encircled by a diadem with long bands falling down on his back and by a string of pearls. Richly decorated garment. Bracelets and ear-rings.

8. The queen on a high chair in a richly decorated tunic with tight ornamented sleeves; the long fringed mantle over it. Soft shoes. Star-shaped ear-rings, neck band, bracelets and a diadem in the shape of battlements. Feather fan on the small table.

9–12. Servant girls in long-sleeved tunics partly covered by a mantle. All garments with fringed borders. Sandals tied together with bands, probably worn over shoes made out of material. Turban-like head gear (fillets). Neck ornamentations and ear-rings. They wave the fan against flies and hold a plate with fruit and also a fringed cloth (possibly a napkin, Fig. 12). Incense burners on the floor.

Bottom Group

13. Armoured archer, shooting with his left hand.
14. Warrior with helmet, broad girdle over a short-sleeved tunic; lance, sword, round shield. The sword is usually fixed in a horizontal position to the sword-belt. The helmet has the small horse-hair curved metal decoration (which was further developed on the Greek helmet).

15. Horseman with pointed helmet in a short tunic, the upper part covered by a short ornamental garment (upper coat of mail). Fringed girdle, armoured hose, knee bands, laced boots, weapons: lance, sword, bow and arrows in the quiver. The horse's cover resembles an animal's skin. Ornamental straps are wound round the neck over the clipped mane. On the head part of the bridle an ornamental hair-tuft. Snaffle (similar to the bridles of today in Western Asia and Turkestan). The background shows how they shot from behind large shields fixed into the ground. According to original monuments in different museums and Layard, Discoveries. Cf. also C. Bezold: *Ninive und Babylon.*

7   WESTERN ASIA IN ANTIQUITY   *Sumerians, Hittites, and West-Asiatics*

(The non-semitic Sumerians about 3000 B.C. in Southern Babylonia; Hittites from the 2nd millennium rulers over Asia Minor as far as Syria; their empire was destroyed about 715 B.C., with the conquest of Carchemish.)

1. Seated figure with tablet on his knees, wearing a Sumerian mantle (From Tello).
2. Head of a similar figure with astrakhan cap.
3. Head of a commander with helmet and skin mantle; from the stele of Egyptian King Echnaton (Amenophis IV.) 14th century B.C., Paris, Louvre.
4. Woman in a shaggy lambskin mantle (arranged in flounces). Alabaster statuette from Ur in Chaldea (old cultural centre of the Sumerians).
5. Warrior from the ranks with axe, the bronze head fixed to a wooden shaft. Time of the Egyptian King Echnaton (cf. 3).
6. The oldest chariot represented in art. A leopard's skin is thrown over the seat. Drawn by four mules. The driver, unlike all other Sumerians, protects part of his head with a wig and wears a beard against evil spirits.
7. Hittite weather-god. Leather shoes with turned-up points as still worn in the Orient. Basalt relief, 2nd millennium B.C.
8. Hittite warrior. Leather shoes as No. 7. Basalt relief from Sendshirli. 2nd millennium B.C.
9. Hittite chief with pointed cap and ear-rings.
10. Cilician god. He wears a horned cap, and in his hands grapes and ears of corn. Leather shoes as in No. 7.
11. Priest praying to a god or Cilician prince. (Cf. the As-syrian sacrificial mantle, Plate 5 which is draped round the body in the same way). One should notice the clean-shaven upper lip of figures 10 and 11. 10 and 11 form a rock-relief in Northern Syria.
12. Arabian warrior in a short tunic, with bow, arrow and quiver. From an Assyrian representation.
13. Hittite warrior with sickle-shaped sword.
14. Hittite prince in a wide mantle, the borders richly decorated.
15. Deity with peculiar trailing garment (perhaps a mantle held in place round the hips by a girdle. Found at Jerabis.
16. Hittite woman from a procession, wearing a crown in the form of battlements.
17. Hittite woman, in a large wrap which also covers the head, sitting in front of a folding table and holding a metal mirror. Pointed turned-up leather shoes.
18. Hittite figure in a long mantle. From Boghaskoi, the former Chatti (capital of the Hittites about 1800 B.C.).
19. Head of the Armenian king Tigranes I. with an indented crown with animal frieze over the fillet.
20. Head of a Parthian King. Helmet over fillet.
21. Warrior of a sea-faring nation attacking Palestine.
22. Philistine warrior wearing cap with chin-strap and feather-like crest.

8   WESTERN ASIA IN ANTIQUITY   *Phoenicians, Hittites, Syrians (Canaanites)*

The most powerful neighbouring people of the Egyptians in the north were the Hittites (Kheta, Chatti, cf. Plate 7; Kefti: Crete; Retenu: Palestine); this plate also includes West-Asiatic tribes, nomad Bedouins or those in settlements as well as sea-faring nations.

Top Group

1. Man from Kefti with fillet, multi-coloured loin-cloth with tassels, bobs and socks woven in many colours to protect the ankles. Skin-sandals.
2. Hittite or Kheta. Fillet, long, simple garment (as still common in the Orient today), short shoulder cape. Clean-shaven.
3. Man of a desert tribe east of Palestine. Decorated skin mantle fastened on one shoulder. Tattooing on the legs.
4. Man of the Purasate, a hostile sea-faring people from the time of Rameses III. – Feather head dress which does not denote a chief but is worn by every one. The Purasate or Pulasate can probably be identified with the Philistines of the Bible. (Not Semites but probably coming from Aegean countries).
5. Syrian of rank from the interior of the country.

Centre Group

6. Bedouin (nomad hunter and breeder). Loin-cloth woven in gay colours and leather sandals. Bow and arrows, wooden hunting stick for throwing made of hard wood and bent in a special way (cf. the Australian Aborigine's boomerang).

7. Bedouin woman in a mantle woven in many colours; actually a cloth fastened on one shoulder. Fillet, shoes made of one piece of leather. The leather bottle was used for keeping fat, ointment or rouge.

8. Syrian or Canaanite. (According to an Egyptian representation dating from the end of the 18th Dynasty. Perhaps a rich merchant). Yellow tunic with tight sleeves and trousers, covered by a richly embroidered outer garment draped so that the blue and red stripes alternate. Short beard.

9. Man from a South Palestinian tribe.

10. Man belonging to a primitive South Palestinian tribe. The body painted and tattooed in the fashion of primitive people. Fair or dyed hair.

11. Man from *Retenu* (Palestine or Syria) with tassels and coloured borders.

1–11. Partly according to Egyptian representations in *Manners and Customs of the Ancient Egyptians* by Wilkinson, London 1878.

Bottom Group

12–17. Hebrews.

12. Hebrew in a short sleeved long fringed woollen tunic, an oblong piece of material worn over it and decorated with tassels at the lower corners (according to Mosaic law). He wears a pointed cap of bands wound round the head.

13. Street vendor wearing an outer wrap with fringes.

14. Priest with the vessel for the sacrificial blood (cf. 15).

15. High Priest. The priestly costume consisted of breeches or a loin-cloth (second book of Moses 28, 42), a white linen tunic with long sleeves, a long girdle wound several times round the body; the head-dress consisted of a band wound round a large tube (or open cap). During the ritual he was bare footed. In addition, the High Priest wore a sleeveless mantle reaching down to the knees and over that the *ephod* or shoulder garment made of two seperate back and front parts and fastened on the shoulders by means of onyx brooches and round the waist by a girdle made out of gold and coloured threads. Four rows of three jewels were fixed to the breastplate of the *ephod* as emblems of the twelve tribes of Judah. Besides the fillet a golden plate was worn by the High Priest with the inscription: Holy to Jehovah Yahweh).

16. Hebrew with prayer mantle and prayer strap, the longer tassels of the mantle manifesting his great piety and obedience to the law.

17. Ordinary man in a fringed tunic with sash and high boots (According to reliefs on the black Obelisk of Salmanassar in the British Museum, 9th Century B.C.). 1 and 2 according to the same reliefs.

MYCENAE, CRETE, CYPRUS *(Aegean and Phoenician Cultures 2000–500 B.C.)*

1–11. Mycenae.

1. Fragment with representation of warriors and woman. National Museum, Athens.

2. Warriors with large leather shields. From a Mycenaen sword blade.

3–7. Ornamental objects made of gold plate, frequently used as decoration on garments.

8–11. Female figures from gold and copper signet rings, Mycenae.

12–18. Crete.

12. Bronze statuette of a woman wearing flounced skirt.

13–16. Snake goddess with bodice and frills. Flounced skirt.

17. Statuette similar to No. 12.

18. Women carrying pails of water, a harpist behind. Painting on a sarcophagus from Crete. The Crete male figures (bull-fighters, equilibrists, etc.) are mostly represented as naked, pale or reddish as, for instance, the harpist, but they wear a sort of coat of mail round the hips or a loin-cloth corresponding exactly to the women's, who, however, wear in addition the flounced skirt and the bodice which leaves the breasts exposed.

19–23. Cyprus.

19 and 20. Cyprian warrior, terra-cotta statuette.

21. Cyprian prince with double loin-cloth and ornamental collar, cyprian hat (Egyptian style).

22. Man's head (Cyprus).

23. Woman's head with ear-rings, diadem covered by a veil. (Terra-cotta in Creek style).

24. Man's head with a Cyprian straw hat or cap as still worn today.

25. Cypriot wearing a sort of himation (cf. Greece) with ornamental border. (Early Greek period). According to Bossert, *Altkreta*. Berlin, 1937, also F. Winter, *Kretisch-mykenische Kunst*, 1913.

PERSIA IN ANTIQUITY AND THE EARLY MIDDLE AGES

Top Group

1–15. Ancient Persia 6th–5th centuries B.C.

1. King Darius in a long trailing Median outer garment, the superfluous length of which is pulled up at the left side and allowed to fall down in rich folds. Wide sleeves. Stick as carried by the Assyrian kings (cf. Plate 5) and a bunch of flowers in his hand. Long beard which was a royal privilege all other men wearing a short round beard. Regal cap richly decorated and serrated at the edge which is worn by the body guard in similar form. All ancient Persian caps are worn so as to show part of the hair over the forehead.

2 and 3. Fan and canopy-bearers according to ancient Assyrian court custom.

4. Companion of the king with fillet and carrying spear and bow.

5 and 6. Bodyguard. The bodyguard consisted of a whole army mostly dressed in Median garments. Arms: spear, bow, oval shield with semi-circle cut out at the sides. Ordinary warriors carried round shields.

Centre Group

7–9. Warriors in ancient Persian knee-length tunics with girdle and long trousers. Leather cap and shoes fastened on the instep with bands. Short broad sword (or dagger) hanging from the belt. Figure 7 carries the peculiar Persian case for the short bow and arrows.

10. Distinguished Persian in a long Median outer garment with wide sleeves and pleated cap. Beard and medium long curls. Laced leather shoes.
11. Persian in travelling costume with mantle open in front.
12. Court servant in a long outer garment with fan for flies and combined cape and hood consisting of a large piece of cloth wrapped round the neck and head.
1–12. Mostly from representations found in the ruins of Pasargadae and Persepolis, the palaces built by Cyrus (died 529 B.C.), Darius (died 485 B.C.) and Xerxes (died 465

B.C.). Another source is the Mosaic at Naples, an imitation of a much older picture.
13 and 14. Men's heads from Xerxes' reign (485–465 B. C.).
15. Woman's head from the same period, with a veiled mouth as is still customary with Armenian women.
16–25. Persian at the time Khoshu II. (591–628 A.D.).
16. Servant girl in a long tunic.
17–19. The ruler with servants and pages.
20–25. Persian Ambassador according to cave paintings from Ajanta (formerly Berlin, Museum für Völkerkunde).

11   SCYTHIANS AND INHABITANTS OF ASIA MINOR *(Early Greek Culture)*

The Scythians (Saks) often mentioned by Herodotus were a mounted stock breeding people north of the lower Danube and in modern southern Russia, who invaded Asia Minor in the 7th century.
Presumably they are a European tribe of the Iranians and related to the Persians, thus being Indo-Europeans.

Top Group

1–6. Scythians according to representations in tombs. Leningrad, Ermitage.
1. Archer in a leather tunic with long embroidered leather trousers, decorated with small metal plates, called Scythian leather trousers, and soft medium-high leather boots. Band round the long hair.
2. Warrior with a conical cap tied under the chin. Trousers like No. 1.
3–6. Archers with large pocket-like quivers. Cap like 2, trousers like 1. Also two warriors in similar costume.

Centre Group

7–11. Phrygians, i. e. a people related to the Armenians, thus they were Indo-Europeans living in Asia Minor. Agricultural people of a certain cultural standard, they lived partly in towns and cultivated handicrafts, (especially carpet weaving and embroidery).
7. Phrygian shepherd. (A representation of the mythological Attis or Atys, the Phrygian Adonis, who was usually re-

presented as a youthful shepherd and was the favourite of the goddess Cybele.
8. A similar figure from a West Asiatic relief of hellenistic times.
9. Girl in a Phrygian patterned costume as seen on Greek vase paintings, wearing the so-called Phrygian cap.
10. The Trojan Paris in a Phrygian costume with long hose and hood-like head-dress (Phrygian cap).
11. Amazon from a Greek vase painting. It shows her wearing the Phrygian cap, hose and high laced boots. She carries a battle-axe, a small shield (and also often a bow).

Bottom Group

12–21. Costume and arms of Asia Minor.
12. Medea wearing a gaily coloured Phrygian costume, her home being in Colchis in Asia Minor. According to a vase painting of the later classical Greek period.
13. One of the body guard of the Persian king in Phrygian costume. According to the Greek vase, called Darius vase; Naples Museum.
14–21. Arms from Asia Minor according to Greek vase paintings.

12   GREECE. *Early Period (6th and 5th centuries B.C.)*

Top Group (According to black vase paintings)

1, 2, 4, 6. Women and girls in the archaic stiff Doric chiton *(tunic)* which reached down to the feet and was decorated with bands of ornaments and patterns. A girdle was worn round the waist. Chest and shoulders are covered by a short jacket or kerchief which, however, is often produced and arranged by way of pulling the superfluous length of the chiton up through the girdle and allowing it to fall down over the upper part of the body. It was usually fastened with safety-pins and brooches on the shoulders.
This upper part of the garment, when dresses became softer and fuller (linen instead of wool), gradually develops in a way to fall down in a baggy fold which is the beginning of the later forms of garments. In addition the himation, a loosely wrapped cloak, is worn and is sometimes drawn over the head by women.
3. Man in a dignified long chiton with flower patterns and a himation. The borders of both garments are ornamented. Beard and long hair.

5. Youth only wearing a short mantle called chlaina (without chiton).

Centre Group (according to later vase painting. 6th–5th centuries.)

7–9. Women and girls dressed in garments made of thinner material (linen or crêpe, byssus or cotton) and arranged in fine narrow pleats, many bulges and folds, falling down on the upper or lower part of the body. The pleats were produced by stitches on the upper seam or by pressing and ironing. The garment, originally sewn and meant to be pulled over the head like a tunic, is later wrapped and draped round the body (cf. bottom group). A himation is worn over head and shoulders.
10–11. Youth wearing a short linen chiton fastened on the shoulders and held together by a girdle.
11. With the short mantle *(chlaina)* and the petasos worn on journeys (or a travelling hat).
12. Man wearing a long chiton with many folds and a draped mantle *(himation)* having little lead weights at the ends.

13 and 14. Women assisting at a burial and death ritual.

15. Woman putting on the Doric woollen chiton (cf. upper group) with part of it falling down from the shoulders.

16. Girl (before dressing) wrapping a band or girdle round her breast.

17. Girl in a short-sleeved linen chiton draping the mantle, Chlamis and fastening it with brooches or safety-pins on the shoulder.

GREECE. *Great Period of Greek Art. (5th and 4th centuries B.C.)* 13

Top Group

1–4. Examples showing different ways of draping the outer garment *(himation)* without the chiton.
1. According to a tomb stele from Orchomenos.
2. According to a statue.
3. Roman marble copy after a Greek bronze statue of Demosthenes, about 280 B.C.
4. After a statue of Sophocles about 340 B.C.

Centre Group

5. Short chiton, pulled over the left shoulder, in order to leave the right arm free. Craftsmen's costume. The left shoulder and arm are covered by a small wrapper. (Statue of Hephaestus, god of fire and the smiths.

6. Apollo Citharoedus and conductor of the Muses in a long woman's peplos. Roman marble copy after a Greek original of the 5th century B.C.
7. Pallas Athene in a woman's peplos with an outer wrapper, the Aegis, the mythological goat skin with the Gorgon's head (so-called Athena Lemnia. Bronze statue by Pheidias).
8. Delphic charioteer in a long chiton with a girdle (Bronze statue in Delphi, about 470 B.C.).

Bottom Group

9. Amazon by Polycletus in a short chiton with girdle (Bronze statue from Delphi about 470 B.C.).
10 and 11. Attic tomb relief: woman and servant.
12. Resting pugilist wearing a chlamis similar to the Abyssinian mantle *shama*.

GREECE. *Armour, Banquets, Games and Music* 14

1. Chariot which replaced the cavalry in Homer's description according to a later representation. Coat of mail with metal shoulder plates. Helmet with cheek-guards which can be turned up.
   The sword is strapped very high to the belt.
2. Tomb stele of Aristion (end of 6th century). A star on the shoulder plates; a lion's head on the breast plate. The coat of mail is decorated all round with three ornamental metal bands. The short chiton can be seen on the upper arm and the thighs.
3. Achilles bandaging the wounded Patroclus who is sitting on his shield with his helmet taken off so that the felt hair cap can be seen. Coat of mail with movable shoulder plates and studded leather or linen elongations hanging down from the coat of mail for protection of the lower part of the body. Under the coat of mail the short chiton. The cheek-guards on Achilles' helmet are turned up. The armour is that of the time of the Persian Wars.
4. Heavily armed soldier.
5. Heavily armed soldier with greaves connected by springs. Oval shield cut out at the sides.
6. Warrior with spear. Large crest on his helmet, turned up cheek-guards, decorated greaves. The coat of mail protecting the ships consists of several layers.
7. Helmet with fixed cheek-guards and two crests placed across the helmet.
8. Helmet of the late archaic epoch before the great period of art.
9. Banquet *(Symposion)*. The members wearing garlands on their heads, the one on the right with a cup *(skyphos)* the one on the left holds out the goblet to the young slave with a jug. The ornamental border of this painted vase shows cooling vessels, jug, goblet and shoes.

10. Banquet, the man lying, the girl sitting.
11. Member of a banquet wearing a garland and holding goblet and drinking horn.
12. Cup *(Kantharos)* with large rounded handles used for official ceremonies.
13. Bowl without handle *(phiale)* which was filled from a jug.
14. Tumbler *(rhyton)* in the shape of a bull's head, through the nostrils of which the wine flowed into the mouth.
15. Bowl with handle and stem.
16. Jug with handle.
17. Greek woman carrying honey in the comb with the left hand and a kantharos in her right hand.
18. Female tumbler in a loin-cloth moving on her hands between pointed swords.
19. Male figure from the retenue of Dionysus (Bacchus).
20. Wandering minstrel with flute and lyre.
21. Man blowing the flute and wearing a fillet to which the flute can be attached. He wears the peculiar ceremonial garment: the long chiton with a sleeveless jacket. So-called *aulet* (derived from *aulos*: flute with mouth-piece, usually applied to a twin flute).
22. Pipes *(syrinx)* the simple natural instrument of Greek shepherds, each pipe of different length.
23. Woman playing the *psalterion*. (This was the old lyre with strings.)
24. Lyre *(psalterion)* with a roundish sounding-box.
25. Woman with a string-instrument (in the shape of a *kithara*, which was being plucked by the *plektron*.
26. Woman tuning her lyre.
27. Harp *(trigonon*, called thus from its three-cornered shape). The sounding-board faces the harpist.

of the Hellenistic period on painted Terra-cottas of the 4th Century B.C. (mostly from Tanagra, Boeotia)

1. Female dancer in a flounced skirt.
2. Boy wearing a *petasos* (wide, soft sun-hat).
3. Boy wearing chiton and chlamis, as well as *petasos*.
4. Girl in a full-pleated chiton and mantle *(himation)* and well dressed hair (front view).
5. Girl wearing a mantle and pointed sun-hat (so-called Thessalian hat), white and red border.
6. cf. 4 (side view).
7. Girl (Artemis with her hunting dog) wearing a costume suitable for sport and similar to that of the Amazons: Chiton and pink chlamis. The doe skin of the hunter (nebris) over it is fastened by means of a blue girdle. High hunting-boots fastened by bands cross-laced. From Tanagra, 4th century B.C.

8. Two girls putting their arms round each other and wearing the so-called sleeveless Doric chitons and over it a short mantle *(himation)*, the right one being blue, the left red. The girl on the left has her hair combed up carefully, the one on the right has thick plaits laid round the head. From Corinth.
9. Young woman with Eros, wearing chiton and himation.
1–6. According to original statuettes from the Munich Collection of Antiques.
7 and 8. According to A. Furtwängler, Sabouroff collection, vol. 2 (Berlin 1883–87).
9. From a photo in the Loeb collection, Munich.

1, 5, 11 and 18. Woman in a long close-fitting dress. (1, back view, 5, front view).
2. Woman's shoes made of one piece with holes for laces.
3 and 12. Woman with a conical head-dress and with a spiral garment decorated with flowers and the ends of which are pulled over the shoulders from the back and allowed to fall down over the chest.
12. back view.
4 and 7. Golden ear-rings.
6 and 9. Man before arranging his garment and after having draped it round the body (9: is a free drawing in order to illustrate the way the garment is worn).
8 and 16. Ear plates with gold pendants.
10. Head of a female statuette with hood and neck bands.

13. Bronze votive statuette, for protection and healing.
14 and 15. Heads from Etruscan mural paintings from the tomb-grottoes near Corneto.
17. Terra-cotta sarcophagus (from Caere, now Cervetri) a leather wine bottle is placed near the couple on the couch.
19–24. Home-coming warriors, Samnites, enemies of Rome, who, in the 5th century B.C. pushed part of the Etruscans out of Southern Italy (Mural painting from a tomb in Ruvo di Puglia, now in the Museum at Naples).
25–35. The two lower rows: Etruscan banquet: a memorial feast for the dead. The participants lie next to the table, and in addition there are the usual servants, flautists, jugglers and dancers, both male and female (Mural painting from an Etruscan tomb, now in the Vatican Museum, Rome).

---

1. Toga draped over the tunica in the old simple way. According to a so-called statua togata, statue representing an Etruscan in peace time attire.
   Priest (Pontifex) performing a sacrifice. His toga drawn over his head.
3. Dealer of sacrificial animals or sacrificial attendant (victimarius).
4. Inhabitant of Gabii in Latium wearing his toga in a special way: the end of the toga is drawn tightly round the waist thus forming a girdle (cinctus Gabinus). Left: coin showing Julius Caesar's head with a laurel garland. Right: coin of Aurelian with the emperor's crown as worn at the time.
5. Julius Caesar addressing his soldiers. The *paludamentum*, the general's mantle only worn in war-time over the armour, covers the coat of mail with its bronze decorations. It was longer than the simple war mantle, the *sagum* and was fastened on the right shoulder with a brooch (according to a statue in Naples).
6. Julius Caesar wearing the *toga pura* or *virilis*, the simple white toga as worn by men from their seventeenth year (according to a statue in the Alte Museum, Berlin).

7. Dignitary in the stance of an orator in the *toga praetexta* which had a purple border to indicate high office.
8. Emperor wearing the long military mantle *(paludamentum)*.
9. Lictor, i. e. attendant or honorary guard who were attached to the high officials in different numbers. In his hand the fasces (bundle of rods).
10. Emperor wearing the long trailing purple toga, originally worn by the censors. (Since the Emperor Domitian it became the customary imperial garment.)
11. Emperor with the purple mantle embroidered with gold threads over the toga fastened by a girdle.
12. Emperor performing a sacrifice wearing tunica and paenula (mantle) thrown back over both shoulders (cf. Plate 19, fig. 5).
13. Youth wearing paenula.
14. Cape with hood *(cucullus)*.
15. Sun-hat with a narrow point similar to the woman's hat on the statuette from Tanagra (Pompeiian representation) cf. plate 15: Hellenistic costume.

Top Group

1. Auriga (charioteer in the arena in a coloured tunica, carrying victor's palm.
2. Man in the long sleeveless, full *tunica talaris* (ankle length).
3. Peasant wearing a tunic made of sheepskin with high boots and broad-brimmed hat.
4. Fisherman wearing the *exomis* (a short tunic exposing the right breast).
5. Representation of the *paenula* (cloak with hood), back view. Pattern of the north African burnous (cf. Plate 187–88, Algeria and Tunis as well as text: African peoples).

Centre Group

6. Slave wearing a tunica with a girdle and sandals with straps wound round the ankle and calf.
7. Sacrificial attendant (Camillus) wearing a tunica with a girdle. Long hair adorned with a garland.
8. Woman wearing a mantle thrown back over one shoulder and showing a short tunica with a girdle. The under-

garment is a long tight-sleeved *tunica interior* or also called *subucula*.

9. *Tunica recta* made of one piece of material and reaching down to the feet. Long veil and a crown on her head.
10. The wife of Drusus.
11. Women wearing the tunica with a girdle *(tunica muliebris)* the customary garment for women.
12. Veiled vestals with mantle drawn over the head, over long tunica.
13. A middle-aged vestal (priestess of Vesta).
14. The empress Agrippina the Elder (wife of Germanicus and the mother of Caligula, who died 33 A. D.), wearing pleated tunica with half-long sleeves and a mantle thrown over. Wig with plaits hanging down at the sides.

Bottom Group

15–19. Roman women in different stances wearing the *palla*, a sort of himation or mantle draped in various ways.

GREECE AND ROME. *Hair styles and head-dresses* 19

1. Greece

The man belonging to early Greek culture wears locks and plaits skilfully arranged in various ways often intertwined with the fillet or hair band (1–7). Only from the 5th century is men's hair shorn or cropped and arranged in a simpler way (Fig. 8). Women in early times have their hair dressed in a very elaborate way with locks and plaits (11–14), obviously produced by curling-irons or by means of false locks. Probably these elaborate and painfully created styles were not worn every day, as some representations – also from the 9th century – show much simpler styles. Bands and kerchiefs were amply applied (Figs. 15–19).

Men's head-dress was the plain cap and the soft more elongated woollen cap with the edge turned up. The well-known Phrygian cap is only a special form of this kind, which by the way is still worn today by Italian or Portuguese fishermen in red or black colours. The stiffer hat with a turned-up brim has probably developed from the soft cap. The pointed hat with a narrow brim (*pilos*, fig. 10) and the one with the wide brim called *petasos*, the Greek travelling hat, represent the main types of hats. The *petasos* could be hung over the back by its bands (fig. 8).

2. Rome

Already at the time of Ovid (in the reign of the emperor Augustus), the hair styles of Roman women must have been extremely varied, as ladies of rank kept several slave girls for the purpose of dressing their hair. Those who were not in a position to do so had to resort to simpler styles or kerchiefs. Women with simpler styles wore a parting and gathered their hair in a knot similar to the Greek fashion. But it was the women of rank and the elderly women who prefered the more elaborate styles. Fig. 28 has a parting and her hair is laid round the head in a complicated way, interlaced with a ribbon and ending on the head (*nodus*). Besides ribbons they wore hair-nets, fillets and diadems or simple metal bands. Fig. 26 (Bust in the Capitoline Museum, Rome) wears her hair set in waves according to Greek fashion. Figs. 27, 23 and its back view 25 show the way plaits were fastened on the head. There were numerous variations in which little round curls were arranged in tight rolls on the heads of noble Roman women, of which figs. 20, 22, 23 are examples; fig. 20 has, in addition, two long locks hanging down at the sides. Elaborate and majestic (resembling battlements) is the empress Messalina's hairstyle (fig. 21) according to a bust in the Capitoline Museum, Rome.

FOOTWEAR in ANCIENT TIMES 20

At first the shoe served only as a protection with the Greeks; people went bare-foot at home; it was only in the streets that shoes were worn. The Romans as a rule travelled and marched more frequently than the Greeks, also entered colder countries more often and therefore gave more attention to footwear.

The Greek woman, mostly confined to the house, is seldom represented with shoes. She prefers soles fastened with straps, or sandals. Later on, as shown by the Tanagra statuettes, dating from the 4th century B.C., more elegant shoes were worn by women, for instance red ones with yellow edged soles. There were no special types of shoes. There were many forms varying from the simple sandals to the high laced boots partly with rich decorations and slits as can be seen on Greek representations.

The simplest form is the *karbatine* (fig. 16) worn by both Greeks and Romans which consisted of a piece of cow's hide turned up around the foot and fastened by straps. It is in fact the old strapped shoe as also worn by the Teutons and up to the 16th century by German peasants and even today by Rumanians, Slovaks, and other peoples. The main part of all footwear remains the sole (fig. 5), the solid support of the foot as a protection against the cold, dampness and rough ground; then the straps for fastening were added, later the toe-caps and finally the upper part of the shoes, which according to need or taste have slits or are decorated (figs. 9, 10, 12). Figs. 9, 10, 12–16, also 1–3 show Greek styles. These represent the kind called *krepis* or *krepide*. In fig. 17 the foot under the strap is bandaged with linen bands. Figs. 13–15 and 19 resemble more our shoe and boot, but are not of a more recent Greek origin. Fig. 22 is a type between the two, as the toes are exposed again. The simplest Roman footwear were the *soleae* (fig. 5). Figs 7 and 8 show the Roman *calceus*. The colour of fig. 4 is red as a sign of distinction for the high officials of the Republic (*mulleus*). The *calceus* when worn by the soldiers is called *caliga* (figs. 11 and 23) and is represented here as a heavy hobnailed sandal. Fig. 6 has been drawn after an original from a museum in the Rhine Province. Fig. 21 is again the Greek *krepide*, worn by a Roman, fig. 20 is a Roman example from the time of the Imperium. Figs. 24, 26 and 27, 29, 32, 34 are Coptic footwear (slippers, sandals of all types); fig. 28 represents a Coptic straw sandal, 26 is a Coptic laced shoe. Fig. 25 is a late Roman slipper from the time of the Emperor Justinian, 30 is a Roman boot (similar to fig. 20, fig. 31 is a Roman spur).

The Coptic shoes are represented according to *Antike und früh-mittelalterliche Fußbekleidung aus Achmim-Panopolis* by Frau-berger. Düsseldorf, 1896.

21 TEUTONS. *Prehistoric and Early Historic Periods*

1–5. Teutons in Jutland and Schleswig-Holstein. Bronze Age about 2000 B.C.
1. From the finds at Borum Eshöi (Jutland).
2. Girls garments from the finds at Egtved. Linen tunic and outer garment reaching below the hips, a cord gathering this short tunic at the waist.
3. Man's costume from the finds at Trinohi. Oval shaped woollen mantle. A short tunic-like garment is wrapped round the body, the ends of which are knotted at the back.
4 and 5. Women's and men's costume according to the reconstructions in the Copenhagen Museum. No description can be given of the linen undergarment which was probably worn (like fig. 2 where the linen tunic has been added) as all the linen has perished in the wooden coffins. The outer garments were mostly made of brown shorn wool.
6–10. Teutons in Northern Germany.
6. Frisian youth after the find by Max Etzel. Sleeveless short tunic, short breeches. Laced shoes.
7. Man of the Marcomanni tribe in a short tunic with sleeves gathered at the waist by a girdle and wearing mantle fastened on the right shoulder and long hose. Under his coat he carries a sack on his left shoulder.

8. Girl dressed in a long sleeveless tunic with a girdle and a broad richly decorated sash-like band passed over one shoulder. According to a find near Hamburg.
9. Teuton with short tunic and breeches similar to 6. In addition hose (or high gaiters). Find at Oberaltendorf.
10. Man dressed in a long sleeved tunic, putties, mantle fastened on the right shoulder and collar hood. Find at Bermethsfeld near Hanover.
11–15. Eastern Teutons of the Roman period.
11. Cymbric warrior (according to a find at Gundestrup, near Cassel).
12. East Germanic warrior (according to finds reconstructed in Silesia).
13. Fettered warrior belonging to the tribe of the Bastarnae (now settled in Rumania) wearing very long pleated hose as still worn in Rumania.
14. Captive of the Daci tribe (province of Dacia) in the retinue of a prince. (Figs. 13 and 14 according to the Tropaeum-victory memorial monument – at Adamkliss (Dobrudja).
15. Man belonging to the tribe of the Bastarnae (cf. fig. 13). He wears, like fig. 13, a tunica with girdle and over it the narrow paenula (cf. Roman costume) and the Roman hair style.

22 TEUTONS. *Roman Period, partly older*

1. Figure of the *Germania*. The legs covered like those of warriors. The lozenge-shaped pattern has also been found on materials on the bodies found in the moors. Relief from the stone rampart of the *practorium* in the legions' camp at Mayence. Time of the emperor Vespasian (died 79 A. D.).
2. A man of the Suevi tribe, half naked, (with breeches), over-thrown by a Roman horseman. Tombstone of a Roman horseman.
3. Kneeling, imploring Germanic youth covered with hose which have fallen down in front from the girdle; hair gathered in a tuft at the back of the head, mantle and shoes. (Roman bronze figure. Paris. Bibliothèque Nationale.)
4 and 5. House urns.
6. Daci wearing long hose tied at the ankles, tunic with girdle, mantle, oval shields. From Trajan's column erected 113 A.D.
7. Man with a sling. Man of the tribe of the Marcomanni. Relief from the column of Marcus Aurelius, Rome (after 173 A.D.). Similar to fig. 6.
8. Warrior with sword, with the upper part of the body exposed and wearing shaggy woollen trousers. Statuette on an ivory box from Frankish-Merovingian Gaul (about 6th–7th century).

9. Teuton wearing mantle or cape-like sleeveless garment made of wool or fur and with a hole for the neck. Roman triumphal relief in the Vatican Museum, Rome.
10. Germanic woman (so-called Thusnelda) dressed in a Graeco-Roman garment with the left breast exposed as described by Tacitus in the *Germania*. Roman marble statue, now in Florence, Loggia dei Lanzi.
11. Woollen tunic of a Germanic body discovered in the moors, from Thorsbjerg (Jutland). The sleeves are sewn on and show lozenge pattern.
12. Woollen trousers found in the same moors. The foot part of one leg is sewn on.
13–15. Bronze helmets and bronze cap found in Germany but of uncertain origin.
16. Shoe found in the moors. It is in one piece, and is fur-lined. It is the shape of the ancient laced shoe worn by German peasants until the late 16th century.
17 and 18. Shoes found in Swabia, flattened out.
19. High woollen cap, found in the moors, Jutland. Copenhagen Museum.
20. Frankish axe.
21. Short sword, dagger.

22. Axe with shaft, natural shape. According to a find near Reichenhall.
23. Head of one axe with loop and socket.
24. Axe; old emblem of dignity and office. Instead of a blade, a hammer is often attached. Find from Schleswig.
25. Blade of an axe from near Osnabrück. 1–25 according to photographs in *Deutsche Geschichte* by Heyck. Vol. I.
26 and 27. East Teuton with tuft of hair gathered on one side of the head (seen from the two angles).

28 and 29. Men belonging to the tribe of the Bastarnae from the *Tropaeum Trajani* at Adamkliss (Rumania). Cf. plate 22.

30 and 31. Teuton's heads according to Rhenish finds.

32 and 33. Marcomanni from the Column of Marcus Aurelius. (Max Tilke says of the woman's costume that Indian women of Arizona still wear a similar primitive garment). 26–33 according to *Tracht der Germanen* by J. Girke (Leipzig 1922).

PERSIA. *Sassanian Period in the Early Middle Ages (227–636 A.D.).* 23

1. Head of a deity.
2. King Narsahe (Narses) 293–302 A.D.
3. Companion of the king.
4. Official, according to a seal in the British Museum.
5. King on horseback wearing a garment and very wide trousers.
6, 7 and 10. Parthians dressed in tunics and long, close fitting trousers (5) or wide trousers (10), according to Sassanian reliefs.
5–7 and 10. according to *Kostümkunde* by Weiss.
8. King or prince hunting. (From a silver vessel in the Paris Collection of Coins).
9. King Ardeshir.
11. The god Ahura-Mazda, Ormuzd (right) gives King Ardeshir the ring of sovereignty. Rock relief near Naksch-i-Rustam.
12 and 13. Statue of King Sapor from a grotto near Shapur. According to Texier.
14–17. Parthians wearing different helmets and fillets.
18–24. Parthian according to Iranian rock reliefs. The relief representations according to *Iranische Felsreliefs* by Sarre-Herzfeld, 1910.
25. Long-sleeved original garment of a Parthian, wool dyed green. Discovered by Max Tilke in the former Berlin Museum für Völkerkunde (about 600 A.D.).
26. Sassanian horseman.
27. King with halo over the crown placed on a head with long curls.

GAULS, VIKINGS AND NORSEMEN 24

Top Group
1–10. Gauls.
1 and 2. Gallic warrior (1) with leather cuirass over the short tunic.
3. Gallic woman wearing a long blouse without a girdle.

Centre Group
4 and 5. Gallic peasants with hooded collars *(cucullus)*.
6–8. Warriors, the middle one with a bronze trumpet similar to an alpine horn, (6) wearing a *sagum*.
9. Chief with insignia.
10. Warrior. Reconstructed from preserved pieces of weapons and ornaments by French experts (perhaps not quite correctly). The special Gallic breeches *(bracca, braca* = Celtic word, in German *Bruch)* reach only down to the knees.

Bottom Group
11–14. Vikings.
11. Viking wearing skin trousers.
12. Viking (Norseman) with bronze helmet wearing a gaily bordered tunic. (11 and 12) according to bronze plates from Öland.
13 and 14. Scandinavian Norsemen from the 7th to 10th centuries wearing iron or bronze helmets of different shapes. (14) wearing bronze helmet with movable front piece, a coat of mail and carrying a wooden shield mounted with bronze. Copenhagen Museum.
15. Norseman (warrior) with jagged leather coat (from Britain, 9th century A.D.). (11–14) partly according to A. von Jenny: *Germanische Frühkunst*, 1937.

ROME. *Equipment of Army and Gladiators.* 25

Top Group
1. Soldier of the Roman legions with leather cuirass, leather breeches, studded girdle, rectangular shield *(scutum)*, sword attached to the sword-belt *(balteus)*, javelin *(pilum)* and metal helmet *(cussis)* with a crest *(crista)*.
2. Soldier of the Roman legions (similar to those represented on Trajan's Column). The leather cuirass mounted with iron bands *(lorica segmentata)*.
3. Ensign (standard-bearer) (signifer, vexillarius) vexillum-bearer, wearing lion's or bear's skin, coat of mail, leather cuirass with sword, dagger and round shield *(clipeus)* made of mounted leather and with a handle on the inner side.
4. Standard-bearer with the insignia of the legion (4200–6000 men: 10 cohorts, each consisting of 3 maniples). With scale armour *(locica squamata)*. Sword and dagger. In camp the eagle was stuck into the ground.

Centre Group
5. Captain (centurio) of a century or half a maniple with scale-armour, over it decorations of merit (silver phalerne), decorated greaves *(ocreae)*, doubled wrap or mantle and vine-wood stick, the mark of a centurion. Next to 5: helmet with crest placed cross-ways (cf. 1), sword in its scabbard.
6. High officer (Trajan's Column) mantle made of fine purple woollen material. Crest like a caterpillar, round metal shield (in early Greek style).

7. Horseman with leather cuirass and oval leather shield with six corners and elaborately mounted; horseman's spear and long sword (spatha), used by horsemen from 100 A.D. onwards.
8. Soldier of a Germanic auxiliary tribe (auxiliaris) with loin-cloth, girdle, the outer garment (paenula) is fastened up and has a hood. He carries an oval shield, sword, dagger and two javelins (According to a tombstone in Mayence). 1, 3–5, 7 according to Lindenschmit: *Tracht und Bewaffnung des römischen Heeres*, 1882, – 2 and 6 after photographs of Trajan's Column.

Bottom Group

9. Horn-blower with the cornu, a large, round metal horn, dressed in the tunica with wide border in the middle.

10. Net-fighter (retiarius) who tried to throw his net over his opponent, for instance the heavily armed gladiator with sword (gladius) and tried to pierce him with long trident. He is only slightly protected by his bandaged left cuirass sleeve which is widened on top into a metal shoulder plate. Otherwise only girdle with loin-cloth, greaves with bands wound round them.
11. Gladiator (myrmillo), armed in the Gallic way with vizor helmet, shield, belt, leg protection and sword.
12. Fencer in Thracian armour (thrax) with the same protective armour as the myrmillo (11), but two greaves and the short Thracian dagger (sica).
13. Fencing-master (lanista) at the gladiatorial games, with official's rod and wide tunic decorated with two stripes; he is raising his hand to stop the game. Half-open sandals.

26   EARLY CHRISTIAN PERIOD. *300–600 A.D.*

Christianization of the Roman Empire in the 4th century did not change costume decisively. The early Middle Ages developed the traditional forms and added some features different from those of the Antique. The classic folds had partly to give way to the preference for ornament and gay colours. From the Romans came the name *clavus* (stripe) for the striped ornament on garments which originally were reserved for Romans of rank. This clavus ran down from the shoulders to the seam of the garment. There was also the round clavus. All these stripes were either sewn or embroidered on, or woven or inserted into the material. Christian initials were also used as inserted decorations, i. e. the Greek X and P, which mean Ch and R (Christ's initials) or the anchor cross, i. e. X and P to which were added *A* and *Ω* (alpha and omega), beginning and end, furthermore the cross † with X and P and the old T-cross (Anthony's cross) in addition with *A* and *Ω* (A and O).

Top Group

1. Lady wearing a dalmatica as an outer garment first worn in the East Roman Empire. This became the official costume of deacons. Wide head band the ends of which fall over the shoulders (Catacomb painting, 4th century).
2. Evangelist in the costume of the 5th century (Mosaic at Ravenna).
3. Elderly Christian woman wearing a mantle in the shape of the casula, the costume of officiating priests. Kerchief.
4. Lady of rank wearing striped dalmatica.

5. Youth wearing a tunica (shirt-like garment) with round stripes. Sandals with straps.

Centre Group

6. Shepherd with girdled tunica, bands wound round the legs and protective collar.
7. Apostle according to the conception of the Early Middle Ages wearing a dignified large toga-like mantle.
8. Elderly woman (really a picture of the Virgin) with fringed mantle.
9. Young woman wearing tunica and dalmatica as well as head and praying with uplifted arms.
10. *The good shepherd* with the ancient reed-pipe or Pan flute (like 6). (1–10) according to catacomb paintings and mosaics of Early Christian times. Cf. R. Forrer, *Reallexikon der prähistorischen frühchristlichen Altertümer* (1907).

Bottom Group

11. Richly decorated sleeved tunica partly covered by the so-called hoodless *pluviale*, both woven of fine wool.
12 and 13. Late forms of the antique toga. The upper part is narrowly pleated. Time of the Emperor Justinian (527–565).
14. Warrior in a leather cuirass with mantle tied up on one shoulder. Phrygian cap and round shield. Mosaic in San Marco, Venice.
15. Woman wearing very wide woman's tunica with slits for the arms.

27   BYZANTINE EMPIRE. *4th–11th Centuries.*

Through the destruction of the Ostrogothic kingdom in 552 A.D. Italy was re-conquered by the Byzantine Empire. Ravenna became the residence of the Byzantine governors and is today a major source of our knowledge of Byzantine culture and costume. This is characterized by great magnificence; much silk, gold, jewelry and gaily coloured and patterned materials.

Top Group

1. The Emperor Arcadius (since 395 A.D. Emperor of the Eastern Empire, i. e. Byzantine Empire). The imperial orb was originally the imperial Roman emblem of the earth and world dominion. Later the Christian cross was added as an attribute of the western Emperors.

2. Consul from the first half of the 5th century. Consuls, although of no importance any more since the institution of emperors, were still nominated by the Senate. The years were named after them (until 541). From then on the emperor became *Consul Perpetuus*.

3. Galla Placidia, sister of the emperors Arcadius (Eastern Empire) and Honorius (Western Empire), wife of Athaulf, king of the Visigoths, lived at Ravenna after his death. (Ivory carving in the cathedral of Monza).

4. The Emperor Valentinian III. (435–455 A.D.) of the Western Empire, son of Galla Placidia.

5–11. Figures important for their costume from the choir of the Church of San Vitale, Ravenna. Mosaics after 552 A.D. The Emperor Justinian (9) and the Empress Theodora (11) with offerings accompanied by their retinue. 5. Companion of the Empress. 6. Lady in waiting to the Empress. 7. Distinguished courtier. 8. Weapon-bearer of the Emperor. His magnificent shield studded with jewels and decorated with the initials of Christ: X and P (Ch and R).

9. The Emperor Justinian. 10. Bishop Maximinian in the Emperor's retinue.

11. The Empress Theodora.

12. Byzantine warrior (7th–8th centuries). According to an ivory carving in the cathedral, Aix-la-Chapelle.

Bottom Group

13. The Emperor Nicephorus III. (died 1081) wearing a rich

outer garment exposing the lower part of the tight sleeves of the tunic. Triangular neck and shoulder collar, from the 10th century on, part of the ruler's official costume. Beard (in fashion in the Byzantine Empire from the 7th to the 14th centuries). Crown with ornamental chains.

14. Dignitary from the same period (11th century) wearing a mantle in the shape of the Greek chlamis. Red socks, sandals with white straps.

15. The Emperor Romanus II. (died 963).

16 and 17. The Emperor Nicephorus III. (cf. 13) and his consort in official costume; the emperor wears the *pallium* wrapped round shoulders and hips, originally a clerical garment. It is made of coloured brocade (in contradistinction to the clerical pallium, which was white and decorated with crosses). The empress, too, wears the insignia of a ruler: pallium, sceptre, crown.

MIDDLE AGES. MONASTIC ORDERS AND ORDERS OF KNIGHTS. 28

Top Group

1–5. Orders of Knights.

1. Templars. The Order of the Knights Templar was founded at Jerusalem in 1119 by French crusaders. Their headquarters were south from the Mosque of Omar on the Temple site from whence they derived their name. Red cross on white linen mantle.

2. Armoured Templar: coat of mail covered by a girdled tunic with sword, belt and sword.

3. Knight of the Teutonic Order. Representation of 1243. It was in 1189/90, during the third crusade, that crusaders from Bremen and Lübeck laid the foundation of a hospital near Acre, whose brethren were raised to the rank of an Order of Knights by German princes in 1196. The order consisted of knight-brethren and priest-brethren. In 1211 the order received as a gift the district of Burgenland in Transylvania and later on the Kulmerland and parts of East and West-Prussia. White mantle with black cross.

4. Knight of the Order of the Hospitallers of St. John of Jerusalem (16th century). Originally founded about 1048 in Jerusalem for the purpose of nursing sick pilgrims (Hospital and hostel near the Church of the Holy Sepulchre). After the first Crusade the hospitallers were raised to the rank of an Order of Knights, the oldest of such orders, in 1113 was reorganized and received special rules. The order consisted of three classes of brethren: knights, priests, serving brethren. Their first headquarters were in Ptolemais, from 1291 in Cyprus, 1309 in the island of Rhodes (hence called Knights of Rhodes), 1530–1798 in Malta (Knights of Malta), 1826 in Ferrara, 1834 in Rome. Oldest costume of the Order: black mantle with a white linen eight-cornered cross.

5. Lady of honour of the Order of St. John of Jerusalem. Costume of a later period (18th century).

6–16. Monastic Orders.

Centre Group

6. Dominican. The preaching order of the Dominicans was founded in 1215 by the Castilian Dominic. Costume: white garment, white *scapulary*, large cloth made of two pieces,

covering back and chest and a hole for the head. Black hooded mantle.

7. Franciscan. The order was founded by the layman Francis of Assisi in 1208. The Franciscans' garb is the brown cotton cowl with a rope in place of a girdle and sandals on bare feet.

8. Augustinian monk. It was not until 1244, after having been founded years, that the Augustinians had their rule formally confirmed. Indoor garment: white woollen cowl and *scapulary*. Outdoor garb: wide black cowl with long wide sleeves and hood. Through Luther, who had been an Augustinian monk, this garment was adopted by the Reformers and Protestant preachers.

9. Benedictine monk. The order of the Benedictines was founded by St. Benedict of Nursia in 528 as the first residential monastic order at the monastery of Monte Cassino near Naples. His statutes became the foundations of the whole monastic life. They vowed obedience, chastity and poverty. The abbot was the head of the monks whose time was divided into periods of prayer and labour (*ora et labora*). Later on science and art as well as teaching children were some of the tasks of these monks. Their garb, although differing according to districts, consisted in the main of a black cowl, mantle and *scapulary*.

10. Carthusian monk. The order of Carthusian monks was founded in 1084 by St. Bruno of Cologne at Chartreuse near Grenoble. The rule of the order demanded an ascetic life and silence outside the Holy Service, forgoing meat dishes and living in solitary cells. Costume: white cloth cowl with leather girdle, white *scapulary* both parts connected by a broad strip of material at the back and front, black mantle. The order exists in France, Italy and Switzerland.

11. Capuchin monk. The order of Capuchins is one of the many branches of the Franciscan order (cf. 7) also called Minorites, founded in 1527 in Italy. They are named after the pointed brown capouch attached to the cowl. The mantle reaches down to below the arms. In place of a girdle they wear a knotted rope. The cowl was rather tight, just wide enough to allow it to be slipped over. Sandals, socks only in emergency. The costume is brown. They wear a beard and carry a rosary.

12. Carmelite monk on outdoor costume. The order was founded on Mount Carmel in the Holy Land in 1156 by the South Italian crusador Bertold and confirmed by the Pope in 1226. Among the younger branches of the order the Observants, or barefooted Carmelites follow a more severe rule. The picture shows a shoeless Carmelite monk in a brown woollen cowl and *scapulary*. Outer garment: a tight white hooded mantle. Rosary.

13. Carthusian monk in outdoor garb: soutane (cloth tunic), white *scapulary*. black hooded mantle which is gathered at the shoulders. Black shoes.

14. Carthusian monk wearing indoor garb: white cowl, white scapulary with hood (cf. 10).

15. Carthusian nun during the ceremony of investiture when taking the veil. Ornaments for this special occasion: Over the white woollen garment the scapulary held together by

bands. Full white mantle, white neck-cloth. Brown veil. Blue stole with golden crosses. Blue maniple hanging over left arm. In her left hand she carries a burning candle and wears a five pointed crown on her head. Doyé in *Die alten Trachten der männlichen und weiblichen Orden.* (Leipzig, 1929), says that "*this garb, if historically true, was worn against the rule.*" The indoor outfit consisted of white skirt, white scapulary and neck-cloth, white veil which was also lined with white material. Black shoes, white cloth mantle.

16. Nun of the order of the Visitation, so-called Salesian nun. The order was founded in 1610. Black pleated dress of coarse wool with long, fairly wide sleeves which are turned back exposing tight sleeves underneath. Silver cross attached to a black woollen ribbon hanging down over her breast. White neck-cloth *(barbette)* tied round the neck. Black fillet, black veil. The Salesian order, like numerous others, followed the Augustinian rule.

29 ECCLESIASTICAL COSTUME AND ORDERS OF KNIGHTS. *1400–1800.*

Top Group

1. Roman Deacon (1450) wearing a long white dalmatica *(subucula)*.

2. Flemish Deacon (1460) wearing a short outer dalmatica over the long *subucula*.

3. Priest about 1470 wearing vestments for the mass with chasuble (round bell-shaped mantle, cut out at the sides) and stole only the fringed ends of which are visible over the dalmatica.

4. Bishop wearing double chasuble over the dalmatica and alba and a mitre, a bishop's crozier and maniple (originally a linen sudarium). According to Matthias Grünewald's painting in Munich, about 1525.

5. Pope in ceremonial costume, that is as a bishop of the Lateran church, Rome. His mass vestments consist of a shoulder wrap *(humerale)*, an alba (white gown), a cingulum girdle, not visible in this picture), a tunicella (fringed dalmatica reaching down below the knees) and outer and more richly decorated dalmatica, a stole (a narrow band), a chasuble, embroidered gloves and mitre (the papal tiara consisting of three crowns). Crozier with double cross. According to a Low-Rhenish painting about 1480.

Centre Group

6. Bishop of the 17th century wearing ceremonial robes with richly decorated chasuble. Bands *(fanones)* are hanging down from the mitre. Dutch (After a painting by Rubens).

7. Pope Pius VI. (1775–99) pronouncing the benediction in Vienna and wearing the white chasuble over the stole, tunicella and alba, as well as the mitre.

8. Bishop wearing canon's vestments: violet soutane and over it a surplice. Over the shoulders a short cape *(manteletta)*. Violet beret *(biretta)*.

9. Pope when appearing in public (not at holy service), wearing white silk soutane, surplice, red velvet cape *(mozetta)* richly trimmed with ermine, red gold-embroidered stole. Red velvet hat. In addition to the white papal garments he

wears the scarlet of a cardinal in his position as Cardinal-bishop of Rome.

10. Priest of the Order of the Knights of Our Lady of Mount Carmel and St. Lazarus in Jerusalem. Costume as 8.

6–10. After Schwan, *Abbildungen der geistlichen Orden*, 1791.

Bottom Group

11. Lady of Honour or *Lady of Devotion* of the Order of St. John in the 18th century, wearing black garment with black mantle, tight-fitting linen cap over the shorn head and over this a black stiff veil like a cap with lappets. (The veil is the symbol of betrothal to Christ. The linen headdress is a reminder of Christ's shroud). White cross on breast and left side of the mantle.

12. Knight of the Spanish Order of St. James of the Sword, founded in 1170 by King Ferdinand of Leon and Galicia, 14th century. White garment with girdle. Mantle fastened by a cord. Gauntlets. Beret with St. Andrew's scallop shell. Red cross on white mantle.

13. Knight of the Order of the Golden Fleece (18th century), founded in 1429 by Philip the Good, duke of Burgundy at Bruges (in remembrance of the ancient Greek legend according to which the Argonauts sailed off to Colchis to carry home the Golden Fleece (ram's skin). Bright red robe and wine-red wide mantle lined with white material and richly embroidered. Golden chain of the Order with the golden fleece *(toison d'or)* pendent on it. White shoes with red heels.

14. Knight of the Order of St. Stephen, Hungary, founded in 1764 by Maria Theresia, the robe resembling the costume of the Hungarian magnates.

15. Teutonic Knight of the 18th century (the Teutonic Order was founded in 1189). The costume reflects the rococo fashion but the colour of the material is black without pattern or embroidery. The special costume of the Order is represented by the white mantle (with lapels) ornamented with a black cross, the simple scarf and the high boots (cf. Doyé, *Die alten Trachten der Orden.* 1929).

Top Group

1–3. Frankish noblemen of the Merovingian and Carolingian times. Long-sleeved tunic decorated with silk braids or embroidered patterns. Girdle. Mantle fastened on the right shoulder by a brooch. Long hose bound with bands at the knees and the lower part of the leg bandaged according to old Germanic fashion leaving the toes exposed. Otherwise soft leather boots.

4. Frankish warrior with round shield with the buckle fixed on the crossed iron frame. Carolingian iron helmet with crest. Breeches. Bands wound round the legs and sandals. About 850.

5. Warrior with helmet and the rest of the head protected by armour. Coat of mail with skirt studded with metal plates. About 900–950.

Centre Group

6. Frankish woman in a long-sleeved tunic the borders gaily decorated. Mantle fastened on the breast by a brooch. Soft pointed leather shoes in the Roman fashion.

7. Frankish noble lady wearing two garments, the one underneath with long tight sleeves, which are visible. Embroidered long mantle pulled over the head.

8. Charles the Bold (youngest son of the Emperor Louis the Pious (le Pieux) first King of France (Western Frankish kingdom 840–877).

9. A Princess. 8 and 9 according to a miniature. (Bible of Charles the Bold).

10. Carolingian king according to a relief on a book cover.

11. The German king Henry II. (1022–1024) according to a miniature.

12. Frankish man of the 10th century (cf. 1–3) wearing boots.

13. Frankish woman wearing linen kerchief over her head.

Bottom Group

14. The Emperor Rudolph of Swabia (chosen in opposition to Henry IV. of Germany, died 1080) in coronation robes. According to a tombstone at Merseburg.

15–17. Women's costume of the later 11th century. Girdled garments which are slipped over long-sleeved tunics. 15 and 17 wear a long fur-lined mantle, fastened over the breast with a cord. 16 wears an unusual undergarment which is open in front and exposes the long tight-fitting hose.

18. Sword-bearer of the time of the crusades with parti-coloured garment; two pieces differing in colour sewn together down the middle.

19. Noble youth in a long tunic with high collar and gathered by a girdle.

Top Group

1 and 2. Men of the earliest Middle Ages (according to ivory carvings) in Florence, 4th century.

3. Warrior in the late Roman costume (ivory carving from the episcopal throne of St. Maximilianus at Ravenna).

4. South European man of rank (according to an ivory carving).

5. Warrior (according to the mosaics of San Marco, Venice).

Centre Group

6. Man of rank of the 10th century (ivory slab in the museum at Milan. The Emperor Otto I. and his family kneeling).

7. Woman of rank of the early Middle Ages with the draped veil-like mantle. (Mosaic in San Marco).

8. The Emperor Honorius, 5th century (ivory slab at Aosta).

9. Figure (servant girl from the mosaics of the church of Santa Maria Maggiore, Rome. Triumphal arch, 5th century).

10. Warrior (according to an ivory carving formerly in the Kaiser Friedrich Museum, Berlin).

Bottom Group

11. Greek (Byzantine) patriarch of the 9th century. The ecclesiastical stole is seen hanging down. It was a wide band put round the neck, made of gold thread. The shoulders are covered by a cape (instead of the palladium), woven through with gold threads. Along the right leg hangs the so-called *hypogonation*: the bag with tassel of the higher clergy.

12. Bishop (Pontifex) of the Greek church with the *pallium*. With the Romans the pallium was originally a mantle which in clerical costume was reduced to a wide band (similar to the stole). In the Roman Catholic Church it was bestowed by the Pope on the archbishops, rarely on bishops, as a special sign of distinction. The bishops of the Greek church generally wear it. The ecclesiastical pallium is always white with red crosses.

13. Representation of a priest of high rank wearing a pallium (but with black crosses for a religious festival). From the mosaics of the Church of San Marco, Venice.

14. Byzantine monk with a tunic arranged in folds and mantle. High leather boots over the patterned hose.

15. Greek-Byzantine empress from the time of the first crusade about 1096.

---

1. Woman of rank in a long close fitting garment with tight sleeves above the elbow, and falling down wide and open below it. 12th century.

2. The Emperor Frederick I. (Barbarossa) as a crusader (according to a miniature from Northern Italy, end of 12th century).

3. Woman of rank wearing a short-sleeved tunic-like garment over the long under garment with long ermine trimmed sleeves. Shoulder mantle. Kerchief. Late 12th century.

5. Peasant in a girdled tunic with pleated skirt. Long hose. Hood.

5. Jew with a long girdled tunic and mantle trimmed with yellow stripes. Pointed yellow hat (Jew's hat).

6. Vagrant minstrel with fiddle wearing a furred tunic.

7–19. Costumes from the so-called *Manesse-Liederhandschrift* (a manuscript of songs) in the University library of Heidelberg.

7. Princely minnesinger.
8. Man of rank.
9. and 10. Woman and girl belonging to the court.
11. Man in travelling attire.

12. The Jewish minnesinger Süsskind with the pointed *Jew's hat* as prescribed by the Lateran Council of 1215.
13–17. Ordinary minnesingers, dancing and playing instruments.
18 and 19. Minstrels.

33   FRANCE IN THE MIDDLE AGES. *900–1400.*

1–6. French Costume in the 11th century (partly according to frescos in the vaulting of the Abbey Church of St. Savin at Poitou). The peculiar pointed conical caps partly with the point bent down, (similar to the ancient *Phrygian* cap) are striking. Similar in shape is the helmet with bands (3 and 6): Knights in the coat of mail over the tunic.

Centre Group

7. Knight wearing scale armour over coat of mail and a flat iron hat.
8 and 9. Squires in girdled tunics with caps also covering the ears and tied under the chin.

10. Knight with battle-axe wearing a material garment over the coat of mail.
11. Elderly man with sleeveless tunic falling in folds down to the knees and a hood attached to it.
12. Falcon-bearer with a head-dress tied under the chin (similar to 8 and 9) and wearing long hooded cloak and gauntlets.
13 and 14. Youth and woman in hooded cloaks (13 shows the hood hanging down over the back; 14 has drawn it over the head.
15. Girl in long-sleeved garment, the upper part close-fitting.
7–15 Miniature paintings from the 12th–13th centuries.

34   NORMANS AND ANGLO-SAXONS. *11th to 14th Centuries.*

Top Group

1–9. According to representations on the embroidered tapestry at Bayeux (Normandy) after 1066 (Battle of Hastings).
1. Fully armed Norman horseman. The coat of mail consists of material with rings sewn on. The legs are protected in the same way. Over the hood of mail is the basinet reinforced by bands with nose guard. Wooden shield, lance.
2. Light-armed Norman. The hair at the back of his head shorn in the Norman fashion.
3. Dismounted horseman from the army of the Anglo-Saxon King Harold. Armour like No. 1. Legs bandaged with leather bands. Buckle shield.
4. Anglo-Saxon warrior with club and large wooden shield.

Centre Group

5. Norman warrior with battle axe (not used by the Anglo-

Saxons). Scaled hawberk, mantle fastened by a brooch, calves bandaged.
6. Light-armed Norman in a short girdled tunic.
7. Anglo-Saxon archer. The small conical cap covers half long hair.
8. Norman with a large wooden shield.
9. Light-armed Anglo-Saxon with a moustache and long hose.

Bottom Group

10–12. Norman peasants (12th century).
13 and 14. Peasant women (13th–14th centuries); 14: hood with nape protection.
15. Man of rank in fur-lined travelling dress. Hood with collar and fur cap (14th century).

35   ARMOURED KNIGHTS *(800–1300)* CRUSADERS *(1100–1300).*

Top Group

Protective armour: helmet, coat of mail, shield.
Offensive weapons: lance, sword, dagger, battle-axe and mace.
1. Knight with iron helmet over leather cap, scaled coat of mail (iron plates fixed on leather doublet) over pleated leather skirt; round buckler, lance, long sword, calves bandaged, shoulder mantle *(sagum)* from the Carolingian period about 800.
2. Knight wearing helmet with iron bands and nose guard *(nasale)* chain mail (with hose all in one piece). Elongated, large three-cornered shield with rounded corners. Short sword.
3. Knight with iron helmet and short chain hawberk. Round shield and battle-axe.
4. Knight covered by barrel helmet (flat-topped helmet; *heaume).* Over the ringed coat of mail *(byrnie)* the girdled and sleeveless surcoat falling down to the knees and called *cote armure.* Small pointed shield.
5. Knight wearing on his head a basinet with nose-guard *(nasale* cf. 2). Surcoat over coat of mail. Large shield. Horn.

Centre Group

6–12. Crusaders.
6. Crusader, wearing helmet, strengthened by a band, from the time of the German Emperor Henry VI.
7. Crusader from the time of Barbarossa. Barrel helmet. The horse's trappings ornamented with coat of arms.

Bottom Group

8. Knight wearing chain mail. 12th century.
9. Saracen warrior with two lances and large round shield. Short girdled and quilted tunic over loin-skirt. In front of him the small Saracen fist-shield. On his head a turban.
10. Knight covered by an iron hat. 13th century, time of the crusades.
11. High helmet resembling bishop's mitre.
12. Knight wearing ringed mail *(byrnie)* with hood under the surcoat. In his right hand the barrel helmet. 13th century.

Burgundy, France, England, Italy, Poland

Top Group

1. Burgundian armour about 1450. Plate mail over chain mail. Barrel-like cap made of jagged pieces of cloth. From the girdle hang the then fashionable bells.
2. Burgundian armour about 1425.
3. English armour. 15th century. Plate mail which replaced the older chain mail in England about 1450. Battle-axe for beating and pushing, still in use with lance and sword. The long handle indicates the further development towards a *partisan* or halberd about this time.
4. English armour. 14th century (Edward, the Black Prince, died 1376). Chain mail with hood of mail, rerebrace of plate to defend the arms and greaves to protect the legs, close fitting surcoat. It is decorated with the owner's coat of arms.
5. French armoured horseman, archer. He wears *brigantine*, i. e. plate armour. About 1450. At this time the cross-bow replaces the bow in battle.

Centre Group

6. Young Burgundian knight, 14th century, with upright

wings or *ailettes* fixed as shoulder or neck pieces to the ringed or chain mail.
7. Knight with bells hanging from the girdle, about 1350.
8. Polish archer. 14th century. From his girdle hangs the hook to stretch the bow.
9. Polish nobleman. 15th century.
10. Horseman alighted, about 1375.

Bottom Group

11–16. Italian battle dress in the 14th century.
11. Armoured soldier protected by numerous plates.
12. Condottiere (Italian general) in mangnificent ceremonial outfit, with field marshal's baton, chain mail covered by plates, surcoat, beret. Decorated horse trappings.
13 and 14. Foot soldiers, mercenaries.
15. Italian knight.
16. Mercenary wearing ringed mail under the *brigantine*. Naked legs. Calves and feet bandaged over pieces of material, narrow shield. Partly after paintings in the Campo-santo at Pisa (about 1350–60).

ENGLAND IN THE MIDDLE AGES. *10th–15th Centuries.* 37

Top Group

1. Anglo-Saxon, 10th century in a long-sleeved tunic gathered by a girdle with a short cape-like mantle fastened by a clasp or brooch on the right shoulder. Hose (in fact stockings sewn together) bandaged with straps or bands. Shoes made of soft material or leather.
2. Irish monk, 10th century.
3. Warrior of the 11th century (time of the Norsemen's invasions) in a thick armoured coat with small iron plates sewn on and a hood attached to it. Underneath tunic reaching down to the calves. Helmet with chinstrap and nose-protection. High soft leather boots.
4 and 5. Women of the 12th century in long-sleeved garments with small girdles and mantles fastened by a cord, a costume which was also common in Germany at the time of the

Hohenstaufen. The hair was gathered in the nape by a net. A *chapel* (crown-like cap with cheek and chin band).
6. Girl of the 13th century in a short-sleeved outer garment (cf. the *Suckenie* of the German costume of that period) over the long under garment with tight sleeves. Hooded collar for protection.

Centre Group

7–13. English costume of the 14th century, on the whole corresponding to the prevailing Burgundian-French fashion of the continent.

Bottom Group

14–20. English costume of the 15th century, also following the fashion on the continent. According to examples in Strutt: *Dress and Habits of the People of England*, 1862.

ARMOURED KNIGHTS. FRANCE AND GERMANY. *15th Century.* 38

Top Group

1–5. French.

1. French knight about 1405 in the earlier plate armour. Basinet with movable vizor, underneath the hood of mail with large camail. The plating of the armour which is laced at the back consists of small studded plates on which the skirt of tonlets is fastened as a protection of the loins.
2. French foot soldier under Charles VII. at the time of Joan of Arc about 1430 during the Hundred Years' War.
3. Archer from the same period.
4. French knight of the same period in plated armour. Helmet in the shape of a *salet* with vizor, shield with three buckles, battle axe.
5. Ceremonial armour from the time of King Louis XI. (1461 to 1483).

Centre Group

6–15. German

6. Armour in the princely armoury at Sigmaringen, supposed to have belonged to Count Eitel Friedrich I. of Hohenzollern (died 1439).
7. St. George from the altar by Hans Multscher (died 1463) in Sterzing, Tyrol.
8. St. George (after the wood carving of about 1420, formerly at Kaiser Friedrich Museum, Berlin).
9. St. Gereon (according to a painting in the Museum at Cologne).
10. Knight Konrad of Schauenburg (according to the tomb by Tilman Riemenschneider at Würzburg).

11. Johann von Eschbach (according to the tomb at Lorch on the Rhine).
12. St. Victor (according to a wood carving in the museum at Wiesbaden).

13. Plate armour about 1450.
14 and 15. Fluted harnesses about 1500. So-called Maximilian armour.

39 ITALIAN MONUMENTS REPRESENTING KNIGHTS. *13th to 15th Centuries.*

1. Statue of a horseman representing Mastino II. (died 1289), by Perino Milanese. 13th century, Verona, tomb of the Scaliger near the church of Santa Maria Antica, Verona.
2. Statue of a horseman, representing Can grande da Verona by Giovanni da Campione. 1329.
3. Tomb of Guglielmo Berardi near the church of Santissima Anunziata at Florence. 14th century.
4. Relief of a horseman (St. George with the dragon) with two

bearers of coats of arms. The armour in the antique tradition. Door lintel (sopraporta) on the palace at Vico Mele, Genoa. Lombard school. 15th century.
1–3. Show battle horses with large wide partly decorated trappings. The armoured knights wear 1. the high barrel helmet, 2. the basinet with a barrel helmet hanging down on the back, 3. the iron helmet over the hood of mail and 4. the *salet* with neck plate and vizor.

40 GERMANY. *Garments of People of Rank as represented by 13th Century Sculpture.*

1. Margrave Hermann von Meissen (died 1032) and his consort Reglindis. Statues in the west choir of the cathedral at Naumburg about 1250–70. Both wear the girdled long tunic with close fitting sleeves. The slit to widen the hole for slipping over the head is fastened on the breast by a brooch. Hermann also wears as an outer garment a sleeveless mantle (*Schaperun*) with six ornamental buttons and without girdle. The wide semi-circular mantle is kept in place by means of a band over the chest with flat brooches on both sides. The woman's hair is veiled by a kerchief passed round the chin. Over it she wears the *chapel* in the shape of a cap held in place by a crown-like fillet.
2. Margrave Ekkehard II. von Meissen (died 1046) and his consort Uta. Statues in the west choir of the cathedral at Naumburg. Costume like 1. The man in a long girdled tunic with mantle. The soft cap on his head does not entirely cover his curly hair. The woman's mantle has a high collar. Over the barbe (cf. 1) the cap-like *chapel* but a higher crown-shaped fillet.
3. *Foolish Virgin* and prince of the world as seducer. Statues on the south portal of the west façade of Strasbourg cathedral in Alsace (about 1280–1300). Both their garments

consist of the long-sleeved long tunic gathered by a girdle (not visible) which is covered by a wide sleeveless outer garment, the so-called *schaperun*, that of the man having short wide sleeves hanging down from the shoulders as well as ornamental buttons on the chest. The outer garment has slits at the sides which are fastened by buttons. Both wear the fillet-like *chapel* on their heads. The one of the man decorated like a crown.
4. *Synagogue* (Old Testament) with broken rod and veiled eyes. Statue at the side of the *princes* portal on the northern aisle of the Bamberg cathedral. About 1250. Long trailing garment of finest diaphanous material gathered by a girdle. A brooch at the base of the neck.
5. The Emperor Heinrich II. and his consort Kunigunde, the founders of the cathedral at Bamberg. Statues on the left jambs of the south-east portal (Adam's gate) of the cathedral at Bamberg. About 1240. The woman wears a long outer garment (*schaperun*) with girdle over the long girdled tunic, the man wears a mantle draped over one shoulder.
6. *Ekklesia* (the Church, the New Testament). Girdled garment with brooch like 4, covered by a shoulder mantle held by a band across the chest.

41 ARMOURED KNIGHTS. GERMANY AND BURGUNDY. *14th Century.*

Top Group

1–8. German.
1. Over the chain mail short leather doublet reaching down only as far as the loins; breast plate, helmet and helmet-protection. Legs cased in plate; knee cops.
2 and 3. Chain mail covered by leather doublet with chain sewn in.
4. Knight in indoor costume. Doublet, short close fitting cape over chest and back.

Centre Group

5. Knight wearing ermine coat and iron *knee cops* which are attached separately. They later on developed into greaves.
6. Leather doublet down to the loins, leather hose, knee cops.
7. Leather doublet worn over complete chain mail.

8. Doublet with pleated skirt both decorated with embroidered or woven coat of arms.

Bottom Group

9–12. Burgundian.
9 and 9a. Burgundian knight (about 1380) covered by a steel basinet with movable vizor. This form of helmet was called *Hundsgugel* in Germany. Small shield cut out at the side.
10. Knight from Neufchatel, without vizor, about 1370, wearing basinet with camail edge.
11. Standard-bearer about 1300 with the insignia of a crusader who has taken the vows (cross and pilgrim's staff). Flat topped helmet (*heaume*) with the vizor screwed on.
12. Knight's armour about 1370. Lance, large shield for horsemen who had alighted and tried to protect themselves with several of such shields against archers, etc.

Plate armour consisted of the following pieces: helmet with gorget, shoulder plates with pieces connecting them with breast and back plate casing for the arms, elbow cops, gauntlets, coat of mail with steel bands, loin covering, knee cops, greaves, iron shoes (following the fashion of the wide shoes after 1500). This armour of overlapping and movable plates and greaves was even more perfected under Maximilian I. by fluted plates which increased the power of resistance against attack. These coats of mail were called Maximilian armour or Milan armour.

1. German armour made of polished iron with movable iron bands. The metal is either polished or tarnished by oxidizing or applying acids or by painting it black.
2. German steel armour about 1515 with high shoulder plates (French: *passe-gardes*). The right shoulder plate is much smaller and appears as a sort of free-standing disk in order to leave room for fixing the jousting lance. The steel tonlets are rigid, not overlapping and movable.
3. Italian armour. The polished iron decorated by patterns produced by etching.
4. Italian round shield, made of six pieces, similar to the ones in use in Germany about 1500. In France called *rondache*.
5. Heavy helmet with vizor of polished iron (cf. plate 43).
6. Helmet with ear-like appliances standing out (called horse's face, i. e. *Roßstirn* in German). Iron, studded with brass nails and a thorn.
7. Burgundian helmet of polished iron with crest, with protruding nose and nape guards and cheek plates.
8. Iron cap with cheek guards.
9. Pointed iron cap, (called *Birnenhelm*=pear-shaped helmet in German).
10 and 11. Sword hilts with the so-called ass's hoof, ornamental bands surrounding hilt and blade.

Bottom Group

Tilting over the lists with coronet on the end of the lances (cf. plate 43). On the right: Frederick, Count Palatine; on the left: Duke Wilhelm IV. of Bavaria. According to the *Turnierbuch* (Tournament book) of the Bavarian Dukedom 1510–18. Original miniatures. Munich, Bayrische Staatsbibliothek.

EUROPE. MIDDLE AGES. *Helmets and Swords.* 43

1. Pointed helmet with nose guard *(nasal)*.
2. French copper helmet of the 12th century.
3 and 4. Flat topped helmet *(heaume)* with movable vizor, 1280.
5. Painted flat topped helmet *(heaume)*, 1240.
6. Italian flat topped helmet *(heaume)*. About 1250.
7. Head protection from a picture of the 9th century.
8 and 9. German swords 1100–1400.
10. Bassinet with vizor, a close fitting round cap. 1310.
11. Pointed helmet with side wings. French and English. About 1270. Not used after 1325.
12. German basinet. 1370.
13. Pointed basinet with vizor.
14–16. and 21. Northern swords. From the Copenhagen National Museum. 1000–1450.
17. Basinet with nose guard *(nasal)*. 1350.
18. German helmet worn for tilting. 1370.
19. Spanish basinet.
20. English basinet. 1380–90.
22. French sword. About 1375.
23. French basinet with vizor. 1350–90.
24. Spanish sword. 1480.
25. *Salet* with the Wittelsbach crest. 1449.
26. Danish sword. 1400.
27 and 29. Early spear heads of Norsemen.
28. French helmet. 1430.
30. Tournament helmet for fighting with swords and maces. About 1450.
31. French *salade* or salet. 1420.
32. Iron hat. 1460
33. Iron hat, Danish. About 1475.
34 and 36. Salets resembling more modern helmets.
35 a and b. Salets with *mentonnière*, chin protection. 1480.
37. Striped helmet *(armet)* with simple vizor. 1506.
38. Striped helmet *(armet)* with chin guard *(mentonnière)* and vizor.

Bottom Group

39. German knights tilting, from the end of the 12th century. (Reign of the Emperor Heinrich VI.). Helmets with nose guards *(nasals)*; Italian nasale; cf. fig. 1. Small shields, lances with pennons. Right: large horse-cover. From the manuscript of a south-Italian Norman.
40. Spanish knight in the tourney yard. According to a representation in the Alhambra near Granada.
41. Knight, jousting. Beginning of the 14th century. The spear of the opponent (whose picture has not been preserved) is not pointed but shows the little coronal usual at tournaments (sometimes a pointless metal end was fixed). Crested flat-topped helmet *(heaume)*. Surcoat and large horse cover (French: *housse*). From the Codex Balduini Trevirensis about 1330.
42. Helmet with crest (in the shape of a dragon) of King James I. of Aragon (died 1276). Imitating Oriental forms. Madrid. Armeria Real.

As to the development of helmets: The conical form of the 11th century develops into a large flat-topped (barrel-shaped) helmet *(heaume)* in the 12th century. This flat-topped helmet wrought in one piece is worn over the basinet which, from the 13th century replaced the hood of mail. From about 1300 onwards the basinet is worn without the heaume, developing into a more conical shape in the 14th century and later on becoming more pointed, and is completed by a nose-guard *(nasal)* and vizor. – The iron hat (32–33) is an old independent shape of helmet disdained by knights but worn by the ordinary soldiers, vassals, archers and cross-bow men. When later adopted by knights two slits were pierced into the front brim, through which the horseman with his head bent could look. This is the origin of the salet (French: salade = bowl. 35 a and 35 b) of the late 15th century which adopts the long horizontal slit for the eyes from the iron hat but has a less projecting brim. It also adds the *mentonnière* (35 b and 25) as a characteristic novelty. This mentonnière, a movable chin protection, is the forerunner of the vizor, also the neck guard of the salet, which originally is a rigid protecting part of the helmet (see figs. 31 and 35 a) becomes a movable joint made of several plates (36) – Tournament helmets vary according to purpose whether for tilting or jousting and often have the vizor made of steel bands or trellissed rods

(30). (They were specially favoured in heraldry). – In the time of Maximilian I. the so-called knight's helmet appears. It originated from the basinet, but the camail of the basinet gave way to the rigid steel plates, the gorget (as a protection of the neck) while the vizor consisted of two movable overlapping parts: the chin-guard and the vizor proper, which turn on the same pivot.

44 FRANCE. *14th Century.*

Top Group

1. Youth in a semi-long girdled doublet, hooded shoulder cape, hose and pointed shoes.
2. Girl wearing a long outer garment gathered by a girdle just below the breasts with wide low neck and sleeves hanging down to the knees. Her hair braided at the sides. (1 and 2 according to ivory tablets).
3. Princess wearing a long trailing garment with long sleeves and outer garment gathered at the waist in rich folds.
4. Prince wearing a close-fitting short doublet fastened in front by buttons and a low belt. The long open sleeves expose the long and patterned sleeves of the under garment. Hooded cape and parti-coloured hose (so-called *mi-parti*).
5. Courtier wearing jagged coat with jagged hooded cape (cf. German *Gugel*, plate 53, 9 and 10).
6. Girl wearing parti-coloured outer garment slashed open at the sides, with long hanging sleeves.
7. Figure similar to 5; back view, the hood *(gugel)* pulled over the head.

Centre Group

8. Knight wearing a girdled short close-fitting tunic with hood and a tight fitting hat with the narrow brim turned up.
9. Similar to 3, the garment shows a close fitting bodice.
10. Dandy in a short tight-fitting coat buttoned down the front, a belt round the hips, a collar with hood ending in a long liripipe.
11. Woman of rank wearing a long garment with long sleeves hanging down to the ground and having slits for the arms.

As an outer garment she wears the so-called surcoat, a sleeveless low-necked jacket which looks like a shoulder cape on this figure.

12. Prince at the court of Charles V. of France (died 1380) with a cloak-like outer garment with long padded sleeves (so-called *tabard*). On his head a cap with a liripipe worn round the neck. The high, upright collar is attached to the short tunic under the coat.

Bottom Group

13. Women of rank in a long-sleeved gown with a girdle right under the breasts. Head-dress: the new-fashioned conical hat (steeple cap) with a long flowing veil.
14. Judge wearing a long fur trimmed tunic *(tabard, cf. 12)* slashed open at the sides, slit sleeves padded at the shoulders. Narrow-brimmed hat.
15. Youth wearing the new-fashioned short and close-fitting jacket with wide sleeves exposing the tight sleeves of the under garment.
16. Prince wearing the knee-length bell-shaped outer cloak *(heuque* or *huque*; in German: *Hoike* or *Heuke).* Slit sleeves over the short tunic with standing collar. Hat with liripipe.
17. Distinguished citizen in a long wide outer cloak *(tabard).*
18. Young courtier in a short, girdled outer jacket with half open hanging sleeves over the short under jacket which has standing collar and tight sleeves. Turban-like cap. (The short jacket was called *jacquette* in French and *Schecke* or *Hänslein* in German.)

45 BURGUNDIAN FASHION *represented in Flemish Book Illustrations (Miniatures) of the 15th Century.*

Top Picture

Reception and banquet at the court of the Duke of Burgundy. Miniature from the *Geschichte des Karl Martell* (history of Charles Martel). Painted at Bruges 1470 by Loyset Liédet. The ladies on the left wearing the high conical Burgundian steeple cap *(hennin)* and long trailing gowns girdled under the breasts; the men wearing either the short jacket or long coat with padded sleeves *(mahoîtres)*, high or medium high hats with narrow brims, long pointed shoes without the wooden sandals attached (cf. plate 51).

Bottom Picture

Coronation ceremony with retinue. Miniature from Jean

Mansel's *Fleur des histoires*, painted about 1425–1435 by the so-called *Mansel Master.* Most of the women wear the high head-dress made of kerchiefs and drawn out at the sides to the form of a pair of bull's horns wide veil, and a long fur trimmed outer garment draped in such a way as to expose the gown beneath. Short low-necked bodice. The kneeling woman on the left as well as two others in the outer court wear, in place of the short low-necked bodice, an ermine jacket with pieces cut away under the arms and on the hips. These jackets were worn by princesses, only on ceremonial occasions and weddings, in the 15th century. (Photographs by Prof. Dr. Friedrich Winkler.)

46 BURGUNDY. HEAD-DRESS. *15th Century.*

1. Middle class woman with a large linen head-dress, covering the hair. According to R. van der Weyden.
2. Distinguished Italian merchant (representing his country in Bruges) wearing high Burgundian beaver hat, 1434, accord-

ing to Jan van Eyck's double portrait of Arnolfini and his wife.
3. Burgomaster's wife from Bruges, 1480, in a medium high Burgundian cap with veil (so-called *hennin*). According to Memling.

4. Man with conical cap.

5. Learned man with hat made of a roll of material from which folds of cloth hang down (cf. 6 and 8). According to Quentin Massys.

6. Burgundian man of rank in the new-fashioned turban-hat. 1433. According to Jan van Eyck.

7. Duke Philip the Good of Burgundy (died 1467) with cropped hair giving the impression of a wig.

8. The same merchant Arnolfini in a hat made of a roll of stuff from which on one side the liripipe is hanging down and from the other a piece of material (cf. 5). According to Jan van Eyck. 1439.

9. Youth from Bruges with long curled hair falling down to his shoulders. According to Hans Memling. 1487.

10. The Count of Croy with his hair cut like 7. According to Hans Memling.

LATE MIDDLE AGES. FOOTWEAR *(Pointed shoes and wooden under-shoes).* 47

1. Pointed shoe with wooden under-shoe.

2. Pointed shoes with the point turned up and wooden under-shoes.

3 and 4. Pointed shoe in the museum of Colmar in Alsace (about 1460). (The under-shoe is a later and incorrect reconstruction).

5. Pointed shoe in addition to greaves and spurs.

6. Pointed shoe, part of the armour.

7. Ordinary wooden under-shoe, seen from above.

8. Pointed under-shoe. Side view.

9. Elongated flat under-shoe, side view.

10. Elongated under-shoe seen from above.

11. The same shoe seen from below.

12. Pointed boot of king James I. of Scotland.

13. Pointed boot with short under-shoe.

14. Short pointed shoe seen from below.

15. Pointed shoe.

16. Shoe as part of the armour, similar to 6.

17. Flat under-shoe showing the straps.

18. Thick under-shoe with wide strap in front. (According to originals and works by Hefner von Alteneck, Weiss, von Falke and Heyne). These pointed shoes (French: poulaine = prow) are already mentioned at the Synod of Reims 972, it is true but they only became fashionable in the 14th century, originating in France they were imitated in Burgundy, from there went to Germany, England and Scotland. During the whole of the 15th century they were considered a requisite of distinguished costume. The points were sometimes turned up or held up by bands or chains. The wooden under-shoes worn as a protection against the dirt and mud of the unpaved streets were mostly raised by thick heels. We hear from a chronicle of 1480 that the fashion of the pointed shoe disappeared about this time and that shoes with broad toes came into fashion which after 1500 remained in use for about a generation.

ITALY. EARLY RENAISSANCE. *1485–90 according to Mural Paintings by Domenico Ghirlandaio.* 48

Top Picture

A Florentine woman of rank (Ludovica Tornabuoni) and her retinue visiting a woman in childbed. *Birth of Mary*, mural painting by Domenico Ghirlandaio, choir chapel of Santa Maria Novella, Florence (left wall) 1486–90.

Bottom Picture

Birth of John the Baptist. Mural painting by Ghirlandaio (as above, right wall).

Both pictures show characteristic costumes of Florentine women and girls of different classes towards the end of the Early Italian Renaissance.

GERMAN KNIGHTS' *apparel about 1500–1515.* 49

1. Knights riding to take part in tilting, i. e. display of fighting by several combatants. Plate harness with overlapping pieces at the joints. Lances with blunt points. They were not manipulated by the hand alone but they were supported by two hooks, attached to the armour, one holding the lance from below and the one in front from above to keep it in a horizontal position. The horses, too, (strong stallions) had plates of armour on their heads. In addition, there were the magnificent tournament trappings, often embroidered with symbolical pictures and letters. The shape of the surcoat with long wide skirts corresponds to men's fashion

about 1500. (From the tourney book by Hans Burgkmair, the Younger; formerly in the possession of the Princes of Hohenzollern.)

Bottom Picture

Tournament with pointed lances. Knights jousting. On the left Duke William IV. of Bavaria (died 1550), on the right Ritter von Egloffstein. (According to the tourney book of Duke William IV. of Bavaria.) Original miniatures in the Bavarian State Library, Munich about 1515.

FRANCE. *First Half of the 15th Century.* 50

Top Group

1–4. Young men of rank hawking; 1 and 2 wearing wide and long fur-trimmed girdled coats, open in front over short *pourpoint* or *jacquette*, small beret with ostrich feather over the tight fitting cap *(calotte)*. 3 and 4 wearing short skirted coats, conical hats with narrow brim, tight hose and soles attached under the feet.

5 and 6. Youths wearing short fur-trimmed jackets with slits

for the arms, exposing the long sleeves of the tunic. Soft pointed shoes, 5 with under-shoes, high heeled wooden soles as a protection against the mud in the streets.

Centre Group

7. Similar to 1 and 2 with specially long sleeves.

8 and 9. Elderly men in long gowns (slipped over the head).

10. Lady wearing the sleeveless surcoat slipped over the head over the wide-sleeved outer garment, showing the narrow sleeves of the undergarment.
11. Lady wearing a veiled coif drawn out into two points at the sides and a short-sleeved outer garment over the patterned under-garment which has wide sleeves sewn onto it.
12. Princess wearing a low-necked trailing and girdled outer garment over the long-sleeved undergarment.

FRANCE. *(Charles VIII., 1483-98, Louis XII., 1498-1515).*

Top Group

1. Lady wearing a somewhat shorter garment over a trailing under-garment and a head-dress in the Italian style covering ears and nape.
2. Man of rank in hunting costume with a horn hanging from a belt and wearing a beret, a knee-length coat with turned up cuffs and richly decorated borders. The shoes are slightly pointed (forming the transition to the broad toes of the 16th century).
3. Queen with a long trailing outer garment with slits for the arms and a veil falling down from her head.
4 and 5. Ladies in waiting wearing draped outer garments with low cut neck exposing the fine Frisian linen. The woman on the right wears a head-dress covering the nape with a sort of roll on top.

Centre Group

6 and 7. King in a long sleeveless fur-trimmed mantle over the long pleated skirted doublet, close-fitting cap under the beret. Shoes with broad toes. Behind him the squire carrying his sword (6) wearing an outer garment which is fastened up at the front.

8. Man of rank, sitting with a flute. Mantle with long sleeves hanging down to the knees. Medium length hair. Beret.
9. Lady of rank in a trailing gown with long wide hanging sleeves with slits for the arms, showing the sleeves of the undergarment. Velvet turban-like cap fastened under the chin.
10. Man in a ceremonial costume: under-garment with scarlet sleeves, over it long sleeveless trailing gown, slashed open at the sides and fastened by means of ribbons. Red chain round his neck made of tassels. Medium length hair, cut straight over the forehead. Flat broad shoes.

Bottom Group

11. Lady in mourning. Hood-like veil with pleated kerchief in front, so-called barbette. Long fur-lined gown.
12. Old man wearing wide mantle with cape-like collar. Berte with ostrich feather. Wide shoes with slits (about 1510).
13. Messenger with sealed letter. Coat as worn by heralds (shape of the dalmatica) with embroidered heraldic designs. The staff is the emblem of the messenger.
14 and 15. Distinguished couple wearing garments similar to 4 and 10.

BURGUNDIAN FASHION. *1425-90.*

Top Group

1 and 2. Courtiers about 1470 wearing a long *houppelande*, i. e. the long ceremonial girdled garment, open in front mostly with long sleeves and padded shoulders *(mahoîtres)*. High padded conical caps.
3 and 4. Ladies of the court, in long trailing gowns with high girdles and low cut neck. They wear the high Burgundian caps (steeple caps) with veils or fine linen kerchiefs forming an elaborate decoration (3). The under-garment *(cotte)* can hardly be seen.
5. Young Burgundian Duke (Charles the Bold) wearing a medium-length girdled outer coat over the short doublet *(pourpoint)* with collar and long sleeves. Fur beret with ostrich feather.

Centre Group

6. Queen Charlotte (of Savoy), consort of Louis XII. of France, wearing a Burgundian costume with steeple cap *(hennin,* cf. 9).
7. Young courtier wearing long fur-trimmed *houppelande* open in front with low cut neck (cf. 1 and 2). Attached to his girdle is the bag for alms *(aumônière)*.
8. Duke Philip the Good (died 1467) wearing the costume of the Grand Master of the *Order of the Golden Fleece.* The characteristic liripipe is hanging down from the cap.
9 and 10. Archduke Maximilian of Austria (later Emperor

Maximilian I) and his betrothed, Maria of Burgundy, daughter of Charles the Bold. 1477. (According to a drawing in the Germanische Museum, Nuremberg). Maximilian wearing the *houppelande* open in front over the laced jacket. Shoes with broad toes, no longer the pointed shoes. Maria is wearing the well-known Burgundian costume.

Bottom Group

11. Young man (about 1425) in a half-length jacket with skirt, consisting of four overlapping pieces which are jagged at the edges and embroidered with gold. Out of the sleeves, at the wrists, fall long white jagged linen streamers. The fashion of jagging (i. e. indenting the borders) spread especially from Burgundy at the beginning of the 15th century. His shoulders are covered by a red velvet cape. He wears a wide-brimmed hat made of material with feathers and tightly sewn hose on his legs, as well as wooden undershoes (cf. plate 50). His hair is cut short round the head giving the impression of a cap.
12. Lady in a long trailing girdled gown. On her head a gold-bordered piece of cloth, a flat bag fixed on top of the cap (similar to the kerchief of Italian peasant woman in modern times).
13. Man going hawking, wearing the heavy sleeveless *hoike* (bellshaped coat) which is slashed open at the sides and ornamented with jagging. It is made of velvet and lined

with fur. The gauntlet for hawking, made of stag-leather, has large cuffs. Gaiters round the calves. Pointed shoes. Cap made of a bag and a piece of cloth hanging down, both jagged.

14. Duke Philip the Good of Burgundy. Padded cap with long liripipe. The ringed mail-coat can be seen at the neck under the plates of the armour. Fur-trimmed surcoat and cape

round his shoulders are decorated with armorial designs.

15. Young man of rank wearing fur-trimmed *hoike* with wide sleeves fastened on the left shoulder with three jags by means of three buttons. When unbottoned the garment can be slipped over the head. The lower part of the legs is covered by a kind of gaiters. Hair cut straight in front (cf. 11).

Top Group

1 and 2. Italian princes. 1. wearing a long tunic buttoned down the middle and along the sleeves with lined cloak. 2. wearing a short close-fitting sleeved doublet with a girdle round the lower part. This short doublet, fashionable in Burgundy and France since 1380, exposes the long hose. Shoulder mantle buttoned on the right shoulder according to older fashions. (From the Florentine painting of the *Adoration of the Kings*, about 1375 to 1400, formerly Berlin, Kaiser Friedrich Museum.)

3 and 4. Queen and princess. Back part of the head and the neck covered by the so-called *Rise* made of linen. Short-sleeved outer garment with ermine trimming over the long-sleeved under-garment. (According to a miniature, Naples 1352).

5 and 6. Lady (6) with servant (5) both wearing a high-girdled coloured outer garment with semi-long wide sleeves over a longer under-garment. The lady wears a wide cloak over it. (According to Giotto's frescoes in the Capella dell'Arena at Padua about 1305–8).

Centre Group

7. Municipal mercenary wearing a short girdled coat with sleeves and a basinet.

8. Man of rank wearing a cloth hat with the ends of the cloth capuccio sticking out. Underneath a white cap covering the cheeks. Long wide mantle with wide sleeves (the costume of learned men) about 1350.

9 and 10. People of rank in a short girdled tight coat with hanging sleeves and a hood which was worn with the liri-pipe (originally only worn by lower-class people, in German called *Gugel*) about 1350.

11. Lady about 1320 wearing a richly draped outer garment with wide sleeves over the trailing tunic with buttoned sleeves and a narrow high collar which is sewn on. Veil-like kerchief.

12 and 13. Man of rank (side and front views) about 1320. Under-garment reaching down to the knees. Right: open mantle with a hood sewn on, decorated with a long liripipe.

Bottom Group

14–16. Noble ladies about 1340 wearing long trailing gowns with narrow braid trimming around the neck. 15 and 16 wear an outer garment with wide or hanging sleeves over the long-sleeved under-garment. Over the fine plaited hair 14 wears a round cap with the ends of the pleated cloth standing up, 16 wears a draped veil with lappets.

17. Musician (knight) in a long coat (slashed open at the sides) over a tight-sleeved under-garment. The garland of the Minnesingers on his head.

18. Young lady of rank wearing a medium-length sleeveless outer-garment over the long tunic with long and tight-fitting sleeves. Plaits arranged like garlands on the head.

19. Citizen in a long garment and a shorter outer garment (like 18) slit at the sides with a hole for the neck. Cap over the linen cap with lappets.

20. Ordinary citizen in a short girdled coat and cap, the cloth ends hanging down.

21. Gentleman about 1370 wearing a fastened-up cloth coat with jagged seam and hood with collar attached on to the coat. According to small sculptures and paintings of the 14th century, partly according to frescoes of the Campo-santo at Pisa.

Top Group

1–4. Heralds in short outer garments, some with girdles over a shorter jacket recognizable only by the tight sleeves.

5. Man of rank (king) in a long coat with hanging sleeves.

6. Youth in a short quilted garment with wide sleeves decorated with emblems.

7 and 8. Youths in dark mantles, on their heads caps made by pieces of cloth wound round the head and with liripipe according to the fashion of the Burgundian turban caps.

Centre Group

9. Falcon-bearer wearing a girdled mantle slashed open at the sides which is slipped over the head, so-called giubberello (cf. fig. 1).

10. Very short jacket with sleeves cut wide on top. Outer garment (like 9).

11–15. Group of soldiers. 11 and 14 officers wearing surcoat (cut like 1 and 2) with short sleeves over the plate armour. The soldiers in short jackets some with mantles. Helmets; 11 iron hat, 13 conical pointed basinet with chin-strap, 14 and 15 flat iron caps. 1–8 from Masaccio's (Florence) paintings *Birth of the Virgin* and *Adoration of the Kings*. 11–15 from the *Martyrdom of St. Peter and John the Baptist* by the same artist (about 1425). 9 according to Vittore Pisano's (called Pisanello) *Adoration of the three Kings*, 10 according to Domenico Veneziano, both about 1450.

Bottom Group

16. Duke of Mantua in a girdled mantle (like 9) over short jacket with slit sleeves. Brimless cap (according to Man-tegna's frescoes in the castle of Mantua about 1475).

17. Italian knight wearing wide brimmed straw-hat and plate armour over the middle part of which the feather or fur-trimmed surcoat is worn (according to Pisanello's painting: *St. Anthony and St. George* about 1450).

18 and 19. Men's costume from Viterbo. Fez-like caps with or without brim, light sleeveless mantle (similar to 9), the one of the youth on the right is open in front. Slit sleeves with tags (according to Lorenzo da Viterbo's *Marriage of the Virgin*, fresco 1469).

20 and 21. Venetian men's costume made of magnificent material. 20: Fur-trimmed mantle, ambassador's chain, bracelet. 21: Magnificent richly ornamented pleated coat with girdle *(giubbone)* and hanging sleeves. Large hat with fur-brim. Hair falling down to the shoulders.

55 NORTHERN ITALY. EARLY RENAISSANCE *(1440–90) under the Influence of Burgundian Fashion.*

Top Group

1 and 2. Elegant Veronese youths about 1440.

1. In a simple mantle, the *giubberello* in the shape of a *poncho* slit at the sides and without girdle.

2. Wearing a short pleated and quilted jacket with wide winglike sleeves. He wears the originally Burgundian cap which is made of material draped round the head. (1 and 2 according to Pisanello's *Adoration of the three holy Kings*.

3. A representation of a scholar wearing a white fur beret with liripipe.

4. Venetian woman about 1470 wearing an outer garment with slit sleeves, a low neck, double roll cap with veil.

5. Young man with spurs, perhaps a messenger in a short coat trimmed with bells.

Centre Group

6–11. Lombard rich ceremonial costume (according to Vivarini's *Adoration of the three holy Kings*).

6. Groom.

7. Flautist wearing a jagged mantle (cf. Fig. 1: giubberello) over a short brown jacket with parti-coloured hose *(mi-parti)*.

8 and 11 wear the long bell-shaped, fur-lined surcoat *(tabarro)* with open wing-sleeves, partly jagged.

8. One of the kings, 9 and 11 distinguished companions of this king.

9. He wears a half-length jagged outer coat *(giubbone)* with a low belt. On his head the short liripipe *(mazocchio)*.

10. Herald.

Bottom Group

12–14. Venetian costume about 1490 (according to Carpaccio's *Ursula* series, Venice, Academy).

12 and 13. Page and falcon-bearer.

14. Podestà, i. e. burgomaster in a long, wide *houppelande* with wide fur-lined sleeves.

15 and 16. Venetian youths, members of a distinguished guild, the *Compagnia della Scalza* (meaning: stocking), i. e. a sort of *maître de plaisir:* 15 with a short jacket and parti-coloured hose. 16 wearing a long trailing mantle (according to Carpaccio's painting *The Wonder of the Cross*, Venice).

56 ITALY. EARLY RENAISSANCE. *1350-1500*

Top Group

1. Young florentine man about 1350 in a long girdled parti-coloured robe of former fashion (according to Taddeo Gaddi, Florence).

2. Hooded cloak over a short tunic with low belt. Close fitting hose and pointed shoes. 1370.

3. Long hooded cloak fastened by buttons.

4. Cloak with wide sleeves. The hood is attached to a special shoulder cape. The liripipe goes out of fashion before the end of the 14th century.

5. Head of the hospital at Siena wearing a long robe and a mantle made of watered silk. Beret (beretto) worn by officials. About 1375.

Centre Group

6. Florentine nobleman about 1400 in a cap shaped like a bag and a long girdled cloak with wide sleeves.

7. Gentleman wearing a short-sleeved cloak over a long-sleeved garment. Gloves with the cuffs extended to a bag. Cap made of a roll of material, the ends falling down onto the shoulders. According to a painting by Fra Angelico about 1450.

8. Lady about 1420 wearing a girdled outer garment with long wide hanging fur-trimmed sleeves. Round cap made of a roll of material over the hair which is arranged in a roll round the head.

9. Young man of rank about 1420. Girdled outer-garment with wide pleated and fur-lined sleeves. Hat decorated with a feather.

Bottom Group

10. Archer wearing small round cap with feather.

11–14. Venetian youths in different attire.

(10–14) according to paintings by Vittore Carpaccio about 1495.

57 ITALY. EARLY RENAISSANCE. *Head-dresses and Hair Styles.*

At the courtly time of the *minnesingers* Latin races preferred fair hair (as had the women of Imperial Rome, who wore the imported fair hair of the Germanic women) and this fashion was still fostered during the Renaissance from the 14th to the 16th centuries. This is specially apparent in Venetian portraits of women who took great pains to bleach their hair. Shaving the eyebrows and the hair of the forehead, sometimes up to the middle of the head in order to show *an egg-like moulded brow* was fashionable in the Middle Ages, and was especially brought to perfection in Italy in the 15th century.

1. Woman's head by Sandro Botticelli with yellow-brown curls and plaits entwined with pearls.

2. Maddalena Doni, née Strozzi. According to a painting by Raphael.
3. Woman's head. Painting by Piero della Francesca.
4 and 5. Venetian courtesans. Details from a painting by Vittore Carpaccio. Venice about 1505.
6. Piero de' Medici, father of Lorenzo (8), died 1469. After a medal.

7. Young woman. Painting by Domenico Veneziano about 1458–60.
8. Lorenzo de' Medici, son of Piero (6). After a medal.
9. Giuliano de' Medici, brother of Lorenzo (murdered in 1478 by the party of the Pazzi). Painting by Sandro Botticelli.
10. Angelo Doni. Painting by Raphael.
11. Self portrait of the Venetian painter Gentile Bellini.

GERMANY IN THE LATE MIDDLE AGES. *Costume of Craftsmen and Burghers* 58

Top Group

1–7. After drawings from the so-called *Mittelalterliche Hausbuch* (mediaeval housebook), an illuminated manuscript in the possession of the prince of Waldburg-Wolfegg (about 1480).
1. Copper-smith with turban-cap and wooden under-shoes under the pointed shoes.
2. Man of the lower classes wearing a round brimmed hat.
3. Woodcarver wearing short sleeveless outer jacket.
4 and 5. Peasant and peasant woman.
6 and 7. Young distinguished couple. She is wearing a trailing garment with laced bodice, he has a short shoulder mantle over a short sleeved jacket.

Centre Group

3. Wearing a long fur-lined gown open in front (German: *Schaube*) and a fur beret.
4. Distinguished burgher wearing a half length coat with skirts and long sleeves wide at the ends. Beret over tight-fitting cap, broad flat shoes.

10–13. People taking part in a ball, the women in long trailing garments. 10: With long trailing sleeves. 11: With Burgundian steeple cap; the youths: 12 in a short jacket laced by cords over the low-cut neck, pointed shoes; 13: In a long skirted coat with a low-cut neck. (After a copperplate by Israhel von Meckenem in Westphalia, died 1503.)

Bottom Group

14. North German peasant with spade and shepherd's staff. Sickle in his girdle. (According to a Lübeck woodcarving.)
15. Mercenary with halberd, armour and sallet (vessel-like helmet). According to a chronicle at Bern about 1485.
16. Executioner's assistant (with wooden logs) wearing pointed cap. (After woodcarvings by Michael Wohlgemuth.)
17. Jew with the yellow ring to mark his race. (According to woodcarvings by Michael Wohlgemuth.)
18. Archer (mercenary) wearing *iron hat*.

SPAIN IN THE MIDDLE AGES. *(Late 13th to 15th Centuries)* 59

Top Group

1 and 2. Burghers about 1275. Outer-garments with wide three-cornered sleeves with light border decoration. Hooded shoulder-capes.
3. Knight (caballero) about 1300. Shoulder cape with decorated border.
4. Lightly armed horseman in a sleeveless surcoat without girdle. Small leather-covered wooden shield studded with metal.
5. King about 1350 (Painting in the Alhambra, Granada).
6. Knight about 1375. Helmet with vizor, ringed coat of mail, parti-coloured doublet covering the loins and slit open at the sides, low-belt made of gold-plated pieces of metal. Light coloured morocco leather shoes.

Centre Group

7. Knight about 1375. Blue and white turban-cap, red hood with collar and long liripipe, white tight-fitting coat reaching to the loins. Low gold-plated girdle, yellow hose, shoes like 6.
8. Court lady wearing long red gown with blue sleeves and

white sleeveless outer garment with gold braids. Necklace and earrings. On her head a garland.
9. Court lady wearing a white mantle lined with red material and the borders trimmed with gold braid over a white outer-garment. The under-garment is of reddish-violet colour. Bleached hair. 8 and 9 about 1300.
10. Man of rank about 1400 wearing high pointed hat and fur-trimmed cloak (houppelande).
11 and 12. Soldiers about 1400 wearing *brigantine* and over it a leather doublet. Iron gloves, round shield with hollow for the fist.

Bottom Group

13. Rodrigo de Lauria (died 1314).
14. Lady of rank about 1390. Doña Elvira de Ayala.
15. Spanish Countess 1353.
16. Lady about 1435.
17. Man of rank about 1430.
18. Don Alvara Perez de Guzman, Admiral of the kingdom of Castile. 1394. (13–18) according to *Iconografia Española*.

GERMANY *about 1500* 60

Top Group

1 and 2. Huntsmen.
3. Bag-piper.
4. Nuremberg citizen's wife ⎫
5. Young peasant. ⎪ according to Albrecht
6. Peasant girl. ⎬ Dürer's paintings.
7. Old peasant. ⎭

Centre Group

8–13. Peasants at the time of the Peasants' Revolt 1524–1525 (according to representations by Dürer, H. S. Beham and others).

Bottom Group

14–19. Vagrants (according to Hans Burgkmair's *Triumphzug Kaiser Maximilians* (The Triumph of Emperor Maximilian).

61   ITALY. RENAISSANCE *1520–30. According to Contemporary Paintings*

1. Picture of a young woman called *La Bella* by Francesco Mazzuoli, (called Parmigianino), about 1530. Naples National Museum.
2. Italian nobleman. Painting by Alessandro Bonvicino, called Moretto da Brescia, about 1525. London, National Gallery.
3. Italian nobleman. Painting by Moretto, 1526. London, National Gallery.
4. Woman and child. Painting by Paris Bordone, about 1525. Leningrad, Eremitage.

62   GERMANY AT THE TIME OF THE REFORMATION. *Head-dress (1500–50)*

1. The Emperor Maximilian I. According to Dürer's painting.
2. The Elector Frederick the Wise of Saxony, 1534. According to Dürer.
3. Ulrich von Hutten. 1520.
4. Bernhard Knipperdollinck, a draper and one of the heads of the Anabaptists at Münster, 1534.
5. Duke William IV. of Bavaria, painted in the year of his death, 1550.
6. Leonhard von Eck, 1475–1550, the efficient chancellor and statesman of Duke William IV. of Bavaria (He should not be confused with Johann Eck, who had a disputation with Luther). Engraving by B. Beham. 1527.
7. A 24-year-old member of the Augsburg patrician family of the Welsers, painted in 1533.
8. Sebastian Münster, the scholar and cosmographer who came from Ingelheim and lived in Basle 1489–1552. Painted by Christian Amberger.
9. Katharina von Bora, who married Luther in 1525. According to Cranach.

63   ENGLAND DURING THE REFORMATION PERIOD. *(Henry VIII., 1509–47).*

1. Edward, Prince of Wales, son of Jane Seymour, 15 months old. About 1538. New York. Mellon Collection.
2. Anne of Cleves, later Queen of England, 1530. Paris, Louvre.
3. King Edward VI. as a youth, about 1548. Windsor Castle. (cf. Plate 88).
4. Jane Seymour 1536. Vienna, Kunsthistorisches Museum. 1, 2 and 4 paintings by Hans Holbein, the Younger. 3 Painting by an unknown English painter about 1548, in Holbein's style.

64   SPANISH FASHION. *1550–80, according to Contemporary Paintings.*

1. Philip II. of Spain. Painting by Anthonis Mor. Althorp, Lord Spencer's Collection.
2. Isabella of Valois, Queen of Spain (third wife of Philip II). Painting by Pantoja de la Cruz. Madrid, Prado.
3. Don Carlos, Infante of Spain (son of Philip II.) Painting by Anthonis Mor. Formerly Cassel, Picture Gallery.
4. The Infante Don Diego of Spain (son of Philip II.) Painting by Sanchez Coello. Collection of the Earl of Northbrooke.

65   GERMANY AT THE REFORMATION PERIOD. *Citizen's Costume and Peasants, 1510–1550.*

1. Scholar of the University of Strasbourg. 1516.
2 and 3. Scholar with three distinguished students. 1512.
4. Peasant 1512.
5. Peasant from the Upper Rhine carrying the flag of liberty of the so-called *Bundschuhe* (laced shoes). 1520.
6. Wife of a patrician wearing high cap and pleated mantle (worn out-of-doors). 1516.
7. Couple, patricians from Münster in Westphalia during a wedding-dance. According to Aldegrever's series of copper plates: *Wedding-dancers* 1538.
8. Swabian peasant with hooded shoulder cape and short pleated skirt. 1521.
9. Mayor, member of a court martial. Upper Rhine. 1512.
10. University professor of law. 1549.
11. Merchant of Augsburg. 1539.
12. Patrician's wife from the Electorate of Saxony. 1550.
13. Horseman (servant from Augsburg). 1539.
14. Mercenary officer. 1549.

66   ITALY. RENAISSANCE. *Head-dress and Hair styles (1500–1550)*

Persons of the Renaissance with the typical head-dress and hair styles as well as the characteristic collar fashions of the period.
1. Self-portrait of Raphael (1482–1520)
2. According to Sebastiano del Piombo (1483–1547).
3. According to Francesco Franciabigio (Florentine painter 1482–1525).
4. Lady of the time of the new Duchy of Tuscany. According to Bronzino (1502–1572).
5. Person of rank according to a painting of northern Italy.
6. Venetian woman. According to Paris Bordone (1500–1570).
7. According to a painting by Girolamo Romanini (Brescia 1485–1566).
8. According to a picture by Lorenzo Lotto. (Venetian painter, about 1480–1556).
9. Pietro Aretino, famous and notorious author, ruthless literary money maker and libertine (1492–1557), came from Arezzo, but lived mainly in Venice. According to a painting by Titian.

Top Group

1–8. Participants in a betrothal celebration (Ferrara?). The women 1–3 wearing sleeveless girdled outer garments over long garments with a low-cut neck and long slightly slit sleeves. The betrothed wears her long hair falling down to the knees instead of a veil. The men 5–8 are wearing long cloaks reaching down to the ground and some of them girdled and with long hanging sleeves (8) and with a high collar (7 and 8). The bridegroom (4) has a shorter cloak with slit sleeves and a small cap on his half length curled hair, with the part over the forehead cut in a fringe. According to a picture painted by a Ferrara artist between 1460 and 70. Formerly in the Kaiser Friedrich Museum, Berlin.

Centre Group

9–13. Venetians about 1496. 9, 11–13 in long coats with wide sleeves (9) or with hanging sleeves (12 and 13) over long-sleeved tunics most of them buttoned up to the neck. Narrow-brimmed stiff hats worn over the tight-fitting caps. The youth (10) is wearing a short jacket (giubberello) with wide inserted sleeves open at the sides over a still shorter long-sleeved jacket. Parti-coloured hose *(mi-parti)* and flat

leather soles. This striking hose points him out as a member of the *Compagnia della Calza* (Hose company), a group of young Venetian noblemen. (According to Gentile Bellini's painting of the procession on St. Mark's square, dated 1496. Venice Academy.)

Bottom Group

14. Italian youth with shield and spear in a girdled fur-edged giubberello with the medium length sleeves attached by laces. Parti-coloured hose and soft shoes.
15. Ferrara dandy wearing a somewhat longer fur-trimmed giubberello with trailing sleeves open at the top over a short jacket buttoned up to the neck. Arrow and hoop in his hands. (Part of the fresco by Franc. Cossa), about 1470 in the Palace, Ferrara.
16. Girls' costume at Ferrara: High-girdled trailing brocade gown with a V-neck. Small cap (From the same fresco).
17. Florentine Patrician woman about 1490 in the *giornea*, a sleeveless garment open at the sides and slipped over the head. The garment underneath with slit sleeves. Ingeniously plaited hair. (According to Domenico Ghirlandaio's fresco *The Visitation* at Florence, Santa Maria Novella.)

Top Group

1–8. The Doge of Venice in ceremonial costume with his retinue.
1 and 3. Retinue of the Doge, 15th century.
2. Venetian Jew. 15th century.
4. Cushion-bearer in the Doge's public procession. About 1500.
5 and 6. Venetian Doge with canopy-bearer in a ceremonial procession about 1500.
7 and 8. Trumpeter in the Doge's procession. The shape of the Doge's cap *(il corno* or *beretta ducale)* was developed from the fisherman's cap (similar to the Phrygian cap) and was made of stiff brocade with a crown-like fillet.

Centre Group

9. Young man from Padua. 1508.

10. Recruiting officer wearing a turban. Milan 1505.
11. Venetian negro as a gondolier.
12. Youth from Siena. (According to Sodoma).
13. Venetian about 1505. (According to Giorgione).

Bottom Group

14–16. Young Florentines in short doublets slit in front; long tight-fitting hose, in front cod-piece.
17. The same. – The fashion of slashed and puffed trousers begins to appear.
18. Young student in a half-length coat fastened up to the low-cut neck.
19. Mercenary officer in parti-coloured costume.

Top Group

1. Lady of rank wearing the Burgundian *hennin* (steeple hat draped with veils).
2. Girl wearing a brimmed conical hat.
3. Woman wearing *hennin* divided in the middle. (Bull's horns cap.)
4. Girl wearing a wide trailing outer garment (in German called *Tappert*) with wing-like sleeves and a jagged cap.
5. Merchant in a short *heuke* with long hanging sleeves and hat made of a thick turban-like roll of material. About 1407.
6. Man wearing a knee-length girdled coat with short sleeves over a long-sleeved short doublet.

Centre Group

7. Man wearing a tight-fitting jacket with baggy sleeves (in German called *Schecke*).

8. Knight.
9. Lower Rhenish costume.
10–12. Gentleman and youths in quilted jackets.

Bottom Group

13. Knight in armour.
14. Herald wearing high leather boots. The herald, as an official messenger, wears the armorial designs and colours of his master or his authorities on his coat.
15. Man of rank wearing a wide coat (German: *Tappert*).
16. Young knight with falcon.
17. Dandy.
18. Wife of an innkeeper.

Mercenaries take the place of the technically antiquated knights and form the modern army towards the end of the 15th century. They are recruited from citizens and peasants but partly also from young impoverished knights.

Top and Centre Group

1–9. The characteristics of the costume are: the parti-coloured costume (so-called *mi-parti*), the slashings on sleeves, doublet and trousers. The beret is decorated with feathers which attained their largest size about 1525–30. Leather doublet, mantle thrown round the shoulders, wide, flat shoes. About 1520 the costume becomes more conspicuous with brighter colours; slashes and puffs increase. Weapons:

long pike, partisan and halberds and straight or S-shaped parrying rod. The superiority of fire-arms soon led to the use of the arquebus and musket.

Bottom Group

10. Standard-bearer of the town of Basle about 1520.
11. Mercenary wearing costume with profuse slashing about 1530.
12. Captain of the mercenaries wearing a long skirted coat and a wide beret with feathers.
13. Mayor of the court-martial about 1530, a man versed in the law with the staff of the regiment.

71   GERMANY. *Mercenaries (1520–60). The Wide Trunk-hose*

Top Group

1 and 2. Executioner's assistants.
3. Executioner or *free man* with a red feather on his beret.
4. So-called *harlot's sergeant* who had to see to the sutler-women and soldiers' wives among the camp-followers.
5. His wife, a sutler-woman.

Centre Group

6–13. Shows the later costume with the wide bag-like hose from about 1540 on.
6. Provost, the lower police judge and executive. Wide baggy trunk-hose and short Spanish cape. High hat.
7 and 8. Drummers wearing long wide baggy trunk-hose and big hats.

9. Standard-bearer.
10. Pikeman.

Bottom Group

11. Soldier who receives double pay with arquebus. Richly incised helmet in the shape of a morion (*Marianus*).
12. Executioner with a red feather.
13. Armoured soldier who receives double pay, wearing pointed basinet (pear-shaped helmet).
14 and 15. Pikemen with the pike (formerly called spear). The soldiers who were armoured and those armed with musket or arquebus were entitled to double pay.

72   GERMANY DURING THE REFORMATION PERIOD. *(1500–30)*

Top Group

1, 3 and 4. Nuremberg middle class women about 1500 according to the well-known watercolours by Albrecht Dürer, from the Albertina, Vienna, dated 1500, with the characteristic explanations of 1: *Thus one goes to church in Nuremberg*; of 2: *Thus one walks about at home*, of 4: *Thus the Nuremberg women go dancing*. No. 2 represents (in the same series of Dürer's costume studies) a Venetian woman of 1495 who in contradistinction to the Nuremberg women shows the new fashion of northern Italy: short bodice with wide bands across the low-cut neck. The damask under-skirt attached to the bodice is covered by a skirt slashed open and fastened by two large buttons over the stomach. The false sleeves are laced to the bodice and consist of several parts exposing the fine pleated blouse.

Centre Group

5–8. Costume of Basle middle-class women about 1530, according to the drawings in Indian ink by Hans Holbein the Younger in the museum, Basle. Bodice with long trailing skirt falling down in folds. Underneath the bodice-like blouse and under-skirt. Low cut neck or blouse with pleated collar inserted. 7. Long sleeves with puffs, elongated ruffles or velvet cuffs round the wrists. 5–7. Wear small white embroidered caps covering the hair. 8. Has a large beret decorated with feathers over the hair net. 6. Wears over the low-cut neck the new-fashioned *goller*, a short shoulder

cape with the lapel turned up. Characteristic is the girdle with sewing material, keys, knife and fork, pocket, etc., hanging down from it.

Bottom Group

9. Young man about 1500 in a short doublet with slashed sleeves, a low-cut neck exposing the shirt and laced by bands. Slashed breeches, long mantle thrown over the shoulders. Slightly pointed flat shoes (transition to the broad shoes), slashed plate-like beret. Long loose hair.
10. Old man of rank wearing the characteristic fur-trimmed long sleeveless coat (in German: *Schaube*) over the skirted doublet with wide baggy sleeves. Half-length hair with a fringe (called *Kolbe* in German). Broad flat shoes.
11. Man of rank wearing a short fur-trimmed coat (*Schaube*) and cap. Spade beard.
12. Ceremonial costume of the new Protestant pastors (according to a picture of Dr. Martin Luther by Lucas Cranach the Elder). A composition of the black Augustinian cowl and the gown (*Schaube*) of the university men (*Doctores*). Broad soft closed shoes.
13. Patrician horseman about 1530. Short doublet with slashed and puffed sleeves and a skirt attached. Laced leather leggings. Slit shoes. Beret-like cap with peak over eyes.

Top Group

1. Gentleman in Spanish costume about 1595 wearing short padded trunk-hose.
2. Gentleman (1590) wearing long padded breeches.
3. Gentleman from Görlitz (1591) with only slightly padded long breeches.

Centre Group

4–7. Betrothal ceremony about 1585. 4 in a genuine Spanish costume, 5 wearing breeches according to German fashion but with padded jerkin (in German: *Gänsebauch* – goose stomach); the old gentleman (7) is dressed according to the older fashion with German trunk hose and a large bow in front to hide the cod-piece. But he wears the short Spanish cape and high hat instead of a beret. The shoes are still broad. Similar to the shape called cow's mouth *(Kuhmaul)* about 1520–1530. The betrothed (6) is wearing two stiff Spanish skirts on a stiff under-skirt and a stiff bodice. Close-fitting cap with ostrich feathers.

8. Gentleman in dark Spanish costume: a longish coat and breeches with knee-bands. Tight-fitting soft pointed shoes.

1–8 According to original paintings from contemporary genealogical registers formerly in the department of the Lipperheide costume library of the State Art Library.

Bottom Group

9 and 10. Duke Albrecht V. of Bavaria (1550–1579) and his consort Duchess Anna in the then new-fashioned Spanish costume. According to pictures by Hans Mielich, the Bavarian court painter.

11. Master goldsmith about 1560 wearing the short Spanish cape and the German trunk-hose as well as a high fur-cap,

12. German merchant in German costume; a knee-length coat. soft ruff, cap with ear-lappets.

13. German nobleman in Spanish costume.

Top Group

1–7. Spaniards.

1. Figure and armour in the Armeria Real (armoury at Madrid).
   Supposed to be Charles V. armour: iron hat, ringed coat of mail covered by plate armour, round shield, velvet surcoat with skirt and high tight-fitting leather stockings.
2. A later development of armour as compared with 1(Armeria Real).
3. Fernando Cortez according to a painting in Madrid.
4, 5, 7. Soldiers of Cortez from contemporary paintings in Mexico.
6. Costume of Christopher Columbus.

Centre Group

8–11. Portuguese.
8. Vasco da Gama.
9. Alfonso d'Albuquerque.
10. Nuno da Cunha. 1487–1539.

Bottom Group

11. Pedro de Mascarenhas (discoverer of the Mascarene Islands) as a captive in chains. (8–11 according to Manuscripts and old pictures from S. Ruge's *Zeitalter der Entdeckungen*.)

12–18. Spanish Moors of the 15th century.

12. Huntsman with hunting spear. Cloth coat with sleeves. Hooded cape. Yellow leather shoes over red hose made of soft Cordovan leather.
13. Soldier with iron ringed coat of mail, plate armour, shield with rounded corners and a straight sword.
14. Man wearing turban wound round the head in a simple way.
15. Upper middle-class citizen wearing a sleeved coat, long baggy trousers, mantle, soft shoes and turban and carrying a leather bag.
16. Man with conical embroidered cap.
17. Better class Moorish woman wearing long baggy trousers, pleated garment, white mantle and decorated shoes.
18. Common man wearing a garment with half-long sleeves and wide breeches down to the knees. (According to paintings and sculptured figures in the Alhambra, Granada.)

Top Group

1. French court costume about 1505, still under the influence of Italian fashion before 1500 (Charles d'Amboise died 1511).
2. Costume of French noblemen imitating to some extent the German mercenaries' costume but more refined and less spectacular as far as the slashing and colours are concerned. (Duke Claude de Guise about 1525.)
3. King Francis I. of France (1515–47) wearing short doublet, short trunk-hose, short girdled fur-trimmed jacket, about 1538–39.
4. French nobleman about 1540 wearing a short V-necked coat with skirt and elbow length sleeves, in addition short, padded and slashed trunk-hose and brimmed Spanish hat. (François de la Tremouille, died 1541.)
5. Scotsman in the bodyguard of Francis I. wearing coat with skirt, beret and carrying halberd.

Centre Group

6 and 7. Ladies at the court of King Francis I. in long trailing outer garments with fur-lining and fur cuffs over the equally long under-garments with a square-cut neck. Caps from which falls a piece of cloth.

8. French nobleman about 1550 wearing a knee-length fur-trimmed and sleeved coat. Shirt buttoned up to the chin with small ruff. Small beret.
9. King Anton of Navarra (died 1572, father of the French King Henry IV.) wearing Spanish costume about 1560. Cape with up-turned collar.
10. King Henry II. of France (1547–59) in Spanish costume.

Bottom Group

11. French citizen in a short mantle with folds (resembling the German *Schaube*) with the collar turned up.

12. French citizen with mantle thrown over his shoulders and padded Spanish cap (called *tocque*).
13. Nobleman with a narrow-brimmed conical hat.

14. Lady in out-door costume with the outer garment draped in folds. Tocque (hat) decorated with a long veil.
15. Maid of honour of Queen Catherine de Medici, widow of Henry II. of France.

76   FRANCE. SPANISH FASHION *1560–90 (Charles IX.)*

Top Group

1. Chancellor in ceremonial costume (long wide robe with fur-collar i. e. shoulder cape and small stiff beret).
2. King Charles IX. (1560–74) wearing a round carefully ironed ruff, short sleeved and padded doublet. Short padded trunk-hose, small Spanish mantle, tocque (a shortened beret), tight-fitting cotton hose. (Mechanical stocking knitting was not invented till 1589 by the Englishman William Lee.)
3. Maid of honour. Conical Spanish hooped petticoat. Over the hoop arrangement two garments, the outer one open in front. Neck ruff, cap-like head gear.
4. Officer wearing plate armour over the doublet with hanging sleeves. Helmet *(Morion)* on his head.
5. Arquebusier.

Centre Group

6. Soldier, 1562 with a curved-bladed sword and dagger.
7. Officer, 1562.

8. Arquebusier, 1562.
9. Citizen, 1562.
10. Chamber maid from the provinces, district of Saumur. Cap according to the Anjou costume. Outer skirt slit open in front. The sleeves of the bodice decorated with velvet cuffs.
11. Wine hawker in Paris 1586 as advertiser for his inn.

Bottom Group

12. Street hawker selling shoe polish, Paris 1586, with leather bag and earthenware jug.
13. Peasant woman from Saumur in outdoor attire. White petticoat, blue outer garment, black apron.
14. Peasant from Saumur going to the weekly market.
15. Servant girl carrying pails of water, Paris 1590.
16. Porter, Paris 1590.
17. Paris citizen wearing long cape-like mantle (with velvet collar) 1590.

77   SPANISH FASHION IN FRANCE. *1575–90 (Henry III.)*

Top Group

1. King Henry III. (1574–89) in the costume of the Order of the Holy Ghost (Saint Esprit) founded by him in 1578.
2. His consort, Queen Louise. The former conical shape of female costume now disappears in favour of a more accentuated waist line. The low-cut neck appears in contradistinction to the Spanish fashion. Lace collars are arranged fan-like round the neck.
3. Courtier with the ribbon and cross of the Order of the Holy Ghost (Saint Esprit).
4. Lawyer with a beret with a pompon in a long gown with soft collar. *(Golilla.)*
5. Huguenot musketeer.

Centre Group

6–7. Noble ladies about 1500. Barrel-shaped skirts and the hoop arrangements *(Vertugade* or *vertugalle)* underneath.

Over the outer garment there is a frill attached covering the hips. Slashed and puffed sleeves.
8. The queen's page.
9. Footman in livery at the royal court.
10. Nobleman's footman.
11. Servant or housekeeper out shopping.

Bottom Group

12. So-called *Mignon* in dandy's costume (one of the feeble and effeminate King's favourites, who surrounded and influenced him).
13. French admiral.
14. Duke Louis of Nevers from the house of Gonzaga.
15. French nobleman.
16. *Gentilhomme de la Compagnie* (Gentleman of the bodyguard, 1581).

78   ITALY UNDER THE INFLUENCE OF SPANISH FASHION. *1590–1610*

Top Group

1. Roman courtesan. 1590.
2. Respectable unmarried Venetian woman of rank in outdoor attire hiding head and part of body.
3. Venetian courtesan in a garment made of heavy silk damask with a lace collar standing up fan-like and a handkerchief *(fazoletto)*.
4. The same woman (the front part of the dress being removed) wearing breeches, stockings with gore and stilt-shoes (wood with leatherwork or painting). These stilt shoes *(zoccoli)* were also worn by respectable women. Hair arranged in the shape of a half-moon.
5. Lady from Ferrara, the short sleeves padded to form a roll

on the shoulder. The outer garment slashed open in front. Feather fan. 1590.

Centre Group

6. Venetian lady. 1610.
7. Old Venetian man of rank. 1610.
8. Venetian gentleman dressed in Spanish fashion. 1610.
9. Venetian lady. Outer garment with hanging sleeves. 1605.
10. Young Venetian *Nobile*. 1605 (Spanish fashion).
    According to costume books of the 16th century.

Bottom Group

11–15. Milan ladies and gentlemen performing court dances. 1604.

Top Group

1. King Henry IV. of France (1589–1610). He never wore the beard called *Henriquatre*, but a full short beard. Stiff wheel-like ruff, trunk-hose.
2. Nobleman with pointed beard, flat collar, perhaps in imitation of the collar of the Walloon guards of the 16th century. Stiff short padded trunk-hose.
3. Nobleman with wheel-like ruff, ribbons on knees and shoes, slashed bag-like breeches.
4. Henry IV. in a stiff Spanish hat and short padded trunkhose.
5. Leader of the mercenaries with feather hat, leather doublet and leggings covering the whole legs.

Centre Group

6 and 7. Marie de Medici, wife and widow of Henry IV. shown in different shapes of the Spanish hoop-petticoat, stiff ruff and fan-like high lace collar.

8 and 9. Noblemen in the reign of Louis XIII. (1610–43). The ruff disappears in favour of a flat fine pleated collar. The hair is worn longer. The high horsemen's riding boots come into fashion.

10. Citizens about 1610.

Bottom Group

11. French nobleman *(gentilhomme)*. 1630.
12. The same. 1635.
13 and 14. The same 1635–40.
15 and 16. People of rank in outdoor costume. 1635.
(11–16. According to engravings by Abraham Bosse, died 1678).

SPAIN *in the 16th and 17th Centuries. (Spanish Fashion from 1540–1660)* 80

Top Group

1–10. Times of Charles V. and Philip II. (1540–90).
1. Captain of the Spanish infantry.
2. Spanish soldier.
3. Armour worn at military parades about 1580.
4. The earlier Spanish costume about 1530 (The Emperor Charles V., King of Spain, according to a painting by Titian about 1533. Madrid, Prado).
5. Spaniard of rank about 1550.

Centre Group

6. Spanish Queen (Isabella of Valois, third wife of King Philip II., married in 1559) about 1565.
7. King Philip II. of Spain (1555–98) as a young prince, according to a painting by Titian 1550–51.
8. Lady of rank (the Infanta Isabella Clara Eugenia).
9. Don Juan d'Austria, illegitimate son of Charles V. and half-brother to Philip II. (the victor in the naval battle of Lepanto against the Turks, 1571). According to a painting of 1572.
10. Spanish nobleman and knight of the Order of Santiago (red sword on a black mantle).

1–10. According to contemporary pictures and costume of the Armeria Real at Madrid.

Bottom Group

11–13. Time of Philip IV. (1621–65).
11. King Philip IV. of Spain (1621–65) painted 1644.
12. Infant Balthasar Carlos in hunting costume about 1635.
13. Infant Don Carlos about 1626.
14. Queen Maria Anna of Austria, second wife of Philip IV., painted 1658-60.
15. Infanta Margareta, about 1660.
11–15. According to paintings by Diego Velasquez (1599–1660).

RUSSIA. *16th and 17th Centuries* 81

Top Group

1 and 5. Two warriors of the 16th century. A ringed coat of mail strengthened with plates and worn over the tunic. Helmets with guards over the forehead and with ringed mail attached (1) used as ear guards (5). Shields made of chased metal. Sword, halberd (battle-axe) (1) and mace (5).

2 and 4. Boyar women in ceremonial dress from Torzhok. (The Boyars, meaning fighters, were formerly warriors in the retinue of princes; later on they became the leading aristocracy). The garment made of velvet and brocade. The high head-dress draped with large, fine veils. Torzhok in the Government of Tver is a famous centre of embroidery and lace handicraft.

3. Tsarina (mother of Peter the Great, died 1694) in a gold-brocade garment covered by a mantle of fur-trimmed silk. On her head a narrow pleated cap covered by a fur-cap with hood.

Centre Group

6. Boyar in military costume about 1600.
7. Tsar wearing in-door costume about 1550.
8 and 9. Boyars, 16th century.
10. Boyar, 17th century.

Bottom Group

11 and 12. Cossack of rank in a coat of honour.
13. Tsar in coronation robes, with a conical fur-trimmed gold cap to which the small crown is attached.
14. Boyar (Prince Repnin).
15. Boyar, 17th century.

POLAND, HUNGARY AND UKRAINE. *16th–17th Centuries* 82

Top Group

1. Great hetman, commander-in-chief of the Polish army, about 1600 (According to a picture of the great hetman Stanislaus Solkiewski, died 1620).
2. Young Polish noble lady wearing the national beret.
3. Marshall of Lithuania (end of 16th century). *Szuba* (long coat) taken in at the waist. Ornamental shoes made of yellow morocco leather. The *szuba* is usually a fur-lined coat with a turn-down collar.

4. Polish nobleman, end of the 17th century.
5. Heyduck, old Hungarian warrior used to guard the frontiers against the Turks. Later on also the name of Hungarian foot-soldiers and servants of the magnates and town administrators.
6. Polish peasant, end of 17th century.

Centre Group

7. Armed Polish nobleman.
8. Armed Polish lancer.
9. Polish nobleman about 1580. Over his coat he wears the

Bekiésche. The decorative fastening by buttons and laces is influenced by Hungarian costume.
10. Polish nobleman.
11 and 12. Magyar couple of rank (end of 17th century).

Bottom Group

13. Peasant from the Cracow district.
14. Polish nobleman.
15 Peasant girl from the Ukraine.
16 and 17. Peasants from the Ukraine.

83 GERMANY

Reformation and Spanish Fashion as represented in paintings by Lucas Cranach, Father and Son (1514–64)

1. Prince Christian I., son of the Elector August of Saxony, at the age of four. Painting by Lucas Cranach the Younger. 1564, Moritzburg near Dresden.
2. Prince Alexander, son of the same elector, as a ten-year old boy. Painting by Lucas Cranach the Younger. 1564. Formerly Dresden Museum.
3. Prince Moritz of Saxony. Painting by Lucas Cranach the Elder. 1526. Darmstadt, formerly in the possession of the Great Duke of Hesse.

4. Margrave George Frederick of Ansbach-Bayreuth, painting by Lucas Cranach the Younger. 1564. Formerly Berlin, State Castles.
5. Duchess Katharina, consort of Duke Henry the Pious of Saxony. Part of the painting by Lucas Cranach the Elder. 1514. Formerly Dresden Gemälde Galerie. According to photographs in the Kaiser Friedrich Museum, Berlin.

84 COSTUME OF GERMAN CITIZENS *about 1560–80*

Top Group

1. Craftsman's wife from Dantzig.
2. Maid-servant from Dantzig using a wooden carrier (cut out for the neck) with two chains and hooks for the water pails.
3. Wife of a distinguished citizen from Cologne.
4. Craftsman's wife from Cologne.
5. Wife of a distinguished citizen from Lübeck.

Centre Group

6. Nuremberg woman with a small *Schaube*, i. e. shoulder cape.
7. Nuremberg maid-servant.
8. Patrician's wife from Nuremberg going to a wedding.

9. Craftsman's wife from Augsburg.
10. Daughter of a patrician from Augsburg.
1–10. From *Trachtenbuch* by Weigel 1577. Woodcuts by Jost Amman.

Bottom Group

11–13. Men at the age of 20, 30 and 40 years in German Costume, i. e. slashed sleeves and trunk-hose about 1560–80.
14. Horse-cart driver from Franconia wearing wide high boots which can either be laced to the doublet or let down. According to Amman.
15. Nuremberg burgher wearing Spanish holiday attire.

85 MILITARY COSTUME. EUROPE. *End of 16th Century*

Top Group

1. Spanish soldier, 1555.
2. Musketeer about 1590 with gun-powder bag hanging from the belt.
3. Captain, 1590.
4. Higher officer with gold-inlaid breast plate armour slightly indicating the cod piece (padded front part) without hip plates. 1590.
5. Musketeer with pouch-belt, from which hang wooden boxes or leather pouches containing ammunition. Light helmet *(morion)*. Gun-powder bottle attached to the belt. 1590.

Centre Group

6. Standard-bearer during the war in the Netherlands with the fashionable cod piece (padded front part).
7. Musketeer.
8. Captain.
9. Standard-bearer (6–9) according to engravings by Hendrik Goltzius, Haarlem 1585–87.

Bottom Group

10–13. French soldiers about 1581.
10: Pikeman; 11: Musketeer; 12: Halberdier; 13: Arquebusier.

86 GERMANY. *Head-dress (Spanish Fashion) 1550–1600*

1. Duke Maurice of Saxony, died 1553. Small beret. Forked beard.
2. Otto Heinrich, Elector Palatine, died 1559. Painted by B. Beham.
3. Calvin, Geneva Reformer (died 1564). Tight flat beret over skull cap reaching to the ears.

4. Lady with small *tocque* over caul.
5. Duke William of Jülich, 1566. According to a memorial coin. Ruff under the ring collar.
6. Philippine Welser, 1527–1580. High collar and ruff. Painting in Ambras Castle.

7. The famous goldsmith W. Jamnitzer from Nuremberg, 1568 wearing a fur-trimmed high cap.
8. Merchant from the Meissen district. According to Jost Amman. Ruff. Long pointed beard.
9. William of Orange, the hero of the Netherlands (by birth a German prince of Nassau). According to a painting.

Pointed beard, Spanish hat. Double ruff.
10. The French Admiral Coligny. Added to this plate by the artist for the sake of comparison.
11–15. Heads from Jost Amman's woodcuts about 1570–80.
16–18. Heads from a woodcut representing the Nuremberg rifle association. 1592.

GERMANY, HOLLAND, FRANCE. *Costume during the Thirty-Years' War (about 1630–35)* 87

1. and 5. So-called *alla modo* costume. Germany 1629. According to alla-modo pamphlets. 1. *How a German gentleman should be dressed.* 5. *Gentlemen's alla modo costume and ladies' oddities.*

2. French nobleman greeting someone.
3. Lady playing the spinet.
4. Woman from Cologne. 2–4 according to etchings by Wenzel Hollar, about 1635–40.

ENGLAND. SPANISH FASHION. *(Time of Queen Elizabeth I., According to Contemporary Paintings)* 88

1. Queen Elizabeth I. of England (1558–1603). Painting by an unknown artist. Chatsworth. Collection of the Duke of Devonshire.
2. King Edward VI. of England (1547–1553). Painting by Anthonis Mor. Paris, Louvre (cf. plate 63: England at the Reformation period).

3. James I., King of England and Scotland (1603–25). Painting by a Flemish master. Madrid. National Museum.
4. Mary, Queen of Scots (died 1587). Painting by Frederigo Zuccaro, Chatsworth, Collection of the Duke of Devonshire.

SPANISH COURT COSTUME *about 1630–60. According to Paintings by Diego Velasquez* 89

1. King Philip IV. 1632–35. London, National Gallery.
2. Infanta Maria, Queen of Hungary. 1630. Formerly Berlin, Kaiser Friedrich Museum.

3. Prince Balthasar Carlos about 1639. Vienna, Kunsthistorisches Museum.
4. Infanta Margherita. 1656. Vienna. Kunsthistorisches Museum.

TURKEY. *16th and 17th Centuries* 90

Top Group

1. Turk of rank with the title of Emir held by all direct descendants of Mohammed and some others. Kaftan with scarf worn as a girdle. Coat with long hanging sleeves. Large turban.
2. Commander-in-chief of the janissaries. Brocade garment covered by a sleeveless mantle. High pointed cap of the highest dignitaries, with large turban. Braids for lacing the outer garments are as much in use in Turkish costume as with that of the neighbouring peoples: Magyars and Poles.
3. Cook. Wide baggy breeches as worn by male and female persons; the coat shortened by tucking up as is done with the coats of marching troops. Cap with border decoration.
4. Medical man (Jew) with *tarbush*, so-called Fez.
5. Janissary of the body-guard of the sultan with a high flat-topped cap, a piece of cloth hanging down from it at the back and large feather decoration; the border over the forehead decorated with a wide gold band.

Centre Group

6. Turkish woman in out-door costume. Low decorated *tarbush* (Fez). The women's outfit of this time consists of baggy trousers, cotton or silk undergarment and one or two outer garments. Soft slightly turned-up leather shoes.

7. Middle class Turkish woman at home. Tarbush with turban. Garment covered by a fine, knee-length outer garment, scarf used as girdle.
8. Turkish woman of rank at home. Tarbush draped with a veil, necklaces, woven dress, scarf-girdle, trousers, the naked feet on high wooden sandals.
9. Arabian merchant.
10. Woman of rank from Pera, the residential part occupied by the Franks (Europeans) in Constantinople.
1–10. According to *Raiss und Schiffahrt in die Türkey* by N. Nicolai. 1576.

Bottom Group

11. Lady in out-door dress.
12. Woman of the seraglio.
13. Turkish lady in in-door attire.
14. Imam; leader of the prayers in the mosques. Costume: long outer garment and white turban.
15. Wandering dervish, member of the *Calenderi*, a special order of the dervishes, which requires ceaseless wandering from their members.
11–15. According to pictures of the 17th century.

TURKEY. *17th Century. Costume at the Sultan's Court represented on Miniatures* 91

Top Group

1. Mufti, i. e. judge who studied the secular law and that of the Koran.
2. The Sultan's personal physician having in his left hand a

chain (similar to the rosary) favoured in the Balkans but only used for distraction.
3. The sultan's turban-bearer.

4. The sultan's chief wife.

5. Woman smoking a pipe.

Centre Group

6. High officer of the archers.

7. Archer of the janissaries.

8. Officer of the sipahi or spahi (cavalry).

9. Officer of the Egyptian-Ottoman troops.

10. Janissary from Barbary (North Africa).

Bottom Group

11. Orderly officer of the sultan.

12. Bread-carrier for the advance guard of the army.

13. Officer of the Deli (the word meaning fool; fool-hardy); they were the storm-troops of the armies, mostly stimulated by opium. (Body-guard of the great viziers.)

14. Privy Chamberlain of the sultan.

15. Woman fan-bearer to the mother of the sultan. Her cushion-like cap resembles the head-dress of the Turk peoples in Central Asia. (Mostly according to a Turkish miniature manuscript of the 17th century, formerly in the Lipperheide department of the Staatliche Kunstbibliothek, Berlin.)

92 EUROPE. MILITARY COSTUME *1600–50*

Top Group

1 and 2. Musketeers, 1609. Over the doublet the bandolier (worn from the left shoulder to the right hip) with the bullets in little wooden boxes.

3 and 4. Pikemen. Breast plates with loin-plates attached to them in front.

5. Captain, 1613 with partisan, the weapon of the pikemen's officers. Chest and arms protected by armour underneath. Brocade doublet with skirts.

Centre Group

6. Wallenstein.

7. The Elector Johann Georg I. of Saxony. 1631.

8. The Swedish King Gustavus Adolphus in war costume.

9. Officer about 1635.

10. High officer, 1632.

Bottom Group

11. Musketeer with forked rest for the arquebus.

12. Lancer with the old vizor-helmet. 1635.

13. Cuirassier 1640.

14. Captain 1640.

15. Dutch captain of the rifle-men with sash and pike. 1648.

93 FRANCE AT THE TIME OF LOUIS XIV. *1650–1700*

Top Group

1. Man of rank about 1670 with sword and stick. Large wig, large felt hat with feathers, neck-cloth (called *steenkerke* since 1692). Outer coat *justaucorps* with large cuffs and galloons. Wide pleated breeches giving the impression of a skirt, hose decorated with ribbons at the knees. Shoes with latchets, buckles and red heels.

2 and 5. Officers.

3 and 4. A marshal's wife in a widow's costume and her page.

6. Lady about 1675 in a long trailing outer garment (manteau) draped in folds over a trailing under-garment (robe). Wide cut neck with lace trimming. Hat decorated with ribbons.

7. King Louis XIV. about 1660. White decorative shirt, short waistcoat, mantle, short skirt showing lace breeches (Rhinegrave breeches). Buckled shoes.

8. The same about 1670.

9 and 10. Men of rank. 1664.

11. Man of rank in the earlier costume about 1660. High hat. Wide riding boots richly lined with lace.

12 and 13. Ladies wearing the costume of about 1680–1700. High stiff cap of frilled linen *(fontage)* with veil, trailing outer garment *(manteau)* with baggy folds at the back, laced bodice *(planchette,* German *Blankscheit),* flounced skirt (12) or with cross stripes (13). The outer garment with semi-long sleeves and linen cuffs opens in front over the skirt.

14. Man in a dressing-gown with turban-like night cap.

15. Louis XIV. about 1700 with a later development of a coat *(iustaucorps,* cf. 1) with wide cuffs and large pockets. Underneath a jacket of the same length with sleeves. Large ceremonial wig (Allonge wig). The large brimmed hat is turned up to form a three-cornered hat.

16. Duke Philip of Orléans *(Monsieur)* brother of the king (about 1690–1700).

94 FRANCE. RÉGENCE AND ROCOCO *about 1700–40*

Theatre and Dancers.

Top Group

1–6. According to paintings by Antoine Watteau about 1710–15.

1 and 2. Pierrots of the Italian Commedia dell'arte (cf. pl. 103) from which the comic characters and buffoons originate. Pierrot (or Pierre: stupid Peter) is originally the type of the deceived fool. He appears on the stage of the Italian comedy in Paris at the end of the 17th century, adopting the outfit of Pullicinello, (Pulcinella or Polichinelle).

3. Arlecchino, Arlequin, harlequin in coloured-patched attire (jacket with sleeves, long trousers, bearded mask).

4. Lady of *Crispin* (from the painting by A. Watteau, *L'amour français).*

5. Crispin (Crispino) a French imitation of the harlequin, an impudent and witty valet, appearing about 1600 for the first time. Black (Spanish) costume with mantle, high leggings, leather cap, round hat, wide yellow leather belt, rapier. Title hero of many French comedies, ceasing to appear after 1750.

6. *L'indifférent* (Who is indifferent to his surroundings; melancholy figure on the stage according to a painting by Watteau).

Centre Group

7–11. The dancer Camargo according to a painting by Nicolas Lancret, about 1740.

12–17. The *moulinet* (group-dance). According to the same artist, about 1740.

Examples of the shepherd dances and scenes in high society of the Rococo.

GERMANY. *1625–75. Citizen's Costume, partly under French Influence* 95

Top Group

1. Nuremberg merchant, south German costume about 1626.
2. Jew of the same period with the yellow ring, which Jews were compelled to have on their coat.
3. South German burgher of the same period in travelling attire.
4. Man of rank belonging to the social class privileged to wear a sword. Same period.
5. Man of rank from Cologne, about 1630–35.

Centre Group

6. Cart driver about 1650.
7. Merchant from Hamburg of the same period.
8 and 9. Germans of rank. They wear the French petticoat breeches (*rhinegraves*, cf. explanation of plate 97). About 1670.

10. Burgher about 1675.
According to contemporary engravings.

Bottom Group

11. Augsburg woman in mourning.
12. Artisan's daughter from Strasbourg in wedding attire.
13. Wife of a physician in Strasbourg wearing a skirt with hip frill.
14. Maid servant from Strasbourg.
15. Citizen's wife from Strasbourg wearing special costume for the Holy Communion.
16. Citizen's wife from Strasbourg.
11–16. According to etchings by Wenzel Hollar about 1640–44.

THE NETHERLANDS AND ENGLAND. *17th Century. Contemporary Paintings* 96

1. The family von Hutten; Painting by Cornelis de Vos, Antwerp about 1610. Formerly Munich, Alte Pinakothek.
2. Picture of Helene Fourment (Rubens' second wife) as a bride. Painting by Peter Paul Rubens. 1630. Formerly

Munich, Alte Pinakothek.
3. Portrait of Thomas Wharton. Painting by Anthony van Dyck. Leningrad. Eremitage.

THE NETHERLANDS. *1650–1680, partly under French Influence* 97

Top Group

1–5. Dutch citizen's costume about 1650–60 according to paintings by de Keyser, Terborch and Metsu.
1. Councillor offering a drink of honour.
2. Member of a rifle-association (or officer) in a short cuirass eating his breakfast.
3. Daughter of a distinguished citizen wearing silk dress with short cape.
4. Physician dressed in a doctor's gown.
5. Trumpeter of a troop of horsemen.

Centre Group

6–13. Types of Dutch citizens about 1675–80.
6. High officer wearing high open boots with heels.
7. Cavalier wearing the Rhinegrave breeches or petticoat breeches in French called *rhingraves*, which are said to have

been invented by a Rhinegrave of Salm. (The officer No. 6 wears them gathered by a cord and tucked into his wide horseman's boots).
8. Lady in out-door garments (draped outer garment with a low stiff bodice).
9. Cavalier bowing and wearing wide baggy breeches (resembling plus-fours) and shoes with heels.

Bottom Group

10 and 11. Female skaters with masks for protecting the skin, fur cape and long tube-shaped velvet muffs.
12. Male skater playing ice-hockey.
13. Cavalier with Rhinegrave breeches (petticoat breeches) and wig. Heeled shoes with long, narrow bows. According to the series of engravings by Romeyn de Hooghe: *Figures à la mode* about 1675–80.

THE NETHERLANDS. *Ruffs and Collars, Hair and Beard Styles of the 17th Century* 98

1. Wide, pleated lace collar falling down over chest and back. (According to a picture by Rembrandt 1693).
2. Cape-like collar trimmed with lace and cut away in front exposing the jagged shirt. (According to a Rembrandt picture of 1644).
3. Starched wheel collar made of fine linen and crimped with a crimping iron. (According to a picture by Rembrandt about 1642). The wheel collars appeared first after the middle of the 16th century, at first increasing in size, later on slowly decreasing in width. They were often worn in two or three layers on top of each other. At about 1630 they

went more or less out of fashion and were only worn by older people. Today they are still worn with the official dress of Protestant preachers of some German districts and the Hamburg senators.
4. The Emperor Ferdinand II. about 1625 wearing the wheel ruff, crop head and small pointed beard.
5. The Elector Maximilian I. of Bavaria about 1635. The large wheel ruff has been replaced by a simple linen collar leaving the chin free so that a fuller beard can be worn again.
6. King Christian IV. of Denmark about 1640 wearing a plait of hair hanging down from one side, a short-lived dandy

fashion originating from the time of the wheel ruff. (Painting in the palace of Rosenborg, Copenhagen.)

7. King Charles I. of England 1632 according to a portrait by A. van Dyck. The hair falls down freely and untrimmed and has not assumed the shape of a wig like 17. The beard, too, looks natural and little trimmed.

8–14. French head-dress and hair styles of the 17th century.

8. Rubens' first wife, Isabella Brant (1609–10). She wears a cap under her hat. This hat, really a male head-dress, was then not usually worn by better class women.

9 and 10. Mother and daughter (from a painting by Franz Hals about 1645). The mother still wears the wheel ruff, the daughter has a soft linen collar with lace, falling down on breast and shoulders.

11. Marie Luise of Taxis according to a picture by van Dyck. Hair style influenced by French fashion, about 1630.

12. English woman about 1645 not showing any foreign in-

fluence in her way of dressing. (According to an etching by W. Hollar.)

13. Dutch woman showing the hair style of 1660. (According to a painting by Terborch.)

14. Dutch woman about 1675 (according to a painting by Vermeer van Delft.)

15. Duke Ernst of Mansfeld (about 1625–30). The hair is worn longer after the disappearance of the wheel ruff.

16. Shows the transition from the stiff crimped wheel ruff to the simple turn down collar. The shape of the round ruff is still preserved, but the collar does not fit so tightly round the neck and the stiff pleats are abolished. Nevertheless, there are still several ruffs on top of each other. (According to a picture by E. Pickenoy 1627.)

17. Bernhard of Weimar about 1635. The hair becomes more predominant and longer, the beard smaller.

18. Starched and crimped wheel ruff consisting of three layers on top of each other. (According to a picture by P. Codde 1627.)

99   ENGLAND *about 1640. According to etchings by Wenzel Hollar*

Top Group

1, 2 and 4. English ladies of rank with low-necked lace turn down collars (cf. plate 98: ruffs). Wide pleated skirts (without farthingales as in the late Spanish fashion). Short jacket with skirts and short sleeves with lace cuffs. Feather fan or pleated felt fan.

3. English lady of rank in a winter out-door costume with outer jacket, hoodlike cap, face mask (worn to protect the skin against the weather) and muff. The mask originated in France and became fashionable not only as a protection but also as a sign of good manners and renouncement of vanity (for instance at church processions); it was much used in Northern Italy, not only at Carnival.

Centre Group

5. Citizen's wife from London with broad-brimmed soft felt hat and draped outer skirt.

6. Wife of the Lord Mayor of London with broad-brimmed high stiff hat and the old-fashioned wide Spanish ruff (a sign of her official rank, similar to some ceremonial costume in England and Hamburg in present times). Laced bodice.

7. Citizen's daughter with fastened turn-down collar, apron and linen cap.

8. Craftsman's wife.

9. Citizen's wife (cf. 5) with apron. Wooden sandals under the shoes as protection against the dirt of the street.

Bottom Group

10, 11, 13, 14. English ladies of rank (14 again with a face mask).

12. Wife of a rich merchant.

100   FRANCE. *Fashions at the Court of Versailles according to Contemporary Engravings, about 1700*

Fashions at the court of Versailles after contemporary engravings. Paris about 1700.

1. *Dame de qualité en déshabillé* (Lady of rank in dressing gown). Engraving by Trouvain about 1700.

2. Lady and gentleman at court. Mezzotint by J. Gole about 1700.

3. François Louis, Prince of Bourbon. Engraving by Peter Schenck, Amsterdam about 1700.

4. *Dame de qualité en habit d'été.* (Lady of rank in summer cos-

tume). Coloured mezzotint, Paris about 1695. The men wear the large ceremonial wig, long outer coat *(justaucorps)* with rich braid trimming and large cuffs, kerchief *(steenkerke)*, sash, felt hat with turned up brim and feather decoration, ankle shoes with red heels, tight breeches *(culottes)*. Gored stockings. The women are wearing a high stiff linen cap *(fontange)* and beauty-patches *(mouches)*, a trailing outer garment *(manteau)* over a bell-shaped skirt *(robe)*, small apron, stiff bodice *(planchette)*.

101   FRANCE AT THE TIME OF LOUIS XIV. *1695–1700*

Cavaliers and ladies of Paris society. According to engravings by Sebastian Le Clerc from the series: *Divers costumes français du Règne de Louis XIV.* Paris about 1695–1700. This

plate demonstrates the costume of the courtiers at Versailles, which is characterized by the ceremonial wig of the men and the fontange caps of the women.

102   FRANCE. TIME OF THE RÉGENCE *about 1715–20*

1–4 and 6. Parisian cavaliers.
5 and 9. Parisian women of rank.
7. Woman from Valenciennes.
8. Girl from Paris. Etchings by Antoine Watteau from the

series *Figures de Modes.* Paris 1715–20. This plate shows the transition from the stiff Versailles court dress (about 1700) to the more comfortable and natural costume of the time of the *Régence.*

ITALIAN COMEDY IN PARIS *about 1730*

Some of the typical characters of the Italian Impromptu Theatre (Commedia dell'arte).

1. Scaramuccio Napolitano (the bragging coward).
2. Tartaglia (the comical stutterer from Naples).
3. Dottore (the avaricious, jealous scholar or lawyer).
4. Arlecchino (harlequin).
5. Pierrot (stupid Peter).
6. Pantalone (the old comical Venetian merchant).
7. Pulcinella Napoletano (Polichinelle), the predecessor of the circus clown with fat belly and hunchback.
8. Scapino (Scapin) the former *Zanne*, by Giovanni, the disorderly sly servant or peasant lout.
9. Capitano Espagnole, the boasting Spanish captain. According to engravings by Joullain in Louis Riccoboni: *Histoire du Théâtre Italien*. Paris 1728.

HOLLAND AND ENGLAND. ROCOCO *about 1740–50*

1. Dutch smoker's club. Picture in coloured crayons by Cornelis Troost 1740. The Hague. Picture Gallery.
2. Family group. Painting by William Hogarth about 1740. London, National Gallery.
3. Mariage à la mode (breakfast scene). Painting by William Hogarth 1745. London, National Gallery.

FRANCE AND GERMANY. ROCOCO *about 1730–60*

1. Louis, prince of France (son of Louis XV.). Painting by Louis Tocqué about 1739. Paris, Louvre.
2. Princess Sophie of Prussia and Margrave William of Brandenburg Schwedt. Painting by Antoine Pesne. 1734. Formerly Berlin, Hohenzollernmuseum.
3. Madame Adelaide of France, daughter of Louis XV. Painting by J. M. Nattier, the Younger. 1745. Paris, Louvre.
4. Madame de Pompadour. Painting by François Boucher. 1757. Paris. Rothschild collection.

ITALY. ROCOCO. *Venice about 1750*

1. Preparation for a masked ball.
2. Dancing lesson.
3. Dressing in the morning.
4. Levée of a Venetian woman of rank. Engravings by G. Flipart after paintings by Pietro Longhi, Venice about 1750.

FRANCE. ROCOCO. *Paris Street Life about 1740*

(According to *Cris de Paris* - Paris Street Criers - drawn by Bouchardon, engraved by Caylus)

Top Group

1. Chimney-sweep as street-crier.
2. Copper-smith and tinker from the Auvergne.
3. Female hawker with fresh walnuts.
4. Tradesman with lanterns.
5. Dealer in hare-skins.

Centre Group

6. Man dealing in mouse-traps.
7. Flower seller with bouquets of carnations.
8. Female street-sweeper.

9. Dealer in lottery tickets carrying the winning lists with him to attract buyers.
10. Woman buying old hats.

Bottom Group

11. Man selling knives and scissors.
12. Itinerant musician with large drum and flute.
13. Street musician with primitive barrel-organ.
14. Girl with *laterna magica* and barrel-organ. *(La petite Marmotte.)*

STREET LIFE IN VIENNA AND VENICE. *1770–90*

1–12. Viennese street life and street-criers about 1775. (According to Chr. Brand: *Kaufruf in Wien*. 1775.)

Top Group

1. Flower girl.
2. Girl selling honey and fruit.
3. Viennese chamber maid.
4. Female lemon vendor.
5. Laundress.
6. Man carrying cakes.
7. Man dealing in wooden utensils.

Centre Group

8. Jew selling second-hand goods.

9. Bay leaf hawker.
10. Man selling engravings.
11. Woman selling hats.
12. Casual worker.

Bottom Group

13–17. Street life in Italy about 1785. (According to Venetian engravings by Zamponi.)
13. Street crier selling fish *frutta di mare* and candied fruit. He wears a knitted woollen cap.
14. Theatre attendant at the Venice theatre.
15 and 16. Rag-picker and buyer of old goods.
17. Street crier.

1. Maternal joy.
2. The rendezvous in Marly.
3. The grand toilette.

4. Taking leave. Engravings by various artists, after drawings by J. M. Moreau, the Younger, from the series: *Monument du Costume*, Paris 1776 and following years. State Art Library.

110   ENGLAND. *1770–1800*

Top Group

1. Mrs. Carnach. According to a painting by Reynolds.
2. Mrs. Beaufoy. Costume about 1775. According to a painting by Gainsborough.
3. Mrs. Graham. According to a painting by Gainsborough.
4. The Duchess of Cumberland. 1783. After an engraving.

Centre Group

5–9. English fashions about 1770–95.

8. The London actress Elizabeth Farren, later the wife of Lord Derby. According to a picture by Lawrence, 1792, engraved by Bartolozzi.

Bottom Group

10–15. English fashions at the court of St. James about 1795 to 1800. According to aquatints by Nikolaus Heideloff in *Gallery of Fashion*.

111   FRANCE. LATE ROCOCO. *Women's Hair Styles. 1770–90*

After 1750 the flat and graceful hair style gradually rises upward so that the towering head-dress reaches its summit after 1770. The place of the *friseur* (who curls the hair) is taken by the *coiffeur* who works the former *coiffe* (cap) into the hair (in the shape of ribbons and decorations).

1. Madame Adelaide, daughter of Louis XV. (cf. plate 105). A transition from the low to the high hair style about 1755–60. Hair style with lace cap *(coiffe)*.
2 and 3. Rising toupets *(toupets croissants)*. *Toupet* is the name for the hair style which is attained by combing (brushing) the hair straight up from the forehead. According to Chodowiecki's engravings in an almanac.
4. Woman wearing *dormeuse* (night cap), a large cap worn as a *négligé* at home or by elderly women about 1780. *Négligé* meant free and easy attire in contradistinction to *grande toilette* (evening gown).
5. *Hérisson* (hedgehog) with a *coiffe* or cap on top.
6. *Coiffure à la belle poulaine* (prow of a ship) 1778. Besides such

ships artificial flowers, fruit baskets, cornfields, etc., were fastened on top of the hair.
7. *Coiffure en bandeau d'amour* (love bands) about 1780.
8. *Tocque lisse avec trois boucles détachées* (Plain tocque with three detached curls). All that remained of the original tocque (the tight fitting beret of the Spanish fashion is the narrow cord).
9. *Hérisson avec trois boucles détachées* (cf. 8).
10. *Chien couchant avec un pouf* (lying dog with a large pad of hair).
11. *Coiffure en crochets avec une échelle de boucles* (with curls arranged like a ladder).
12. Loose floating hair with large brimmed hat, so-called *merveilleuse* about 1795 (cf. plates 116 and 117).
13. Woman's hair style with Phrygian cap (revolutionary cap). 1790. Transition from the artificial to the loose hair style.
14. Large felt hat with ostrich feathers on a curly wig, about 1785.
15. Queen Marie Antoinette in a high *coiffure* with turban cap and feathers, about 1780.
16. Large *dormeuse* (cf. 4) on a high *coiffure* about 1780.

112   GERMANY AND AUSTRIA. *China Figures. 1750–75*

Costume according to contemporary china figures.

1. Ballet dancer, 1760 (China figure from Höchst).
2. Shepherd and shepherdess (Frankenthal).
3. Dancing girl. 1760 (Höchst).
4. Viennese woman cutting wood with an axe. 1750–60.

5. Shepherdess (Vienna).
6. Cavalier, 1760–65 (Nymphenburg).
7. Itinerant hawker, 1750 (Meissen).
8. Huntsman in a nobleman's service, 1750. Fayence from Strasbourg.
9. Huntsman of rank, 1750 (Meissen).

113   FRANCE. ROCOCO. *1730–75*

Top Group

1. Lady wearing the so-called *contouche* made of taffeta or silk (1730) which replaced the outer garment of the evening dress (either *manteau* or *grande robe*) from about 1720. It was fitted to the body at the shoulders only and flowed loosely down over the under-garments with the farthingale *(panier)*. On the back an inserted fold (Watteau fold) ran down from the nape to the seam.
2. Costume of Queen Maria Leszczynska, consort of King Louis XV. of France. 1747. Rich white silk garment with gold embroidery, blue velvet ermine-lined coat with gold lilies. Folding fan, not open here. (According to a picture by Van Loo.)

3. Dancing master 1745 wearing the artificially stiffened coat with a contrasting long stiff waistcoat sticking out. (According to a painting by Chardin.)

Centre Group

4–8. Typical figures of 1755. Gentleman, ladies and two *abbés* (ecclesiastics). The outer garments of the ladies are open in front to display the petticoat decorated with frills of delicate pleated material. Small white silk or satin slippers. The gentleman with sword and three-cornered cocked hat. (According to an engraving by G. de. St. Aubin.)

Bottom Group

9–13. Scenes from contemporary French representations about 1760–1775.

9. Lady's maid with a tray, chocolate and letters. (From: *Le Bain* – the bath).

10–12. Cavalier with sword and three-cornered cocked hat and two ladies in hoop-petticoats with trailing outer garments and pointed bodice. High-heeled slippers. (From: *Promenade du soir* – Evening walk.)

13. Lady's maid in a gathered *contouche* with folds at the back (so-called *négligé* attire). High-heeled slippers and small cap (From: *The Wakening*).

FRANCE. LATE ROCOCO. *1775–85*   114

Top Group

1. Lady wearing the wrap-like gathered outer garment with stiff bodice (the so-called *contouche* or *robe ronde* over the short hoop-petticoat), cap tied under the chin on a high *coiffure*.

2. Lady wearing hood-like cap, trailing coat and petticoat without hoops.

3. Back view of a lady in a hoop-petticoat and *caraco* jacket with skirts and short folds on the back. High elaborate hair style.

4. Gentleman wearing cloth tailcoat, short waistcoat, breeches *(culottes)* and gored stockings. Round semi-stiff flat hat according to English fashion, lace frill on the front of the shirt *(jabot)*.

5. Gentleman in a long riding coat (*redingote:* derived from the English word) and stiff two-cornered cocked hat, high neck-cloth, 4 and 5 buckle shoes.

Centre Group

6. Gentleman in the earlier court dress (*justaucorps* – cf. France about 1700) with rather long waistcoat, two-cornered cocked hat in his hand and the sword at his left hip.

7. Courtier with the three-cornered cocked hat under his left arm. Silk sash or *Bandelier*. Stockings with gussets.

8–10. Parisian ladies in indoor dress. High coiffures with caps on top. Coat of various lengths over the round or oval hoop-petticoat.

Bottom Group

11–13. Ladies of the period about 1777–78. .The garments decorated with elaborate frills of silk ribbon (in the rococo style) or flower garlands, bows and lace.

12. *Grande robe* about 1780 decorated in the simpler style of Louis XVI. Lace ruffles, small upright lace collar in the so-called Medici-style. Pearl necklace, high *coiffure à la victoire*.

FRANCE. *1780–89 (Late Rococo)*   115

Top Group

1. Woman in out-door attire. Cap or bonnet, fastened with a ribbon. (This head dress was called *à la laitière:* in the fashion of the dairy maid). Fur-trimmed satin wrapper. Hoop-petticoat shortened for wearing out of doors, with *caraco* or *polonaise* (short jacket) made of the same material. Example of greater simplicity in the fashion of the country woman or burgher's wife as a reaction against the over-decorated, extravagant court fashion. The muff appeared about 1680, disappeared during the period of the Revolution and Empire.

2. Lady with large hat decorated with ribbons. Long *caraco* over ankle-length hoop-petticoat. Low neck.

3. Lady about 1783–84 in a ceremonial costume with large hoop-petticoat. *Coiffure à la Montgolfier* (i. e. named after the newly invented air balloon). According to an English engraving.

4. Woman wearing the so-called *dormeuse* (originally night-cap) fichu (breast kerchief) *en marmotte* (marmot) short hoop-petticoat with *polonaise* (jacket) to match.

Centre Group

5. Costume dating May 1786. Coat and waist-coat made of striped velvet. Black silk breeches *(culottes)*, white silk stockings.

6. Costume dating May 1786. Riding outfit in imitation of the English riding-coat; in French called *redingote*. Round English hat. Buck-skin breeches. Jack boots.

7. Costume of November 1785. Outer garment *à la Lévite* open in front; at first reaching down to the calves, later becoming a trailing garment. It was fastened up over the waist by means of bows, buttons or a sash. A *fichu* over under-garment and *lévite*.

8. Costume dating January 1786. *Robe à la Turque*, the older ceremonial garment. Large satin hat with ribbons and feathers.

9. Costume dated December 1785. Déshabillé garment, called *Pierrot*. Decorated cap, fichu (breast kerchief), short caraco (skirted jacket). Hoop-petticoat.

Bottom Group

10–14. Winter costumes 1788–89.

PARIS FASHION. *1790–95. Revolution and Directory*   116

Top Group

1. Gentleman in a silk tail-coat *à la française* 1790. Short waist-coat with fobs hanging down.

2. Lady with a stiff gray silk hat trimmed with silver braid. February 1790.

3 and 4. Ladies in December 1790.

5. Woman wearing cap under a round conical hat with feathers. September 1791.

6. Gentleman in a cloth tail-coat with silk waist-coat and round silk hat with tricolour ribbons. Short waist-coat with hanging down fobs.

Centre Group

7. Woman in 1791.

8. Woman in July 1792.

9. Man with open tail-coat, the front of which is partly cut away, and a round hat. August 1791.

10. Woman in a tricolour costume with cap.

11. Woman wearing silk dress and conical straw hat.
12. Woman with skirted jacket, short waist-coat, hat with *tri-colour* ribbon, all in a man's style.

Bottom Group

13 and 14. Man and woman in 1795. (*Merveilleuse* and *Incroyable*.)

15. *Merveilleuse* partly suggesting antique pattern. 1795.
16. Citizeness 1795.
17 and 18. So-called *Muscadins* similar to the *Incroyables*. Dandies of the Revolutionary Period. Nouveaux riches and profiteers of the Revolution.

117 FRENCH REVOLUTION, DIRECTORY AND CONSULATE. *1790–1803*

Top Group

1. Member of the Paris revolutionary municipal council.
2. Model costume of the *Liberté* and the revolutionary women. (According to contemporary patterns of 1792–94). – The acute phase of the Revolution ended in July 1794, *Thermidor.*
3. Official employed at the Temple (the state prison where among others King Louis XVI. was kept a prisoner till his execution).

Centre Group

4. Member of the Jacobin Club.
1–4. Wear the Phrygian cap which had been declared an emblem of the people's government. The Jacobin (4) has a fillet attached to it with the inscription: *surveillance* (watching).

5–10. Some characteristic hair styles, head-dresses and neck cloths.
5. Charlotte Corday who assassinated Marat.
6. Marat.
7. Danton.
8. Henriot, 1783. Commander of the Paris National Guard The cockade fixed to the ship-shaped hat.
9. Robespierre.
10. Tallien.

Bottom Group

11 and 12. Ladies wearing antique garments fashionable at the time of the Consulate about 1800. (*Mode à la grecque.*)
13–16. *Merveilleuses* (women) and *Incroyables* (men).

118 GERMANY AND FRANCE. *Uniforms (1680–1790)*

Top Group

1–5. Germany.
1. Musketeer with doublet and pouch belt.
2. Officer about 1685.
3. Grenadier.
4. Corporal of the infantry.
5. Musketeer about 1690.

Centre Group

6–13. France.

6. Royal *garde de la porte* (guard at the gate) 1757.
7. Officer of the body guard of the royal family. 1745.
8. Dragoon 1724.

Bottom Group

9. Officer of the Swiss Guards in ordinary uniform. 1757.
10. Soldier of the French guards in ceremonial uniform. 1757.
11. Officer of the French guards in ordinary uniform. 1757.
12. Staff officer in ordinary uniform.
13. Corporal of the fusiliers in ceremonial uniform. 1786.

119 ENGLAND AND FRANCE. *1800–30. French Empire and English Regency*

Top Group

1–6. England 1800–1813.
1. Man in the national English tail-coat with high top hat, buck-skin breeches and jack-boots. (After a fashion engraving of 1801.)
2. Lady in ankle-length high-girdled tunic and short sleeves over a petticoat with bodice. Flat sandals. 1807.
3. Open mantle with stand-up collar. Pot-shaped hat trimmed with feather. 1809.
4. Long outer garment (open at the bottom) over the tunic. Shoulder cape with fringes. 1809.
5. Short bell-shaped garment with jagged seam and a richly decorated bodice. Low wide neck. 1813.
6. Lady in winter costume. Long cloth garment, short fur-trimmed Spencer jacket with fur collar. Fur muff and hat. 1813.
2–6. Repository of Art. London.

Centre Group

7–18. Paris Fashion 1814–30.
7–10. Fashionably dressed women 1814–15. (According to the

series of engravings in *Incroyables et Merveilleuses* by Lanté after drawings by Horace Vernet.)
11. Lady in a bell-shaped flounced petticoat, short Spencer jacket with long sleeves (rather more a blouse without skirts) high lace ruffle round neck. Feathered hat. Fashion engraving. January 1828.
12. Man in a cloth tail-coat (out-door attire). Short waist-coat, neck-tie, high top hat with slightly turned up brim, striped trousers tapering towards the ankles, fastened with straps under the shoes. May 1823.

Bottom Group

13. Women wearing a dress fastened up to the neck with long sleeves puffed at the shoulders, high neck ruffle, large sunbonnet, fur stole. December 1823.
14. Dandy wearing his tail-coat buttoned up and a wide open mantle with flounces round the shoulders. According to a picture by Ingres. 1823.
15 and 16. Women in 1830.
17 and 18. Well-dressed Parisian couple in 1831.
15–18. According to fashion pictures by Gavarni.

Top Group

1. So-called German costume (Teutsche Tracht) 1815 with a wide turned-up collar, puffed sleeves, stiff hat with feathers.
2. Lady's riding habit 1816.
3. Man wearing riding dress (tail-coat and breeches), with buttoned-up leggings. Small top hat with narrow brim. 1815.
4. Lady wearing evening gown reaching down to the calves and ending in bows. High girdle. Beginning of 1817.
5. Summer dress 1819. Feather hat. Low neck with lace collar.
6. Summer attire. Sun-hat, bell-shaped mantle with long cuffs. Narrow lace drawers showing beneath the dress.

Centre Group

7 and 8. Men in 1819. Trousers exposing part of the gaiters (7) or the striped stockings (8).
9. Woman in 1826.
10 and 11. Costume in 1829. Out-door attire.
12. Lady in evening gown, 1832, with full skirt, ample ribbon decoration. Lace stole. Hair arranged in curls.

Bottom Group

13–17. Fashions at Frankfurt on the Main, November/December 1834. (From: *Journal des Dames*, Frankfurt/Main.)

EUROPE. *Uniforms. 1795–1815. Revolution to the Bourbon Restoration*   **121**

Top Group

1–7. Prussian military men. 1806–13.
1. Cuirassier in the regiment *von Holtzendorf.* 1806.
2. Infantry staff officer. 1806.
3. Grenadier of the 1st battalion of the body-guard 1806.
4. Musketeer (drummer) the King's regiment. 1806.
5. Lancer (uhlan) in the guards. 1810.
6. Fusilier. 1810.
7. Horseman of the Silesian Cuirassier regiment. 1813.

Centre Group

8–14. England, Russia, Austria, Denmark. 1802–15.
8. English sailor. 1814.
9. Imperial Russian grenadier. 1802.
10. Russian infantry general. 1813.
11. Russian artillery officer. 1813.
12. Officer of the Austrian riflemen. 1813.
13. Soldier in the Danish body-guard. 1805.
14. Cossack. 1813.

Bottom Group

15–21. France. Uniforms during the time of Napoleon. 1795 to 1815.
15. Hussar. 1795.
16. Infantry officer. 1806.
17. Grenadier of the guards. 1813.
18. Musketeer. 1806.
19. Foot soldier. 1806.
20. Sapper. 1813.
21. Foot soldier, 1795.

GERMANY (PRUSSIA). *Uniforms. 1730–70.*   **122**

Top Group

1. Infantry regiment *Fürst zu Anhalt-Zerbst* (according to an army recruiting pamphlet about 1740).
2. Frederick the Great on horseback (according to D. Chodowiecki).
3. Soldier from the infantry regiment *Fürst zu Anhalt-Zerbst.*

Centre Group

4. Prussian dragoon. 1750. (According to an engraving by J. M. Probst. Augsburg).
5. Cuirassier in billets wearing sleeved waistcoat. Coat and weapons are hung on the wall, cuirass in front of the stool.

(According to an engraving by E. Bück. Nuremberg. Germanisches Museum.)
6. Soldier of the giant guard of Frederick William I. (According to a painting formerly in the Charlottenburg Palace.)

Bottom Group

7. Hussar regiment von Kleist, 1758–67 (green uniform).
8. First dragoon regiment.
9. Fifth hussar regiment (black uniform with the emblem of the skull on the helmet: Totenkopfhusaren).
10. Trumpeter of the 12th cuirassier regiment.
11. Grenadier wearing red cap with a tin shield in front.

GERMANY AND FRANCE. LATE ROCOCO, *about 1788*   **123**

Women's and men's fashions according to engravings by Riepenhausen from the Göttingen pocket almanac (Göttinger Taschenkalender) 1788. German and French fashions as well as stage costumes are shown in these small almanacs by way of small engravings as early as the seventies of the 18th century, that is to say some time before the appearance of the fashion papers proper (from 1785 on) with their coloured fashion plates.

FRANCE. *Paris Fashions. 1830–35*   **124**

1. Evening cape. Paris, February 1834.
2. Evening dress. Paris, February 1833.
3. March 1834.
4. Visite. Paris, April 1834. According to coloured lithographs by Gavarni from the *Journal des gens du monde.* 1833–34.

1. Paris fashion, January 1850. Coloured engraving by Compte-Calix from *Modes Parisiennes*.
2. Paris fashion, June 1850. Coloured engraving by Compte-Calix from *Modes Parisiennes*.
3. Berlin fashion, March 1858. Steel engraving from *Hermann Gersons Modezeitung* (Gerson's fashion paper).
4. Berlin fashion, September 1858. Coloured steel engraving from *Herman Gersons Modezeitung* (Gerson's fashion paper).

126   FRANCE AND GERMANY. *Fashion 1870–75. The Time of the Tournure.*

1. Paris evening gown. November 1873. Coloured lithograph by Gustave Janet from *La Mode Artistique*.
2. Paris racing dress, July 1875. Lithograph by Gustave Janet from *La Mode Artistique*.
3. Men's fashion in Germany, July 1872. Coloured lithograph from the *Europäische Modenzeitung* (European Fashion Paper) Leipzig.
4. Women's fashion in Germany, October 1874. Coloured steel engraving from the *Illustrierte Frauenzeitung* (Illustrated Women's Paper) Berlin, Franz Lipperheide.

127   SPAIN. *Turn of the 18th and 19th Centuries*

Top Group

1–5. According to paintings by Francisco de Goya (1746 to 1828).
1. King Charles III. (died 1788) as a huntsman.
2. Marquesa de Pontejos. About 1785.
3. The duchess of Alba. About 1793.
4. Self-portrait of the painter Francisco de Goya. About 1795.
5. The actress La Tirana. About 1800.

Centre Group

6–11. According to designs for tapestries by Goya.
6 and 7. Peasant and peasant girl. 1787.
8. Customs official. 1779.
9. Young dandy. 1786.
10 and 11. Andalusian gentlemen. 1777.

Bottom Group

12. *Bandillero* who places the *bandellera* (or *little flags*, decorated sticks with barbed hooks) into the bull's skin. Hairbag decorated with red and green ribbons, green jacket with yellow trimmings, red *faja* white stockings (cf. plate 130, Spain, bull fights).
13. Alguacil. Official of the Court of Justice. Black attire with white collar and gray wig.
14. Abate (abbot). Black attire. A blue and white ribbon round his neck. Jabot (frill on the chest) with ruffles round the wrists. Fobs are hanging down from the waist.
15. Water vendor wearing red cap (*gorra*), linen shirt and breeches, sandals (*alpargatas*). These were also worn by soldiers from 1694 onwards. They were made from home-grown Esparto leaves which were also used for making mats, ropes, bags, hats and baskets.
16. Lower middle class woman in the dress for church festivals. Bodice decorated with pink and golden bows. White stockings. Red and gold shoes. Silver and gold jewelry.

128   SPAIN. *1810–30*

Top Group

1. Muleteer from the province of Segovia in Old Castile. Sleeveless leather doublet, slashed sleeves, *faja* (sash). Velvet breeches. Cloth gaiters. Cocked hat.
2. Peasant woman from the province of Segovia with spindle in her hand. Linen shirt with black embroidery. Skirted jacket with slashed sleeves. Hat similar to 1 and 5.
3. Wine dealer from La Mancha (hilly district in New Castile; cf. Don Quixote). Double sleeves, the longer ones laced on the shoulder. Coloured piece of cloth sewn on to the elbow (shown on the sleeve lying on the ground).
4. Peasant woman from La Mancha (cf. 3).
5. Peasant from the Alcarria New Castile (east of Madrid). Cloth jacket *faja*, low necked waistcoat, leather girdle with pouches.

Centre Group

6. Craftsman from Catalonia, North-Eastern Spain, with wide trousers, similar to those worn by German carpenters.
7. Fisherman from the Mediterranean coast. The turned-down woollen bag-cap is characteristic (worn all along the Mediterranean coast, in antiquity known as Phrygian cap, in the French Revolution adopted as the *liberty* cap).
8. Water vendor from the former kingdom of Valencia (Eastern Spain).
9 and 10. Peasant woman and peasant from Valencia in summer costume. 10: Wide breeches, short stockings (reaching to the calves). Laced sandals.
11. Peasant from the same district wearing winter costume with *capa* (mantle with collar).

Bottom Group

12. Cart driver from the former kingdom of Murcia (now a province south of Valencia) with goad (to drive the oxen), wide breeches and fringed wrap (manta) resembling a plaid.
13. Peasant woman from La Mancha.
14. Peasant from Aragon, lightly dressed without jacket or wrap but with *faja*, silk head cloth, hemp sandals.
15. Woman from the mountainous part of Aragon with upstanding lace collar.
16. Dealer from the province of Santander (on the Bay of Biscay).
17. Peasant woman from Asturias. Red head kerchief. Velvet or cloth shawl, wide shirt sleeves gathered at the wrist.

Top Group

1. Man from Malaga.
2, 3, 4 and 5. 1810–30.
2. Inn-keeper from the Sierra Morena. Sheep-skin jacket with silver fastenings. Cloth trousers with coloured braid. Leather leggings. Cloth wrapped round the head.
3. Wife of a smuggler (contrabandista) from Andalusia. Velvet bodice with silver trimmings. Short leather boots.
4. *Manola* (coquette) from Madrid, velvet mantilla, embroidered skirt, comb in her hair.
5. *Manola* or *ministral* meaning dandy from the lower classes. Madrid.

Centre Group

6 and 7. Andalusian horsemen. Hats with turned up brims and small silver tufts. Headcloths falling down at the back

from underneath the hats, red sashes *(faja)* 6: with *capa* (mantle with collar) 7: fringed plaid *mantalerezana*.

8. Muleteer with turned up trousers, headcloth, hat (seen from above, like 6 and 7).
9. *Capa* like 6. Drinking can *(botijo)* to pour the wine into the mouth.
10. Gipsy king from Granada with bright yellow *faja* (sash). Pointed hat with silver pompons.

Bottom Group

11 and 12. Gipsy women in simple cotton frocks.
13. Woman from the country (Jaen) in Sunday costume. Silk skirt striped apron, printed coloured cloth and *mantilla* fixed to the hair.
14. Lady in a Manila wrap (manton de Manila) pinned together on the breast and lace mantilla. Hair ornaments: silver combs and live pomegranate blossom.

Top Group

1. Matador (famous bull-fighter) with richly decorated mantle *(capa de paséo* meaning: ceremonial entrance) cut in a semicircle with a collar. In fighting this magnificent mantle is exchanged for a simpler and larger one.
2. Espada (fighter), who has to kill the bull in the third phase. He incites the animal with the red square cloth *(muleta)* and kills it with the sword *(estoque)*.
3. Banderilléro. These banderilleros place their *banderillas* (rods with pointed barbed hooks and tinsel decoration) into the bull's neck during the second phase.
4. Torero (bull-fighter) in the *capa de paséo* (cf. 1).
5. Torero with *capote* (the larger fighting cape). Hair style: a larger false pig-tail is fixed to the smaller natural one.
6. Alguacil. (City council servant) who has to maintain order in old Spanish costume.

Centre Group

7. Picador. The picadóres open the fight by attacking the bull

with a lance. They have to sustain his attacking run in which usually the (old and worthless) horse falls a victim. The lance *(garrócha)* has a short triangular point fixed into a wooden knob in order not to wound the bull seriously but only to excite him. Large grey felt hat with a rosette. Under the leather trousers iron greaves. Decorative jacket without the many tassels of the banderilleros and espadas (2 and 3).

8. Assistants of the picadóres. They have to help up the falling picadór, while the espadas try to take away the bull.
9. Picadór with leather outer-trousers reaching to the calves.
10. Bull-fighter in walking suit.

Bottom Group

11–13. Wrapping the silk *faja* (sash) round the waist.
14. Matador.
15. Picadór.
16. Torero or Toreadór dressing. The capote (cf. 3) is hanging on the wall. The ornamental jacket on the chair.

Top Group

1. Peasant about 1820.
2. Woman from one of the provinces in a costume displaying her country origin, but also her wealth. About 1820.
3. Woman street-vendor selling edible mussels.
4. Woman selling milk in the streets.
5. Priest.
6. Huntsman selling game.

Centre Group

7. Dealer in animals (the one naked foot is only to demonstrate the footless stockings). The gun carried for security

on the high roads. The plaid-like wrap resembles the Spanish *manta* (cf. plate 129. fig. 7), but without fringes.

8. Peasant women from the province of Minho, in northern Portugal, with many gold ornaments, about 1875.
9. Carmelite monk.
10. Country girl in national costume.
11. Old shepherd wearing straw tunic and mantle.

Bottom Group

12 and 13. Costume worn in church from Miranda (province of Douro).
14. Milk woman from Lisbon.
15. Ox driver and (16–17) ordinary people from Lisbon and Santarém (on the Tejo).

Top Group

1–5. Northern Italy about 1800.
1. Boatman (barcajuolo) in festive costume.

2. Ordinary woman, dressed up. Genoa.
3. Woman weaver making striped linen. From the Bisagno valley near Genoa.

4. Muleteer from the Bisagno valley.
5. Dealer selling home-knitted cotton stockings. Genoa.

Centre Group

6–10. Papal States about 1830.
6. Woman from the Sabine Mountains.
7. Chief of a band of brigands.
8. Brigand from Sonnino (Volscian Mountains).
9. Woman from the Volscian Mountains.
10. Woman from Frascati (Alban Mountains).

Bottom Group

11–16. Kingdom of the two Sicilies.
11. Peasant woman from Venafro in the Matese Mountains.
12. Man from St. Giovanni a Teduccio (between Naples and Portici).
13. Country policeman (guardacampagna).
14. Woman from the Salerno district.
15. Woman from Pizzo (South Calabria).
16. Woman from the Naples district.

133   ITALY. *1800–30*

Top Group

1. Woman from Lerici, Gulf of Spezia.
2. Peasant woman from the mountainous district near Pistoja.
3. Agent dealing in small holdings and market gardening (District of Florence).
4. Girl from Milan 1810.
5. Ciocciara (inhabitant of the Apennines from Fondi, province of Caserta). 1810.
6. Girl from Padua. 1810.

Centre Group

7–11. Southern Italy. 7: Calabrian brigand. 8: Man from Lecce

in Apulia. 9: Peasant from the Naples district. 10: Woman from the province of Cosenza in Calabria. 11: Man from the same district.

Bottom Group

12–16. Sardinia. 12: Elderly peasant from Bono (in the interior of the island of Sardinia). 13 and 14: Man and woman from the district of Nuoro (central Sardinia). 15: Woman from Ploaghe near Sassari (North-west Sardinia). 16: Shepherd from Gallura (most northern part of Sardinia).

134   ITALY. *Modern Times*

Top Group

1. Girl from Venice.
2. Fisherman from Chioggia near Venice.
3. Woman from Furlo (Friuli).
4 and 5. Peasants from Cascano (Campagna).
6. Woman from the island of Procida near Naples.

Centre Group

7 and 8. Costume of the Campagna near Rome.

9. Shepherd from the Campagna.
10. *Pifferaro* from Calabria.
11. Woman from the Abruzzi.

Bottom Group

12 and 13. Couple from the Cosenza district (Calabria).
14 and 15. Couple from Nicastro (Calabria).
16 and 17. Women from Osilo (near Sassari) in the northern part of Sardinia.

135   ALBANIA

Top Group

1 and 2. Dealer in clothes from Tirana in the costume of the Pelicares (militia).
3. Mohammedan Albanian (Arnaut) during the time of the Turkish sovereignty wearing *fustanella* (cf. plate 139; 12) originally the so-called Albanian shirt which is gathered by a band round the hips and falls down in wide folds to the knees giving the impression of a skirt. (Today a detached loin skirt). Sleeved waist-coat under a jacket with hanging sleeves. Decorated leggings.
4. North Albanian Turk with sleeved waistcoat covered by a short outer jacket and trousers in the Malissori fashion (cf. 9).
5. Woman from Prizren (Wilajet Kossowa) in the characteristic long baggy trousers.

Centre Group

6. Man of the Malissori tribe (mountain dweller) with hood under the cap.
7 and 8. Malissori women.
9. Man of the Malissori tribe with white fez, sleeved jacket

and broad cartridge-belt.
10. Woman of the Malissori tribe from Scutari in the ancient bell-shaped skirt.
11. Catholic peasant woman from the Elbassan district in festival garments.

Bottom Group

12 and 13. Catholic couple from Scutari.
14. Mohammedan girl wearing long baggy trousers and short-sleeved jacket.
15. Arnaut (cf. 3) wearing *fustanella* (loin-skirt) with double waistcoat, short jacket and hanging sleeves, leather shoes with turned up points, leggings all richly embroidered in gold.
16. Albanian woman from Janina in a rich costume. She wears a blouse of silk gauze with embroidered sleeves; from her hips to her feet large light pink baggy trousers with embroidery on the stomach, over it a kaftan (*anteria – entari*) with embroidered hanging sleeves. The outer garment is a shorter sleeveless kaftan. The fez or tarbush on her head decorated with gold cords and tassel.

SOUTHERN SLAVONIA

Top Group

1. Christian peasant from Herzegovina. Felt leggings. Double socks. Animal skin shoes laced with leather or straps, made of intestines of animals. (Shoes and socks together are called *opanken*).
2. Christian peasant woman (from the same district) going to market. *Opanken*; open, sleeveless coat.
3. Christian man from Herzegovina. Waistcoat with crosswise decoration under an outer jacket. Felt gaiters and shoes, the flat cap with black border and red top (not visible here) belongs to the national costume of the Serbs, probably originating from the Turkish tarbush or fez. Belt used as a pocket.
4. Girl from the neighbourhood of Split, formerly Ragusa, Dalmatia.
5. Elderly man from the neighbourhood of Split in a richly embroidered sleeved jacket with a waistcoat over it.
6. Young man from Split in a richly decorated costume. Sleeved jacket, gold braided outer waistcoat; wide skirt-like trousers and leather trimmed leggings.

Centre Group

7 and 8. Women from the Lika (formerly Hungarian district in the Karst along the Adriatic sea on the Lika river, Serbo-Croatian. North Dalmatia.
9. Seressaner (red cloaks). Cavalry regiments established in 1700 among Austrian frontier troops for the purpose of reconnoitring. Red cap, *dolman* (tight laced jacket), blue or red mantle. Long shot-gun, pistol, dagger like that of the Turkish police.
10. Bosnian Turk in a costume richly embroidered with gold, wide bag-like trousers tapering from the knees, in the shape of gaiters. These are fastened by hooks and eyes. In his belt curved dagger with long hilt (Arabian *handschar*, now obsolete). Pistol and pipe.
11. Montenegrin in a large sleeved coat open in front (national costume), woollen fringed cloak, white felt gaiters and *opanken*. The belt holds weapons and utensils.

Bottom Group

12 and 13. Bosnian Turks.
14. Peasant from the Serajewo district (Bosnia).
15. Servian peasant girl in festival costume.
16. Bosnian lady.
17. Montenegrin lady.

HUNGARY

Top Group

1. Rich young peasant from the county of Szolnok, Magyar.
2. Man from the county of Szolnok, Magyar.
3. Farm-servant from the county of Veczprem (district of the Balaton Lake and the Bakony Forest, Magyar).
4. Girl from the county of Veczprem.
5. Magyar. Cowherd (gulyás). Linen shirt and wide linen trousers *(gatya)*. Decorated mantle made of waterproof wool *(szür)*, large round hat, whip. The bottle is made of dried scrotum of a young bull.
6. Magyar. Peasant with sheepskin cap, decorated sheepskin coat *(bunda)* with a more valuable skin hanging down the back.

Centre Group

7. Woman servant from the county of Pesth.
8. Slovak linen dealer.

9 and 10. Men from Lower Hungary.
11. Gipsy in Magyar costume. Shirt, waistcoat with metal buttons, short cape (dolmány), close-fitting decorated cloth trousers of different coloured material, jack-boots with spurs.
12. The same. Laced waistcoat. Longer mantle. Round hat.

Bottom Group

13. Woman from Mezzökewecz.
14. Man from Mezzökewecz with wide open shirt sleeves and wide linen trousers.
15. Woman from Mezzökewecz.
16. Hungarian cowherd (gulyás, cf. 5).
17. Hungarian horse-herder.
18. Hungarian peasant in a long fringed leather cloak falling down in big folds *(suwa)*.

RUMANIA

Top Group

1. Rumanian from Transylvania.
2. Rumanian girl from Transylvania in Sunday dress.
3. Rumanian girl from Transylvania.
4. Girl from the Hatzecker Valley, Transylvania.
5. Armed Rumanian from Transylvania.
6. Rumanian girl from Transylvania.

Centre Group

7. Woman from the Marmaros, Carpathian Mountains, north-eastern Hungary, inhabited by Ruthenians, Slovaks, as well as by Germans and Magyars.
8. Raftsman on the river Theiss, from the Marmaros, wearing opanken (laced shoes cf. plate 136).

9. Woman from the former military frontier in the Petro-varadin district.
10. Man from the Slovak frontier district.
11. Woman from the Banat (the district around Timisoara and south of it) in Rumanian costume. The inhabitants (excepting the numerous German Swabians in the Banat) are partly Rumanians and partly Slovak Serbo-Croats.
12. Man from south-eastern Rumania.

Bottom Group

13. Rumanian peasant woman from Walachia in summer dress. Long sleeved shirt-like tunic *(camasha)*, embroidered with wool and over it the apron in front and behind *(catringa)*. cf. 15.

14. Rumanian, leading his bride at the wedding.
15. Rumanian woman from Walachia. Shirt-like tunic, coloured girdle, apron in front and behind, kerchief, neck decoration.
16. Rumanian in genuine national costume.
17–19. Women from the Bukowina with turned-up apron (17) and woven bag thrown over the shoulder.

139   GREECE. *Modern Times*

Top Group

1–5. About 1800 (according to Stackelberg's work).
1. Albanian.
2. Greek woman from the Islands (Island of Mykonos) with a red velvet cap, a piece of gold material with flower patterns inserted over the breast, tight white jacket without sleeves. Threefold sleeves, knee-length skirt, coloured stockings. Shoes with red heels.
3. Woman from the Athens district.
4 and 5. Women from the Island of Chios.

Centre Group

6–9. About 1825–30.
6. Peasant from the Athens district in festival attire. Striped silk scarf wound round his head. Two long-sleeved waist-coats with gold braid, cords and large silver fasteners. White cotton shirt, knee-length.
7. Janissary from Janina in southern Albania (cf. Turkey, modern time) wearing silk scarf wound round his head fastened in a knot under the chin. Long sleeveless woollen coat, shaggy inside.
8. Officer from Nauplia. 1825.
9. Shepherd from Arcadia.

Bottom Group

10. Greek peasant in goatskin mantle.
11. Greek shepherd in sheepskin mantle.
12. Arcadian deputy wearing the *fustanella*. 1879.
13. Greek woman from Constantinople.
14. Woman from Lala wearing fur-lined, embroidered leather jacket without sleeves.

140   BELGIUM. *19th Century*

Top Group

1. Peasant from the Brussels district (Brabant).
2. Boy from the Brussels district (Brabant).
3. Tinker from Brabant.
4. Woman making bobbin-lace from the Bruges district.
5. Woman from Bruges.
6. Woman from Ostend.

Centre Group

7. Milk maid from Antwerp (Flanders.)
8. Woman selling lace from Antwerp.

9. Maid servant from Antwerp.
10. Milk maid from Bruges.
11. Woman going to church (Antwerp).

Bottom Group

12. Fishermen from Blankenberghe (Flanders).
13. The same.
14. Milk maid from the neighbourhood of Ostend.
15. Peasant woman from the neighbourhood of Ostend.
16. Peasant woman from the Ardennes (south-eastern Belgium) of Walloon type (dark-haired).

141   FRANCE AND GERMANY. *Burgundy, Savoy, Alsace-Lorraine*

Top Group

1. Peasant woman from the neighbourhood of Pont-de-Vaux.
2. Peasant from Bresse (Burgundy).
3. Citizen from Bresse.
4. Middle class woman from Bresse.
5. Peasant from Savoy.

Centre Group

6. Girl from the Vosges.
7. Woman from Lorraine.
8. Man from Hunspach, south of Weissenberg (Lower Alsace).

9. Woman from the *Sundgau* (meaning: South district), southern part of Upper-Alsace.
10. Girl from Schleital on the Lauter river near the border of the Palatinate (Lower Alsace).

Bottom Group

11 and 12. Costume from Truchtersheim, north-west of Strasbourg.
13 and 14. Men from Geispolsheim (south-west of Strasbourg) in earlier costume.
15. Man in working dress; loose blue smock from the Schlettstadt district.

142   FRANCE. *Brittany, Burgundy, Auvergne*

Top Group

1. Women from Saille near Guérande (Brittany).
2. Peasant from Yaradey near Ancénis (Brittany).
3. Peasant woman from Château-Briant (Brittany).
4. Peasant woman from St. Bonnet (Burgundy).
5. Peasant from Upper Auvergne.

Centre Group

6. Girl from the neighbourhood of Riom (Lower Auvergne).
7. Girl from St. Germain Lebron (Lower Auvergne).
8. Girl from St. Germain (Upper Auvergne), with a large decorated straw hat.
9. Peasant from Chamalière (Lower Auvergne).
10. Girl from Latour (Lower Auvergne).

11. Old peasant from Coupière (Auvergne).
12. Old peasant from the Clermont-Ferrand district (Lower Auvergne).

13. Woman from Mâcon (Burgundy) wearing festival attire.
14. Woman from the former county of La Bresse (Burgundy).
15. Housekeeper from the Mâcon district (Burgundy). First half of the 19th century.

FRANCE. *Normandy and Brittany*   143

Top Group

1. Costume from the Granville district.
2. Woman from the Caux territory (Département Seine Inférieure, former province of Normandy) wearing the old coif called *cauchois*.
3. Costume from St. Valéry en Caux.
4. Costume of the Cherbourg district (Département Manche).
5. Costume from Crosville near Dieppe (Département Seine Inférieure, former Normandy).

Centre Group

6. Peasant woman from Vannes (Département Morbihan, former Brittany).

7 and 8. Peasants from Lambelle (Département Côtes du Nord, Brittany) in festival attire.
9. Peasant from Pont'Abbe (Département Finisterre, former province of Brittany).
10. Man from the Cornouailles district in Brittany (Département Finisterre).

Bottom Group

11. Peasant from Quimper
12. Peasant woman from Carhaix   (Département Finisterre,
13. Peasant from Ploare   formerly Brittany)
14. Girl from Morbihan
15 and 16. Live stock dealers from Langolan (Montagnes d'Arrée, Département Finisterre).

FRANCE. *Beginning of 19th Century*   144

Top Group

1. Woman from Harcourt near Caën (Normandy).
2. Costume from Alençon on the Sarthe (Normandy).
3–5. Festival costumes from Pollet.

Centre Group

6. Maid servant from Bordeaux (Guyenne).
7. Porter from Bordeaux.
8. Woman from Bordeaux selling baked apples.
9. Peasant woman from the Dauphiné.

10 and 11. Peasant couple from Auvergne.

Bottom Group

12. Woman from Nice (Provence).
13. Woman from Mâcon (Burgundy).
14. Woman from the district of Limoges.
15. Dock worker from Avignon on the Rhône.
16. Young woman from the Aure valley (western Pyrenées).
17. Peasant from Savoy.

NETHERLANDS   145

Top Group

1. Young peasant from the Island of Walcheren.
2. Woman from Volendam.
3. Woman from the Island of Hok in the Zuider Zee.
4. Lady from Friesland.
5. Fisherman from the Island of Marken.

Centre Group

6–10. Fishermen from the Island of Marken.

Bottom Group

12–16. Fishermen from Volendam.

SCOTLAND SINCE THE MIDDLE AGES   146

Top Group

1. Costume of the MacDougal Clan in the late Middle Ages.
2. Costume of the June Clan in the late Middle Ages. Armour and shield.
3. Costume of the Laurin Clan. 15th century.
4. Warrior of the Quaries Clan about 1600.
5. Bagpiper of the Cruimin Clan, 17th century. The medieval weapons were used by the Highlanders together with modern ones up to present times.

Centre Group

6. Man of rank of the Robertson Clan about 1670.
7. Man of rank of the McIntosh Clan. Beginning of the 18th century.
8. Man of rank of the Ogilvie Clan. Middle of the 18th century.

9. Soldier's uniform with the tartan of the Kennedy Clan. End of the 18th century.

Bottom Group

10. Man from the Ross Clan, not fully dressed.
11. Member of the Buchanan Clan.
12 and 13. Woman and boy of the Mattheson Clan. The woman in a more elaborate costume with valuable decorative buttons on the cuffs. The ends of the plaid are tucked into the girdle *(arisaid)*.
14. Girl from the Sinclair Clan. Plaid woven from wool and linen pulled over the head.

Clans are small Scottish tribes the members of which claim a common ancestor. They are led by a traditionally distinguished family. The women's costume was developed (like the kilt of the men) from a loin-cloth.

Top Group

1. Boat-woman from the Lake of Zug. 1824.
2. Peasant girl from the canton of Vaud (Village of Charnay near Clarence).
3. Milk man from the canton of Bern.
4. Peasant woman from the canton of Bern.
5. Man from the canton of Schaffhausen.

Centre Group

6 and 7. Young couple from the canton of Bern. 1804.

8 and 9. Couple from the canton of Aargau. 1804.
10 and 11. Couple from the canton of Fribourg. 1804.

Bottom Group

12. Girl from Knonau in the canton of Zurich. Earlier costume.
13. Canton of Zurich.
14. Canton of St. Gall.
15. Canton of St. Gall.
16. Appenzell, Inner Rhodes, (the catholic half canton near the Sentis).

Top Group

1. Peasant woman from Olten, canton of Solothurn.
2. Bride from Guggisberg, canton of Bern.
3. Girl from Guggisberg in working dress.
4. Woman from the Simmenthal, canton of Bern, going to church.
5. Peasant woman from the canton of Lucerne.

Centre Group

6. Peasant woman from the canton of Unterwalden.
7. Earlier costume from the canton of Schwyz.
8. Married (German) woman from the canton of Fribourg.
9. Woman from the canton of Valais.
10. Alpine dairy maid from the canton of Ticino (Italian frontier).

Bottom Group

11. Girl from Appenzell, Outer Rhodes (the half canton around Herisau and Trogen, where people adhere to the Reformed church).
12. Girl from the canton of Thurgau.
13. Girl from the canton of Aargau. Costume of the former Austrian Fricktal near the Rhine (cf. the costume of Hanau in Baden).
14. Girl from the canton of Zug.
15. Peasant woman from the Schächental, in the canton of Uri, in working dress. The so-called Uri-shoe consists of a thick wooden sole with heel, turned up rim, and four slits through which leather straps are passed and tied over the instep.

Top Group

1. Costume worn by women going to Holy Communion on the Island of Amrum (17th–18th centuries).
2. Costume worn on the island of Sylt in 1644. *Haud-dock* (white kerchief), *Siist* (full white linen skirt lined with fur), *Kardem* (shorter black skirt with low cut bodice). Mittens.
3. Costume worn by Sylt women going to Holy Communion in 1644. The head dress made of cardboard and covered with embroidered velvet, red cloth garment, fur coat with cord and metal ornamentation. Ceremonial handkerchief.
4. Bride from the island of Sylt (17th century). Head dress *huif* with large fringed cloth. *Siist* (cf. 2), sleeved jacket, black woollen outer skirt rolled up to the hips.
5. Costume at Wyk on the island of Föhr, 1798. Kerchief and neck scarf. Laced bodice. Spencer jacket. Elaborate breast ornaments.

Centre Group

6. Sunday costume from the island of Föhr, 1800. The kerchief (as a protection against the sun) also worn with festival costume.

7. Sunday costume from the island of Föhr 1850, closed bodice (like 8) over sleeved jacket.
8. Costume from the islands of the Halligen, 1850. Pointed girl's cap.
9 and 10. Festival costume on the island of Föhr, 1858 and later kerchiefs and breast cloths, elaborate silver ornamentation. Spencer jackets.
11. Costume from Heligoland. Small Frisian cap (cf. Holland).

Bottom Group

12. Costume worn at Holy Communion in the Wilstermark (Holstein). High wheel cap, laced bodice (like 8). Sleeved jacket. Fur muff.
13 and 14. Peasants' costume in the Probstei, Holstein (about 1800–10). The girl in a low-cut bodice, cap with ribbons, linen blouse, pleated skirt. The man in the old-fashioned citizen's costume of about 1786. (Long coat, short waistcoat, striped breeches, buckle shoes.
15. Milk maid in Glückstadt (Holstein) dressed in the new Empire fashion.
16. Costume from Itzehoe (Holstein). Patterned Spencer jacket over blue-striped skirt and apron, carrying a strange basket-like umbrella of wicker work over her head.

Top Group

1–4. Fishermen from Mönchgut (Island of Rügen). Short jacket, multi-coloured peaked cap, wide open linen trousers. 3: Black open cloth trousers; 4: High conical cap over a white one.

5 and 6. Fishermen's wives from Mönchgut. 5: Lined conical cap with silk ribbons, laced bodice, embroidered breast-cloth. Straw-hat over cap with ribbons.

Centre Group

7–12. Pyritzer Weizacker (Pomerania); striking colours (especially blue and red). 7 and 9: Blue silk cap with ribbons hanging down, sleeved jacket, coloured breast cloth, red woollen stockings with coloured gores, knee-length pleated skirt.

8 and 9. Blue cloth coat, with red lining (resembling the cut of uniforms). Buck skin breeches. Silk neck-cloth, black felt hat with silk ribbons. 11 and 12: Bride and bridegroom from the Weizacker.

13 and 14. Mecklenburg. 13: Small straw-hat with blue floating ribbons. 14: Similar to 8 and 10.

Bottom Group

15–17. Peasants from the Kreis Lebus (Mark Brandenburg). 15: Red coloured ribbon cap over lace cap: 16: Long uniform coat, red lined top hat; 17: Bodice with flower pattern, large cotton kerchief, and over it gray-black felt hat. White gathered cotton shoulder frill.

GERMANY. *Hanover, Hamburg, Brunswick* 151

Top Group

1 and 2. Gifhorn on the river Aller, area of Lüneburg, small black silk cap with spiked bands on top, and round the chin, and wide bands falling down the back (cf. 16–18). Large white frill round neck and shoulder *(goller)*.

3. Gifhorn. Long black cloth coat with red lining. Flat large-brimmed hat.

4–7. *Altes Land* (the old country) on the lower Elbe (also called *Cherry Land of Hamburg*, area of Stade, Province of Hanover.

4–6. Small coloured silk cap with broad braid and bow on the left side, the ends of which are floating down. Gold embroidered breast front piece, elaborate silver filigree ornaments (chains and buttons).

7. Peasant from the *Old Land* with waistcoat buttoned up to the chin, short coat and peaked cap.

Centre Group

8. Hamburg district. Flat hat with the brim slightly turned up over a narrow white frilled cap surrounding the face and fastened under the chin.

9. Osnabrück district. Round Osnabrück cap, flat linen collar.

10–13. *Vierlande* (district of four parishes) near Hamburg-Bergedorf. Costume of the market people. 10 and 11: Reddish-brown waistcoat and short woollen jacket. Silver buttons, top hat.

12 and 13. Under the straw-hat a black cap with a large striped pleated bow, called *Nessel* or *Krähe* (crow). Elaborate metal decoration and embroidery.

Bottom Group

14. Shepherd from the Brunswick countryside. Long white coat, cocked felt hat, gaiters.

15. Bortfeld near Brunswick. Red cloth waistcoat, short jacket, fur cap.

16. Gross-Denkte near Wolfenbüttel (Brunswick district). Small pointed black silk cap *(Eidopp)*, large stiff frill round the neck, red pleated skirt.

17 and 18. Market women from the village of Bortfeld. Red pleated skirt with green stripe on the border. White blouse *(Goller)* with ruffle visible round the neck. Small padded cap *(Eidopp)* with four broad bands falling down.

19. Peasant from the village of Bortfeld in a long white linen coat with red lining and felt cocked hat.

GERMANY. *Westphalia and Schaumburg-Lippe* 152

Top Group

1 and 2. Girls from the Osnabrück district. White frilled cap, fringed aprons.

3 and 4. Women from the Münster district. 3: Red skirt, cloth covering back, shoulders and breast embroidered with roses, high silk cap, silk belt. 4: Costume worn at Holy Communion, embroidered cap, with flat round piece at the back, flower-patterned blouse. Net shawl draped over shoulders and breast.

5. Girl from the district of Lübbecke. Flat-backed cap with long ribbons. White frill.

6. Old woman from Hille near Minden. Flat cap with broad ribbons.

Centre Group

7. Woman from the Porta Westfalica dressed all in black, flat cap with ribbons.

8. Women from the country near the river Ems. Cap with ribbons, shoulder scarf with flower patterns.

9. Man from Freienhagen in Waldeck. Long double-breasted coat, flat fur cap.

10. Girl from the Ravensburg district. Coloured flat-backed cap with ribbons, white frill.

11 and 12. Couple from Dankersen, district of Minden.

11. High cap, old-fashioned short shoulder cape *(Goller)*.

Bottom Group

13 and 14. Women from Schaumburg-Lippe. High caps with satin ribbons, large stiff frill. 14: *Bückeburg* cap (made of broad ribbons giving the impression of wings). Shoulder cape, the ends tied round the waist.

15–17. Peasants from Bückeburg. Winged caps, man in white coat and fur cap.

18. Peasant from Lindhorst (Schaumburg-Lippe). Buttoned-up double-breasted short jacket. Fur cap like 9.

19. Woman from Bückeburg in a large mantle with flounced shoulder cape. Winged cap.

GERMANY. *Hesse, Brunswick (Harz Mountains), Thuringia* 153

Top Group

1. Peasant from the Marburg district in working dress. Long smock of unbleached linen, knitted peaked cap.

2 and 3. Girls from the Marburg district. Thick woollen skirts.

High caps on the plain hair style. The cap *(Stülpe)* is made of linen embroidered with wool and tied with ribbons under the chin exposing the back of the head with the plaits arranged round the head (fig. 2).

4–6. Peasants from the Schwalm (between Alsfeld and Treysa).
5. Sunday attire with double waistcoat under the jacket and Sunday cap (fur cap).
7 and 8. Girls from the Biedenkopf district.

Centre Group

9. Girl from Nenndorf, Rinteln district.
10–12. Girls from the Biedenkopf district.
13. Boy from Nenndorf.
14 and 15. Earlier costume from the Schwalm. Long black buttoned-up coat (Holy Communion coat), long hair, large cocked hat (two-pointed). Gaiters.

Bottom Group

16. Women from the Harz Mountains. Thick circular coat with stripes arranged at angles, small pointed cap with ribbons.
17. Woman from the Stollberg district in a cotton mantle in which babies are wrapped when carried.
18. Woman from Dannstedt north of Wernigerode. Large cap with ribbons, golden necklaces.
19. Woman from Ettersberg near Weimar wearing a cap with ribbons arranged as wings.
20. Shepherd from the Harz Mountains with red-lined cloth coat decorated with brass buttons.

154 GERMANY. *Lusatia and Silesia*

Top Group

1. Woman from the Spreewald in Sunday attire. Kerchief tied in a way to form wing-like lappets. Sleeved jacket.
2. Woman belonging to the Slavic Wends in the Spreewald wearing festival attire. Large yellow, winged cap with ribbons.
3. Man inviting wedding guests from the Spreewald wearing uniform, sash and two-pointed cocked hat.
4. Protestant woman belonging to the Wends from Hoyerswerda (Liegnitz district) singing Easter songs and dressed in Sunday service clothes with a white fillet over the cap decorated with ribbons (according to a photograph by H. Retzlaff).

Centre Group

5. Wohlau costume ⎫ both with cap decorated
6. Liegnitz costume ⎭ with ribbons and breast cloth.
7. Festival attire from Hennersdorf (Troppau district) wheel-like cap.

8. Silesian festival costume. Ankle-length black coat (Holy Communion coat), felt top hat.
9. Costume from Tannhausen (province of Silesia). Stiff crêpe cap.

Bottom Group

10. Costume from Tannhausen. Cotton cap with wide floating ribbons.
11. Neuland near Neisse (Upper Silesia). Cap with long lappets hanging down at the sides (Barthaube: beard cap), Spencer jacket with flower pattern.
12 and 13. Upper Silesian winter costume (festival garments). 12: Sleeved jacket, shoulder collar; 13: Long coat reaching down to the calves, high fur cap.
14. Costume from Czarnowanz (Upper Silesia). Woollen pleated skirt with different coloured border, low necked bodice, red kerchief with flower pattern.

155 GERMANY. *Bavaria: Franconia, Upper Bavaria*

Top Group

1–5. Franconia (1800–25). 1 and 2: Nuremberg district (central Franconia). 1: Fur cap worn over a cap with ear-flaps. Cloth for protection against the rain. 2: Broad-brimmed felt hat, red waistcoat, knee-length coat. 3: Gochsheim near Würzburg (Lower Franconia), Franconian cap with ribbons, cloth for protection against the rain carried over her arm. 4: Geldersheim near Schweinfurt (Lower Franconia), large linen kerchief with pointed lappets on her head, pleated woollen skirt. 5: Lower Franconian peasant wearing a short jacket over an open waistcoat. Fur cap.

Centre Group

6–10. Upper Bavaria. Peasant from Dachau with chestcloth and cloth jacket. 7: Citizen's daughter from Dachau with ornamented bodice. 8: Peasant woman from Dachau. Short and heavy skirt *(Bollenrock)*. Draped net cap; short stiff bodice,

silk Spencer jacket. Multi-coloured knitted stockings. 9: Aichach. Large silk kerchief, coloured breast cloth, high, stiff bodice decorated with gold braid. Large straw bag. 10: Starnberg near Munich. Long coat with standing-up collar and cuffs.

Bottom Group

11–17, 11 and 12: Bayrischzell. Festival attire with chains and pendants on the bodice *(Geschnür)*, coloured breast cloth, silk apron. Flat felt hat with gold cords. 13: Peasant woman from Seefeld. 14 and 15: Schliersee. Short jacket of coarse woollen waterproof cloth with horn buttons. Buckskin breeches *(Wichs)* knee-length stockings *(Loferln)*, nailed boots, green velour hat, with pressed-in top. 16: Berchtesgaden. 17: Jachenau (tributary of the Isar) district. Longish woollen jacket with green cuffs, green waistcoat with metal buttons, white gored stockings, conical felt hat with silk cord.

156 GERMANY. *Baden*

Top Group

1 and 2. Peasant couple from Hornberg in the Black Forest. 1: Red chest cloth; 2: Shoulder wrap *(Goller)* with laced bodice, straw hat with woollen rosettes.

3–5. From the former county of Hauenstein, southern Black Forest, about 1825. One of the most ancient costumes of all Germany. 3 and 5: Open shoulder wrap *(Goller)* plait. 4: Sleeveless pullover shirt with frill, wide breeches.

6. Girl from the higher part of the Southern Black Forest about 1825. Laced bodice, open *goller*. Straw top hat.

Centre Group

7 and 8. Girl and woman from the Prech valley, Black Forest. Gaily coloured costume. High straw top hats, varnished yellow.
9. Peasant from the Hanau district (Rhine Valley). Cap made of otter's skin, pullover, shirt with standing-up collar. Black cloth coat.
10. Kinzig valley. Long red-lined coat, short red waistcoat, round felt hat.

11. Gutach valley (Black Forest). Long coat, lined red, over an open waistcoat.

Bottom Group
12. St. Märgen (Black Forest). Curved hat *(Schnapphut)*.
13. Girl from the Gutach valley. Hat with round woollen pompons *(Bollenhut)* over the cap; woman wearing black pompons. Goller of coloured silk round the neck (cf. 15).
14. St. Georgen. Swabian cap with embroidered top *(Plätz)*.
15. Gutach valley. Gutach cap with short net veil.
16. Peasant's daughter from the Lehnsgericht with coloured garland crown *(Schäppelkrone; Schäppel:* obsolete word for chaplet).

GERMANY. *Würtemberg* 157

Top Group

1. Near Ochsenhausen (South-eastern Würtemberg). Green waistcoat, green jacket, broad-brimmed round hat.
2. Near Göppingen. Pointed gauze cap, breast cloth, sleeved jacket.
3. Filstal (south of Hohenstaufen). Long blue coat, long red waistcoat, leather breeches, large flat hat.
4. Near Tübingen. Gauze cap, gold ornamented goller round the neck, laced bodice.
5 and 6. Near Ebingen, north of the river Danube. Festival attire. The bride is wearing a gold crown, low cut jacket, laced bodice; 6: Long coat, lined blue, slouched hat.

Centre Group

7 and 8. Betzingen near Reutlingen (near to the Swabian Alb).
7. Small round cap *(Kugelkäpli)*, red laced bodice with green ribbons, pleated skirt with gold braid.

8. Small flat black leather cap *(Schmeerkäpli)*, long white linen coat, red cloth waistcoat, leather trousers.
9. Echterdingen (south of Stuttgart). Simple Swabian cap with small point and cheek lappets.
10 and 11. Bride and bridegroom from Lossburg (Black Forest).

Bottom Group

12 and 13. Rottweil. Wheel-like head dress *(Rädliskappe)* embroidered with metal threads, the wheel-like arrangement fixed on a wire frame, and four large ribbons hanging down the back. Velvet jacket with puffed sleeves.
14. Peasant from Betzingen in a red waistcoat and peaked cap.
15. Schwenningen at the source of the Neckar. Round black damask cap with ribbons, black silk bodice *(Leibli)*, a pointed piece inserted in front, white linen collar with small frill.
16. Peasant from Betzingen in blue coat (for going to church). High felt hat, red waistcoat.

AUSTRIA. *Carinthia, Styria, Salzburg, Vorarlberg, Upper Austria, Lower Austria* 158

Top Group

1. Costume in the Gail valley, Carinthia. White pleated cap *(Petscha)*. Blouse with baggy sleeves, closed bodice, small chest cloth, short woollen skirt, apron, knitted cotton stockings.
2. Costume worn at Ischl (Upper Austria). Linz golden cap, hemispherical in shape with a high wing made of gold brocade.
3. Costume worn at Linz (Upper Austria). Linz golden cap.
4. Costume worn at Lambach (Salzburg Alps). Broad leather belt, broad brimmed top hat, riding boots made of Russia leather.
5. Costume worn near Klagenfurt (Carinthia). Flat man's hat worn over kerchief.

Centre Group

6. Costume worn at Seewiesen (Styria).

7. Costume from the Tulln district (Lower Austria).
8 and 9. Elderly couple from Zell am See, near Salzburg, about 1900. High top hats.
10. Styrian woman from Graz (Styria).

Bottom Group

11. Woman from Bludenz (Vorarlberg) in a pleated skirt, reaching up to the arms and large beaver skin cap.
12. Woman from Montafon (Vorarlberg) in a high cap of gold material *(Schabbale)*.
13. Girl from the upper Lech valley in a costume for attending church with a high stiff cap and long open mantle.
14 and 15. Couple from the upper Lech valley in an old-fashioned costume of the 18th century.
16. Girl from the Ötztal (Tyrol) with lace collar and blue-black round pointed woollen cap.

AUSTRIA AND ITALY. *About 1800–1850 (Tyrol)* 159

Top Group

1 and 2. Bruneck district, Italian southern Tyrol, Pustertal. 1: Short pleated skirt, sleeved jacket. 2: Broad-brimmed felt hat, chest cloth *(Brustfleck)*, short jacket.
3–5. Zillertal. 3 and 5: Man's hat like 4. Long black pleated

skirts, blue aprons, knee-length sleeved jackets, short stockings (covering the calves). 4: Broad-brimmed felt hat with silk cord and tassels. Red chest cloth *(Brustfleck)*. Embroidered leather belt, buckskin breeches, woollen jacket.

6 and 7. Bregenz Forest. 6: Top hat like 7. 7: Felt top-hat. Coat with skirts, red waistcoat, embroidered leather belt.

Centre Group

8 and 9. Pustertal. 8, 9 and 11 hats like 4.

10 and 11. Ötztal (Tyrol). 10: Broad brimmed flat hat.

12. Brenner Pass. The characteristic large conical beaverskin cap.

Bottom Group

13. Kastelruth (Grödenertal, Italian southern Tyrol). Large broad-brimmed hat, pleated wheel collar.

14 and 15. District of Bolzano (Italian southern Tyrol). 15: Picqué hat with waved brim.

16 and 17. Pfafflar (Vorarlberg). 17: high fur cap, stockings covering the calves only.

160   DENMARK. *About 1800*

Top Group

1. Woman from Skovshoved, on the Sound north of Copenhagen.

2. Woman from Tarmby on the Island of Amager near Copenhagen; dressed for church.

3 and 4. Man and woman from Kragerup.

5. Woman from Zealand on her way to milk cows.

Centre Group

6. Woman from Amager descending from Dutch settlers, going to church.

7. Young man from Amager.

8. Peasant woman from the south of the Island of Zealand wearing winter clothes.

9. Woman from Dragör on the Island of Amager, dressed for church.

10. Peasant from Zealand, Copenhagen district.

11. Peasant from Zealand, district of Kjöge.

Bottom Group

12. Peasant from Roskilde.

13. Girl from Amager, on her way to market in Copenhagen.

14 and 15. Mourners from the Dutch village on the Island of Amager. 14: Winter clothes. 15: Summer clothes.

16. Peasant from Amager, in winter attire.

161   DENMARK. *Modern Times*

Top Group

1 and 2. Man and woman from the Island of Amager near Copenhagen.

3. Man from the small Island of Lyö between Fünen and Alsen.

4. Farmer from Hedebo.

5. Woman from the Island of Fünen.

Centre Group

6 and 7. Man and woman from Refsnäs (north-west Zealand).

8. Woman from the small Island of Dreiö, south of Fünen.

9. Girl from the Ringkjöbing district (western Jutland).

10. Woman from Iceland.

11. Woman from southern Jutland.

Bottom Group

12 and 13. Woman and girl from the Island of Fanö.

14. Peasant woman from Skovshoved near Copenhagen.

15. Peasant woman from Agger.

16. Girl from the Island of Bornholm.

162   SWEDEN

Top Group

1–5. Lapps in Sweden. 1 and 2: Man and woman in winter clothes; 3: Hunting attire; 4 and 5: Woman carrying a cradle on her back; underneath: summer boots.

Centre Group

6. Woman from Mora on the Siljan lake (Dalarne).

7. Hawker from Leksand (south bank of the Siljan lake).

8. Woman from Jerrestad (Scania, Skane).

9. Woman from Wingaker, Södermanland.

10. Dalkulle, i. e. girl from Dalarne (Rättwik on the Siljan lake) in winter clothes.

The national costume of Dalarne (cf. fig. 6) is the best preserved and best known in Sweden, as the Dalkulle people go frequently to town to work (servants, green-grocers, ferry-boat rowers, charwomen, etc.). Characteristics are the conical cap and the horizontal stripes on the apron (10).

Bottom Group

11. Woman from Ystad (Scania, Skane).

12. Woman from Jerrestad (Scania, Skane) in a costume formerly worn by a woman for going to church after childbirth.

13. Peasant from Järbo, Gestrikland (west of Gefle).

14. Woman from Wingaker (cf. 9).

15. Woman making hay from Scania in the most ancient Germanic tunic (sark, Old Norse: *serkr*) with breast slit and in multi-coloured girdle, worn not later than about 1840.

163   NORWAY

Top Group

1–6. Norwegian Lapps in summer costume (Northern Norway).

1 and 2. Lapp settlers from Karasjok, district of Tromsö.

3, 4, 6. Nomadic Lapps, reindeer breeders.

5. A Lapp beauty.

Centre Group

7. Fishermen from the Bergen district.

8. Girl from the Hardanger Fjord.

9. Bride from the Jörund Fjord (south of Aalesund).

10. Peasant from Hitterdal (Telemark).

11. Girl from Numedal.

12. Peasant from Sätersdalen, southern Norway.
13. Peasant from Hitterdal (southern Norway) in overalls for working.

14. Girl from Sätersdalen (south Norway) in a costume already worn during the Old Norse bronze period (pleated skirt up to the arm-pits, girdle, sleeved jacket fastened in front).
15 and 16. Costume worn in Telemark.

BOHEMIA, MORAVIA, SLOVAKIA 164

Top Group

1. German speaking Bohemian from the district of Pilsen.
2. Man from the Pilsen district.
3. Bohemian.
4. Man from the district of Eger.
5. Woman from the Pilsen district.
6. Woman from the district of Pilsen.

Centre Group

7. Moravian woman from the south eastern part of the country, of Slav descent. White short skirt *(fertoch)*, really a broad pleated apron fastened in front where it is covered by a second apron. Blouse with sleeves *(rukavce)*, low cut bodice ornamented with braids *(lajdik)*, coloured kerchief (so-called Leipzig kerchief).

8. Moravian girl from the Eisgrub district. German costume.
9 and 10. Slovakian bride and bridegroom.
11. Peasant from the Zemplin district.

Bottom Group

12. Slovakian peasant woman.
13. Farm labourer from the Pressburg district (Slovakia).
14 and 15. Couple from the Zips (district of the High Tatra). The man wears laced shoes (thick natural leather fixed round the foot and laced, a very old form of footwear, especially in Croatian, Dalmatian and Rumanian districts and still worn in modern times).
16. Peasant from Trencin.

POLAND 165

Top Group

1–7. Peasants from Galicia.
1–3. Peasants from the Cracow district. 2: Wearing an embroidered shoulder cape.
4. Girl from Lobzow.
5. Peasant from the Cracow district.
6 and 7. Goralians (mountain dwellers of the Beskiden). 6: Boy making wire nets to protect earthenware vessels (pot knitter).

Centre Group

8. Peasant woman from Lowicz (district of Warsaw) wearing a mantle.

9. Peasant from the same district.
10. Peasant girl dressed for a festival.
11. Servant to a noble family.
12. Coachman to a noble family.

Bottom Group

13. Peasant woman from Lubelskj with a spinning wheel.
14. Man from the government of Warsaw.
15. Young man from the same district.
16. Peasant from the government of Radom.
17. Peasant woman from Lowicz (government of Warsaw) in festival attire.

RUSSIA. *19th Century* 166

Top Group

1 and 2. Village elder with his wife.
3. Greek-orthodox monk.
4. Hackney-coachman *(iswoschtschik)* in a padded costume (also worn in summer).
5. Young Great Russian peasant.

Centre Group

6. Peasant woman from the Tula district at the well.
7. Peasant woman from the Moscow district.
8. Great Russian porter.
9. Peasant woman from Serkonkoff.
10. Kalmuck merchant. The Kalmucks (belonging to the Mon-

golian race inhabit mostly the country south of the lower Volga, i. e. north-west of the Caspian sea).

Bottom Group

11–15. Volga Finns (west of the middle part of the Volga). 11: Woman from the Chuvash Mountains (Chuvash people cf. Mordvinians).
12 and 13. Votiak women belonging to the Finnish stock, the greatest part of them living in the district of Perm. 14: Ersa-Mordvinians from Arsatov (Government of Simbirsk-Ulyanovsk). 15: Moksha-Mordvinian woman from the Government of Penza. (The Mordvinians and Chuvash people belong to the Bulgarian family of the Finns).

EUROPEAN RUSSIA 167

Great Russians (Muscovites), the Slav inhabitants of the northern districts of Russia from the Ural to as far as Smolensk and the Plipsi Lake in the west, in the south as far as Kazan and beyond Nizhni-Novgerod, Koslov and Orel, also have settled in the district of the lower Volga, the Crimea and the greater part of Siberia. – The White Russians, (the smallest of the three European main tribes) live in the western part bordering on Lithuania (till 1772 under Polish rule, therefore inhabited by a certain number of Jews). – Little Russians really means subject to the Great Russians, today called Ukrainians. They live in Volhynia, Podolia and on either side of the Dnieper. The Ukrainians have kept their race purer and preserved their customs more than the rest of the Russian population. The Ruthenians in East Galicia and in districts bordering on Hungary belong to the Ukrainians.

1–4. Great Russians. 1: Great Russian woman.
2. Woman from Nizhni-Novgerod (Volga) and 3: Woman from Archangel.
4. Woman from Orel.
5. White Russian.

Centre Group

6–10. Little Russians (Ukrainians). 6: Little Russian woman from Kherson (Black Sea). 7: Ukrainian peasant woman.

8: Old Ukrainian. 9: Ukrainian woman in festive attire. 10: Young Ukrainian.

Bottom Group

11. Don Cossack about 1813.
12. Country postillon (jämtschik).
13 and 14. Little Russian peasants.
15. Great Russian peasants.
16. Little Russian country girl.

168   BALTIC PROVINCES AND FINLAND. *18th and 19th Centuries*

Top Group

1. Woman from Latvia.
2. Woman from Esthonia in coloured skirt made of material with the same pattern on both sides.
3. Woman from Ingermanland. 18th century.
4–6. Finnish costume (according to figures in the Museum Rissanen, Helsinki).

Centre Group

7. Woman from Esthonia. 18th century (Back view of 14).
8. Finnish peasant woman from the government of Leningrad.
9. Livonian girl from the Island of Ösel. Next to her and in the right corner: front and side view of the horned cap made of straw and covered with cloth.

10. Part view of the *Sarafan* skirt with straps, made of thick pleated and quilted material.
10a. Cloth bodice. 10b. short linen blouse.

Bottom Group

11. Finnish woman in festive attire. 18th century.
12. Finnish peasant woman. 18th century.
13. Finnish peasant. 18th century.
14. Esthonian woman (cf. 7, back view). 18th century.
15. A maiden from Caluga (Russian Government). 18th century.
11–15. From the travelling book by Johann Gottlieb Georgi, describing all peoples of the Russian empire. Petersburg. 1776.

169   TURBAN STYLES *(from India to North-west Africa)*

The turban consists of a cap around which a silk or muslin scarf or cloth is draped. This cloth called *Keffiyeh* in Arabic or *Koffia* in Moorish is a very old Oriental head-dress. Already the Hebrews wore it draped round their heads. Today the hey-day of the turban is passed. The Ottoman officers, soldiers and officials, etc., have worn the red tarbush with tassel without a wrapper ever since the extensive new regulations of Sultan Mahmud II., 1806–39. (The name *fez* used by Europeans for the Arabian word *tarbush* is derived from the Moroccan capital *Fez*. In Persia the *kulah* is worn.

1. Turban of the Sultan Mohammed II., 1451–1481, the conqueror of Constantinople, according to a memorial coin, in the Berlin Münzkabinett.
2. Sultan Suleiman the Great, 1520–66. According to a woodcut of the 16th century.
3. Persian in earlier times.
4. Oriental on a Renaissance painting. Rome, Vatican, Appartamenti Borgia.
5. Quilted linen cap *(takia)* which according to Moorish fashion is worn under the tarbush, or without it by ordinary people.
6. Turkish tarbush.
7. Low crowned tarbush worn in Maghreb (Western country, west of Egypt).
8. Turban from a Venetian representation about 1500. (Carpaccio), sewn or pinned up.
9. Egyptian turban according to a Venetian representation, about 1500. (Bellini). Tightly wrapped round.
10. Egyptian turban with high tarbush and neck protection. (According to Bellini).
11. Green turban. (According to Bellini). Green head bands are

only allowed to be worn by the descendants of the prophet and the emirs.
12. Padded under-cap, green. Museum, Copenhagen.
13. Black under-cap.
14. High cap with a low turban *(saryk)*. According to Bellini. Cf. figs. 34 and 35.
15. High tightly wrapped turban, (Egyptian), according to Bellini.
16 and 17. Turbans according to Vivarini, about 1500. Painting formerly in the Berlin Museum: *Adoration of the Kings.* North African type of turbans.
18. Turban according to Carpaccio, about 1500. Tightly wrapped North African type.
19. Turban according to Carpaccio, about 1500. Loosely wrapped turban with burnous, the hood of which can be pulled over it (for travelling).
20. Turban according to Carpaccio. Moorish.
21. Modern Moroccan, the turban wound in a roll around a tarbush without a tassel.
22. Tunisian turban.
23. Moorish prince in the Middle Ages. According to a representation in the Alhambra. The ends of the Keffiyeh are thrown over the shoulders as a neck protection.
24. Tunisian turban wound loosely in a roll around the head.
25. Thick brown or black camel hair cord wound round a stiff felt cap and white haik covering it. Algeria.
25a. The felt cap belonging to fig. 25.
26 and 27. Silk caps lined in gay colours around which the turban scarf is wound. Turkestan.
28. Turban from Bokhara.
29. Similar to 25 according to an example from Palestine.

30. High tarbush with gaily coloured silk turban scarf. Western Asia Minor.
31. Persian with lambskin cap *(kulah)*.
32. Kurd. The scarf is embroidered (yellow on white).
33. Felt cap worn by Kurds (cf. fig. 34).
34. Kurd with a high cap and coloured turban scarf loosely wrapped.
35. Kurdish low turban wound around tarbush with tassel.
36. Turban, Hindustan.
37. Turban, Afghanistan.
38. Afghan. The cap of quilted gold brocade.
39. Afghan. The ends of the turban scarf hanging down on the shoulders.
40. Afghan. Loosely wrapped turban over felt or linen cap.
41. Baluch.
42. Baluch. Roll-like scarf.
43. Sultan of Zanzibar, 1875. The end of the turban falls down over his shoulder.
44. Imâm, officiating priest of a Mohammedan mosque. 1860.
45. Kashmir prince. Red turban with gold borders, diadem, clasp, heron's feathers. The Turkish pashas and commanders used to wear heron's feathers on the turban.
46. Kashmir, turban loosely draped, white.
47. Kashmir, turban loosely draped and covering the ears, like fig. 36. Coloured.

48. An example from India. Brocade cap. Scarf in one colour.
49. Radhanpur, India, small turban, olive green, red and gold.
50. Brahman. Tightly wound coloured turban.
51. Parsee from Bombay. Turban wound tightly around a conical cap (picture next to the turban).
52. Man from Pondicherry. Red turban with flower pattern and gold stripes woven in. The caste mark painted on his forehead.
53. South Indian stage turban.
54. The same, back view.
55. Merchant from Madras.
56 and 57. Madras shoemaker; turban loosely wound.
58–60. Men from the retinue of the Maharaja of Pudukkottai.
61. South Indian barber with pink turban.
62 and 63. Man from the caste of the chatti of Coromandel Coast. Red turban with gold stripes over the temples, light green turban wound round the back of the head.
64. High priest of a Vaishnava temple at Tirapadi.
65. Marwari merchant, money-lender from Poona. Red turban with gold ribbons.
66. Marwari sorcerer from Poona. Red turban.
67. Coolie from the Malabar coast. White turban. According to photographs and pictures in travel books collected by Max Tilke.

Top Group

1. Bairakdar (ensign).
2. Harbadshi with a turban made of a cloth 40 yards long.
3. Artilleryman.
4. Janizary of the embassies.
5. Provost of the janizaries. The rice spoon in a case fixed to the cap, as worn by the Janizaries during war time.
6. Artillery captain of the janizaries (Oda-bashi – inspector of rooms), at the same time administrator of inns and caravanserais.

Centre Group

7. So-called jamak, representative of the janizaries.
8. Sailor.
9. Peik, member of a body-guard of whom ten to twelve surrounded the sultan on his riding expeditions.
10. Turkish woman (veiled), walking in the streets.
11. Turkish woman wearing indoor costume.
12. Janizary accompanying a vizier. The janizaries were abolished after the rising in 1826.

Bottom Group

13. Great vizier in a fur trimmed costume for attending the council. He wears, instead of a turban, the ceremonial muslin cap (pointed or flat-topped) with a gold ribbon or woven in gold stripes, a cap worn by high officials.
14. Sultan in a taffeta costume with sable trimming and long hanging sleeves.
15. High officer of the body-guard with the janizary cap surrounded by a balloon-like bag. Wide baggy trousers, gaiters up to the knees, fastened by hooks. Fox-fur trimming on the outer coat *(dolman)* and silver belt into which the knout is stuck.
16. Sultan's wife with wide red trousers, green garment, with silver braids, red jacket, velvet fur-trimmed coat with gold braids on the seams.
17. Dancer in the Seraglio, wearing costume of orange coloured cloth with gold ornamentation. Sash.
18. Woman of the Seraglio. Trousers, garment slashed at the sides and outer garment with winged sleeves. Sash with hanging ends, strings of pearls and half moon as hair decoration. Shoes with wooden sandal stilts.

Top Group

1. Turkish *hodsha* in Scutari (Albania). *Hodsha* means: scholar, religious teacher, also: master, mister.
2. Turk from Monastir in Macedonia.
3. Turkish harem woman wearing indoor costume. Istambul.
4. Vendor of comestibles, especially cakes, sweets or ices, in Istambul. The cakes etc. are protected by the glass covers.
5. Dervish from Istambul.

6. Porter from Istambul.

Centre Group

7. Water-carrier from Istambul in summer attire.
8. Turkish lady in the earlier out-door costume. Saloniki.
9. Lower middle class woman in out-door attire. (Istambul).
10. An official (*aga* – illiterate).
11 and 12. Anatolian peasants from the district of Ankara (Asia Minor).

13. Harem woman from Istambul in gold embroidered cloth-jacket with hanging sleeves over the silk. Entari (Kaftan) the two front parts of which are gathered on the hips thus exposing the silk baggy trousers.

14–18. Turks (ordinary people) in front of a popular café, smoking the narghile rented from the proprietor who also serves the coffee.

172 SOUTH-EASTERN CAUCASUS AND ARMENIA

Top Group

1. Caucasian body-guard, about 1870.
2. Tcherkes (Circassian), about 1800.
3. Caucasian village elder about 1870.
4. Man from a south Circassian tribe (Ubyck) about 1850.
5. Tcherkes (Circassian) 1850 in the long national coat *(Cherkesska)*.
6. Man belonging to a north Circassian tribe.

Centre Group

7. Woman in Grusian costume from Georgia or Grusia, the district south of the Caucasus (Transcaucasia).

8. Woman of the Kabardians, Tcherkesses of the Terek district.
9. Armenian peasant from the Erserum district. 1880.
10. Armenian woman from Kars 1880.
11. Armenian bishop in ceremonial robe.

Bottom Group

12. Wife of a Kurdish chief.
13. Kurd belonging to the Yezidis (sect).
14. Tartar women from Nukha.
15. Woman from the Kara-papaks.
16. Man from Daghestan (Lesghir).

173 SOUTH-WESTERN CAUCASUS

Top Group

1. Above – Imeritian with large hair arrangement and the national flat (plate-like) cap.
2 and 3. Below – two Imeritians with high Astrakhan caps.
4 and 5. Armed Adigheh. The *bashlik* draped as a turban.
6 and 7. Mountain Lazes.
8. Young Laze.

Centre Group

9. Armenian woman.
10. Greek woman.

11. Peasant with *bashlik* turban from Trebizond.
12. Horse dealer with patched *entari* (kaftan) from Trebizond.
13. Street vendor selling coffee.

Bottom Group

14 and 15. Armenian women from Akhaltskh. 14: in indoor dress with cloth apron. 15: Bride in festive attire. Government of Tiflis.
16. Monk from the monastery of Gelati near Kutais.
17. Turkish citizen from Kars.
18. Kurdish girl from Alexandropol.

174 CAUCASUS

Top Group

1–5. Mountain dwellers from the high central Caucasus.
1 and 2. Khevsur couple from the high central Caucasus. The Khevsurs (inhabitants of ravines) belong to the Georgians.
3 and 4. Couple belonging to the Tushes (from Tushetia) of Georgian descent.
5. Andijan from Kideri (in the high Daghestan) in sheep skin coat.

Centre Group

6. Shepherd from the Svanetia district (Government of Kutais).
7. Gurian prince in an earlier costume, Georgian inhabitant of the Guria district (Gono-Kutais).
8. Mingrelian in the so-called *Cherkesska* (long coat with two rows of cartridge pouches). The *bashlik* (Turkish word meaning head-dress) is draped as a turban.

9. Grusian dealing with cream cheese. Man from the Tiflis streets (*Grusian* = Russian word for Georgian).
10. Georgian prince from Tiflis in earlier national costume.
11. Ossete of the militia wearing *Cherkesska* (cf. 8), *burka* (outer coat), *papache* (Astrakhan cap), *kindshal* (dagger hanging on the belt.)

Bottom Group

12. Armenian woman of rank from Julfa (Persian border).
13. Armenian peasant woman from Shusha.
14. Armenian in earlier national costume, from Shusha.
15. Armenian inn-keeper from the Tiflis district. 1912–13.
16. Kurdish chief. From the district of Erivan (southern Caucasus).
17. Kurd from the Nestorian mountains (southern Caucasus).

175 TURKESTAN AND IRAN (PERSIA)

Top Group

1–6. Western Russian Turkestan and Bokhara.
1. Man from Bokhara. Tunic made of printed cotton. Silk outer garment (in Arabian: *Chil'at*, in Persian: *Chal'at)* with blended patterns, boots, overshoes and muslin turban.
2. High official hawking. Cap, cloth coat, leather trousers embroidered with silk. Boots.

3. Man of rank wearing a velvet coat ornamented with gold and silver, brocade boots, over velvet, gold-embroidered shoes.
4. Man from Samarkand, cap, garment, sash, slippers.
5. Horseman wearing jack-boots and three different garments: the under-garment made of cotton, the two top ones of silk.
6. Street vendor from Samarkand, in cotton garments.

7–17. Iran.

7. Muleteer. Astrakhan cap, coat, open in front with tight sleeves *(alkaluk)*, sash, semi-wide trousers *(zerejumeh)*.

8. Businessman. Astrakhan cap. Silk *alkaluk*. Outer coat, wide trousers, coloured woollen stockings, green slippers.

9. Worker. Astrakhan cap. Coat with wide skirts and made of striped green silk, tight black trousers.

10. Mullah or Achund (Mohammedan theological scholar) of the principal mosque Mesdshid-i-Shah in Ispahan. Large white muslin turban, long, wide gown covered by a long sleeveless mantle.

11. Falconer. Coat with wide hanging sleeves, slashed open and exposing semi-wide shirt sleeves, wide trousers.

12. A rich man. High Astrakhan cap, lined red, brown gown with narrow sleeves, covered by a red fur-trimmed jacket, over it cloth coat with slits for the arms and hanging sleeves. Woollen socks. About 1820.

Bottom Group

13. Woman from Shiraz. Large kerchief, with a long veil falling down the back. Short wide skirt.

14. Rich woman. Long white trousers of knitted material, short white dress (resembling a crinoline). Shoulder cape. Hair decorated with flowers.

15. Nurse with kerchief. Blouse of diaphanous material, long tight trousers, short skirt.

16. Rich woman wearing turban with the ends of the material hanging down, long-sleeved brocade bodice, sash round the waist, fur trimmed jacket with hanging sleeves, wide baggy silk trousers. Bare feet with green slippers. About 1820.

17. Woman in out-door attire. Wide baggy trousers, being narrowed and forming garters at the ankle. Black cape and large veil in front of face.

18. Dervish (cf. plate 171, 5). Embroidered cap wound round with woollen cords. Alkaluk (open coat) and Zerejumeh (semi-wide trousers); outer garment (similar to that of the Mullah, fig. 10). Sash with the ends falling down. Necklaces, sandals. In one hand the vessel (for the alms given to them) with the brass chains, in the other hand a halberd for self-castigation.

WEST TURKESTAN AND ASIATIC RUSSIA   176

Top Group

1–6. Turkestan and Bokhara.

1. Dervish from Bokhara with bottle-shaped pumpkin and instruments for castigation. The costume of the dervishes varies according to the orders (of which twelve are said to exist). These Mohammedan monks have caps of various shapes and all wear a coat *(chirka)*.

2. Turkoman with lambskin cap.

3. Dancer from Samarkand.

4–6. Women from Samarkand. Fig. 5 has partly taken off the mantle (with the characteristic sleeves like 6) essential as an out-door garment. 4 shows the thick veil like a wire meshing mask.

Centre Group

7–17. Bashkirs, Kirghiz, Kalmucks. The Bashkirs belong to the Ural-Altaic race and are nomadic stock-breeders and bee-keepers. The Kirghiz are Mohammedans and belong to the Turkish tribes of the same race.

7 and 8. Young Bashkir couple, the man wearing a dark kaftan made of cloth or nankin material; underneath: garment with belt and trousers. Fur cap. Woman in silk kaftan, red cap and many ornaments of glass beads, corals, etc.

9. Kirghiz woman in bridal gown.

10. Kirghiz woman from Bokhara with veil-turban and quilted kaftan *(chalat)*, a garment of honour worn by officials of merit etc., a wide silk or cloth outer garment with long sleeves according to central Asiatic fashion.

11. Kirghiz man wearing fur cap, fur-trimmed woollen coat with sash and silk *chalat*. The Kirghiz costume consists furthermore of wide woollen trousers and riding-boots (not visible here).

12. Armed Kirghiz. The Kirghiz are excellent shots, even if only using old-fashioned rifles.

Bottom Group

13 and 14. Tartar women from Turkestan.

15 and 16. Kalmuck couple. The man with his fur coat turned inside out. The Kalmucks are genuine Mongols who during the 17th and 18th centuries left their homeland (Dzungaria) in order to wander westward and settle in various parts of Russia, Siberia and Central Asia.

17. Kirghiz shaman (priest doctor). Head-dress with fur and feathers. On the sleeve-seams long leather strips with jingling metal plates. Pictures over 17: On top, left: Silk Kalmuck cap with fur, below, left: Kirghiz cap, right: head of a Kirghiz woman.

BALUCHISTAN, AFGHANISTAN, MONGOLIA, AND TIBET   177

Top Group

1 and 2. Khans (chiefs) from Baluchistan. Gold-embroidered, fur-lined velvet coats, 2: with turban of tube-like scarfs wound round the head.

3. Soldier from the frontier of Baluchistan and Afghanistan. Round shield, sword of Indian shape.

4. Mountain dweller from Baluchistan. Silk jacket. Rifle with rest.

5. Woman from Kabul (Afghanistan).

6. Hindu from Peshawar. Gold-embroidered and silk-lined cloth coat over a wide silk or cloth garment. The turban is wound round a pointed cap made of Turkestan material.

A painted sign on the forehead. Boots with high iron heels. (Peshawar belonging to India, since 1840. Transit road for the trade between India, Afghanistan and Central Asia.)

Centre Group

7. Lama (Buddhist priest or abbot, also prophet and magician, etc., of the Tibetans, Mongols, and Kalmucks) with a rattle (made of a child's skull covered with skin). Tibet.

8. Lama in a wide mantle with high red cap. Tibet.

9. Costume of part of the Tunguses between Yenissei and Amur.

10. Woman from Tibet with characteristic head-dress.
11. Girl from Tibet.
12. Lama from Lhasa (capital of Tibet).

Bottom Group

13–16. Inhabitants of Kuldja (Chinese district of East Turkestan). The two women in native costume, the boy and the man in Chinese costume with the native national cap.

17. Chief of the Dunganions (Turkomano-Tarars, inhabitants of Dzungaria).
18. Dunganian woman.
19. Buriat (the Buriats: A Siberian Mongolian tribe from the district of Lake Baikal). Fur coat with iron ornaments, bow and silver decorated quiver. The Buriats are stock breeding nomads and hunters, also famous for leather work and weaving.

178 AFGHANISTAN AND INDIA

Top Group

1–5. Afghanistan.
1. Armed villager from the ruling Afghan tribe of the Durani. Rifle with rest.
2. Hindki i. e. wholesale dealer, money changer, in winter clothes.
3. Armed Afghan in summer clothes.
4. Shepherd from the Durani tribe. Felt-like mantle with very long sleeves. Lambskin cap. The beard dyed with henna (cf. Ancient Egypt).
5. Soldier from Kohistan, a mountainous district, in winter clothes. Short sleeved coat made of hide, leather-covered round shield. Rifle like 1.

Centre Group

6–7. India.
6 and 7. Banjar and wife. The Banjari are a tribe in central India, live as nomads under a chief, and do their corn dealing by ox-carts.
8. Maharaja of Dholpur, a state of Rajputana, India.

9. Court official from Kashmir.
10. Hindu from Simla, formerly summer residence of the viceroy in the Himalayas.
11. Man belonging to the Oudh tribe from Lucknow. Oudh is the country where in antiquity early Indian culture flourished and later on Gautama Buddha was teaching. The capital, Lucknow, remained the recognized centre where poetry, learning and music were fostered. The inhabitants are mostly Hindus, the minority Mohammedans.

Bottom Group

12 and 13. Court official and Raja (i. e. prince) from Dirhut.
14. Fakir from Benares.
15. Dancer from Calcutta (*Dewadashi* servant of the gods). Besides the temple assistants there are the ordinary vagrant dancers, who perform their dances for money.
16 and 17. Princes of Brahmin descent from Orissa (the holy district of the Hindus with many temples and situated on the Bay of Bengal.

179 INDIA. *1600–1800. Mohammedan Princes*

Top Group

1. Man of rank belonging to the Rajputs (a caste very proud of their descendancy from an ancient Indian warrior caste, but who in the course of time have intermarried with other races. Most of them live in Northwest India, in Rajputana which consists of several different states).
2. Jehangir, son of Akbar, the great Mogul emperor in India, who resided in Agra. 1559–1627.
3. The last ruler of the Mohammedan dynasty of the kingdom of Golconda, which was overthrown by Aurung-Zebe in 1687. Golconda is situated seven miles northwest of Hyderabad.

Centre Group

4. A ruler of Delhi. 17th century.

5 and 7. Great Mogul of India, Achmed Shah (1748–58) with two servants.

Bottom Group

8. Murad-Bakche, imperial prince, brother of Aurung-Zebe (cf. 3), 17th century.
9. Woman of a rich family, 18th century with ornaments on her ears, nose, forehead, hair and neck.
10 and 11. Mohammedan Indian with his wife. 18th century.
12. Warrior of the Rajputs. 18th century.
According to contemporary original paintings in the respective department of the Lipperheide costume library (formerly in the State Art Library at Berlin and other collections).

180 INDIA. *Modern Times*

Top Group

1. Man from Bombay.
2. Footman from Bombay.
3. Woman from Bombay.
4. Coolie woman.
5. Man of Dravidian descent from Madras. (The Dravidians are the main original population in India who in prehistoric times were pushed back towards the south and the hilly districts of the interior by the Aryans invading the country from the north.)

6. Brahmin from Bengal.

Centre Group

7. Gardener from Poona (Bombay).
8 and 9. Landowners from the same district.
10. Business-man from the same district.
11. Wife of a Mahratta (the Mahrattas being a warrior race).
12. The same costume, back view.

Bottom Group

13–15. Inhabitants of Ceylon.

13. Tamil belonging to a more cultured tribe of the Dravidian population, in the north of Ceylon and the southern part of India.

14. A drummer.

15. Dancer (Devil dancer) with wooden mask.

16–18. Inhabitants of South India.

16. Actor playing a woman's part.

17 and 18. Native elder with his wife.

CHINA. *National Costume and Dignitaries' Costume* 181

Top Group

1. Servant, bareheaded.
2. Ordinary man from Northern China in winter costume.
3. Usher to the court.
4. Street barber with padded jacket.
5. Man belonging to the lower classes.
6. Peasant with felt hat.

Centre Group

7. Officer.
8. Soldier in the ranks.

9. Soldier from Kuldja in East Turkestan. Cf. pl. 177, 13–16.
10. Cavalry general in a costume of earlier times.
11 and 12. Mandarins of high rank.

Bottom Group

13. Lower class Chinese woman.
14. Lower class Chinese woman from Tsingtao.
15. Woman in a modern outfit from Northern China.
16. Bride from Shanghai with strings of pearls hanging down from her head-dress, Chinese silk and gold embroidery.
17. Violin player from Northern China.

CHINA. *National Costume and Dignitaries' Costume* 182

Top Group

1. Judge in a simple tunic and straw hat.
2. Chinese mandarin with tunic under two silk outer garments with a piece of brocade across the chest, long necklace and velvet cap.
3. Chan (prince of Mongolian descent).
4. His official in a long tunic, short sleeveless outer garment and cloth cap.
5. Business man in silk trousers, long under-garment, sleeved jacket and cloth cap.

Centre Group

6. Woman from Northern China.

7 and 8. Girls from Southern China in indoor attire.
9. Woman's costume according to the old national tradition.
10. Woman from Shanghai in festival attire; on top right the crippled women's feet (as produced for aesthetic reasons: a custom not followed in Northern China).

Bottom Group

11–13. Chinese mother with child and servant.
14. Nurse with child carried by means of a cloth slung over one shoulder.
15. Woman from Manchuria.
16. Chinese woman with stilt-like wooden under-shoes.

JAPAN. *National Costume and Stage Costume* 183

Top Group

1. High Japanese officer in out-door costume.
2–5. Japanese women with sunshades made of a bamboo frame and covered with silk, linen or glazed paper.
6. Yakounine (*yakou*: office; *nine*: man): police officer belonging to the lower aristocracy. He also acts as a guide. An emblem of his profession is fixed on his girdle at the back.
7. Japanese of the privileged class in the costume of the students of the University of Yeddo. He carries a sword and wears silk skirt-like trousers and shoes with wooden under-shoes (stilts).

Centre Group

8–11. Japanese actors (figures of the old Japanese stage).
8. Nakamura Utayëmon as *Shirabyoshi Hana* (lady of the court) in the ballet *Dôjôji*.
9. Omotakaya Kinoshi Shikawa Danshiro in *Kanjincho* (as court official).
10. Actor in a woman's part.
11. Ichikawa Danjuro V in the part of a *Daimyo* (territorial prince).

Bottom Group

12 and 13. Buddhist monks with small rosaries, which, origin-

ally larger, were shaped like very big snakes. Alms bag on their backs. Stilted shoes.

14. Musician (girl) with the three-stringed *Sam-Sim*.
15. Young servant girl with a kerchief wound round her head, bare-footed.
16. Japanese woman wearing winter town-costume (full mantle and hood). Her hands are covered by the long sleeves of the mantle.
17. Fisherman in straw mantle and bamboo hat (worn in rainy weather).
18. Lady with fan in a wide quilted kimono with a sash held in place by a narrow girdle with buckles. Long white stockings. The chief dress for both sexes is the kimono, a long open garment, (the women's a little longer than the men's) which draped crosswise over the chest is gathered round the hips by a wide silk sash (women) or a narrow one (men). Under this outer garment men wear close fitting or wide trousers and over them a skirt. The women wear one or two tunic-like silk garments. Shirts are not worn in Japan. Footwear in summer are linen stockings, in winter woollen ones with a space next to the big toe, through which the band of the straw sandal or the wooden stilted shoe is passed. Workers only wear the short knee-length skirt and no trousers.

Top Group

1. Shinto priest (Shintoism has become powerful again as a national cult since 1867–68).
2. Shinto pilgrim in a white costume (mourning) with an alms bell and long travelling staff. A bag thrown over the shoulder for small books. Flat bamboo hat.
3. Japanese in a non-military winter costume with the embroidered insignia of a professional society (perhaps that of doctors).
4. Citizen in a summer costume with large basket-like straw hat and fan for writing down business notes. Long kimono, short over-coat.
5. Lady in town costume. The outer garment with wide hanging sleeves, which serve as pockets.

Centre Group

6–8. Lady carried in a sedan chair. The bearers wearing leather sandals, tight cotton trousers, shirt, short kimono and fillet-like kerchiefs on their heads.

9 and 10. Porter and little girl. The porter in a short kimono with a longer draped one over it. Sandals made of straw and padded leather, kerchief. A rolled-up picture in one hand. The child is dressed in the costume of adults and wears high sandals made of wood and padded leather.

Bottom Group

11. Officer of the archers (old war outfit of the Samurai). White cotton stockings and gloves. No sandals.
12. Officer with bearded mask.
13. Officer with greaves. 11–13. wear leather mail coats.
14. Maid servant in modern dress.
15. Flower vendor. Kerchief, kimono, socks and sandals.

185   BURMA, SIAM, JAVA

Top Group

1. Woman from Mandalay, since 1860 capital of the kingdom.
2. Buddhist priest from Burma.
3. Burmese dancer (girl).
4–6. Siamese royal family in the traditional court costume.

Centre Group

7–16. Javanese costume.
7 and 8. Javanese couple of rank.

9 and 10. Dancer and pugilist, Java.
11. Javanese actress.

Bottom Group

12 and 13. Musicians accompanying dancers, Java.
14. Woman dancer, Java.
15. Woman vendor, Java.
16. Javanese lower class man in the national sarong, the long cotton loin-cloth with coloured *batik* patterns.

186   MOROCCO AND ALGERIA

Top Group

1–11. Morocco (according to original sketches by Max Tilke).
1. Moroccan wearing the jellab *(djellabía)*, hooded mantle with sleeves. The *skarra*, silk embroidered leather bag with woollen cord is slung over one shoulder. Yellow leather *babouches*.
2. Man from the interior of the country wearing burnous (Arabian word), a white or black coarse woollen mantle with hood. A large straw hat is worn over the turban wound round the head and the hood.
3. Moroccan of rank wearing the linen shirt-like garment *chamîsa* (Latin: camisia; Italian: camicia; French: chemise), over it a burnous made of fine white wool. Turban of plain muslin draped round the red cap.
4. Armed man from the interior of the country. Striped woollen *djellabía* over the *djebba*, the generally sleeveless shirt. A red cloth draped round the head without a cap.
5. Berber from the Rif (Northern Morocco) wearing a blue linen *djebba* and trousers of the same material. Leather belt embroidered with silk. Curved dagger and brass gunpowder horn.
6. Moroccan horseman wearing *haik*, a five yard long woollen cloth which is picturesquely draped around the body similar to antique fashion. Red cap with tassels. Leather boots with *babouches* over them. (Cf. pl. 191: Oriental footwear.)

Centre Group

7. Girl in indoor dress, Morocco.
8. Woman of the lower classes in a draped mantle *(haik, cf. 6)*, Morocco.
9. Conjurer, fire eater, snake charmer etc., wearing a red cloth kaftan with 100 buttons. Morocco.
10. Water vendor with a skin container. Camel wool cords wound round the turban. Morocco.
11. Man wearing *haik* and burnous over it. Morocco.

Bottom Group

12–17. Algeria.
12. Arabian peasant.
13. Kabyl of Berber descent.
14. Sheikh (oldest chieftain) of Arabian descent.
15. Arabian sheikh from the interior of the country.
16. Spahi (native soldier) trained by the French as cavalry in Algeria and Tunis since 1834.
17. Servant (in town), Algeria.

187   WEST AND EAST AFRICA

Top Group

1. Rich woman from Senegal.
2. Man of the Fulbe tribe (a Mohammedan stock-raising people) with letter bag of decorated leather.

3. Haussa negro of rank (farmer, artisan and business man). Mohammedan.
4. Negro from Southern Morocco.
5. Leader of a caravan from Senegal.

6–18. Central East Africa (Nubia, Abyssinia, Italian East Africa, Somaliland, Kenya, Tanganyika Territory).

6. Nubian girl dancer with loin-cloth made of leather cords and shells. Ornamental scars produced by tatooing.

7. Abyssinian chieftain with ornamental mantle and shield covered with velvet and studded with silver and gold.

8. Somali woman wearing a cotton wrap as a dress and silver ornaments on her breast.

9. Swahili negro in festival attire.

10. Swahili woman in festival attire.

11. Arab from Zanzibar.

12. Female water-carrier from Zanzibar wrapped in a cotton garment. (The material is printed in Europe.)

13. Warrior from Uganda in war attire. Leather wrap and leather sandals. The hair is dyed red by means of lime.

14. Somali warrior wearing cotton loin-cloth. Shield covered with rhinoceros hide. Dagger.

15. Young Somali warrior in a cotton wrap draped round the body. Shield made of a thick skin with coloured wool tassels. Amulet round his neck.

16. Abyssinian warrior wearing brocade tunic, linen trousers, decorated shield made of thick skin. Next to him: leather basket with shell ornaments.

17. Bedouin woman of the Somali carrying grass to the market.

18. Nubian warrior.

ALGERIA AND TUNIS 188

Top Group

1–5. Algeria.

1–3. Girl dancers or café dancers from Blida, Algeria, some of them with richly decorated head-dress.

4. Woman from Algiers in indoor dress.

5. Kabyl woman.

Centre Group

6. Workman wearing hooded jacket made of rough wool with white cord trimmings. White linen breeches and loin-cloth (*fuddah*).

7. Countryman belonging to the Berber tribes. Thick brown camel hair cap, cotton tunic (*kandura*). Haik wrapped round the body. Burnous (mantle). The haik is worn in Northern Africa and consists of a cloth five yards long and one yard wide and is generally striped. It is wrapped and draped round the body in various ways. About the burnous cf. plate 186, fig. 2.

8. Rich man from Tunis (capital of Tunisia). The turban is wound in three circles round the cap. Kandura (tunic), yellow silk waistcoat, fine mantle made of European cloth, yellow slippers.

9. Coffee-house owner. Shirt made of rather coarse wool, white breeches. Outer garment with V-neck, yellow slippers. Turban similar to 8.

10. Citizen from Tunis. Short blue cloth jacket. Turban band embroidered with gold and yellow threads.

11. Lower class man wearing white waistcoat, brown outer garment, woollen wrap. Turban band with red and white squares.

Bottom Group

12. Moorish girl wearing indoor dress.

13. Jewish woman wearing breeches and ankle stockings. Over the waistcoat short silk tunic with shoulder parts extended. Pointed cap of gold material.

14. Jewess wearing silk breeches. Silver ankle ring, small slippers.

15. Jew in the traditional costume. (Since the French rule was established in Tunis in 1881 the limitations to which the numerous Jews were subjected were abolished.) Black turban band, greyish-blue blouse and black-grey cotton breeches. Wrap thrown over the shoulder. Red sash, black European shoes.

16. Arab from the interior of the country wearing striped kandura over linen breeches. Cotton cord holds the kerchief in place. The haik is worn in the horseman's way. Soft leather boots with over-shoes. The pointed end of the stirrup (next to the man) is used instead of a spur.

17. Man from Tunis (of Moorish descent) in full dress. Artisan or dealer from the *souks* (streets with bazaars). Turban, kandura, haik, burnous.

6–17. Tunis (according to sketches by the painter Max Tilke).

EGYPT AND EAST AFRICA 189

Top Group

1–11. Egypt.

1 and 2. Bedouins from the Libyan Desert.

3. Bedouin woman.

4. Old village elder among the Fellahs with the long rod (*nâbût*) as insignia of his dignity. He wears a woollen scarf (*hîrân*) and the *abâje* made of goat's wool as a long cape. Yellow shoes (*balgha*). The fellah himself (fellah – ploughman) wears very scanty clothes.

5. Runner in front of riders of rank or carriages.

Centre Group

6. Man-servant in the usual simple indigo-dyed national costume with tarbush and blue tassel fixed to it.

7 and 8. Vagrant musician couple; the man wearing close-fitting felt cap (in Arabic: *libde*).

9. Water vendor.

10 and 11. Women with face veil fetching water.

Bottom Group

12–17. East Africa.

12. Man from Kordofan on the White Nile. Kaftan made of cheap silk, linen cap.

13. Man from Bornu, Central Sudan. Sandals decorated with ostrich feathers.

14. Man of the Tuareg, a Mohammedan tribe in Barbary with the curious face cloth (*lisam*).

15. Man of the Tibbu (Tebu, Tubu) tribe in the eastern Sahara greeting guests and wearing white *lisam*. In his hands: lance and iron weapons to be thrown in battle. (Several other weapons illustrated over his head.)

16 and 17. Men of the Tibbu tribe. On right: camel saddle.

Top Group

1-7. Syria.

1. Mohammedan from the Lebanon (Syria) with turban, cloth jacket and silk waistcoat.
2. Fellah (peasant).
3. Druse woman from the Lebanon. The Druses are an old sect belonging to the Syrian-Arabian tribes. Their women (3 and 5) wear a peculiar horn-like head-dress, called *tantur* or *turtur* (cf. Burgundian cap pl. 46).
4. Fellah woman from the Damascus district, Syria.
5. Druse woman from the Damascus district, represented here without veil.
6. Dancer from Damascus.
7. Woman from Damascus with *kabkabs*, protective wooden stilted under-shoes, especially worn in the baths when walking on the hot floors.

Centre Group

8-14. Palestine.

8. Woman from Bethlehem (without veil, as the town is mostly inhabited by native Christians).
9. Bedouin sheikh from the *Hauran*, a district south of Damascus (Syria) inhabited by Arab Bedouins (shepherd nomads), Fellahs as well as Druses. The head-dress is generally the *keffiyeh*, the large kerchief with or without the thick woollen cord wound round it.
10. Praying Mohammedan, Jerusalem.
11. Bedouin woman, district of Jerusalem.
12. Fellah woman, district of Nazareth.
13. Dervish, Damascus.
14. Bedouin, (nomadic shepherd) from Transjordan.

Bottom Group

15-20. Arabia.

15. Man from the lower classes wearing blue cotton tunic (worn in many parts of the Orient) with red sash (*zunnâr*).
16. Man wearing camel hair mantle (*abâyeh*), also used as a cape by Bedouins (nomads and shepherds). Red tarbush (also called fez) with a turban scarf wound around. (The turban is called *shala* or *leffe* in Arabic.)
17. Man of rank in a more Turkish attire.
18. Woman from Mecca with double or threefold veil (open in this picture).
19. Woman from Yemen, the south-western coast district of Arabia.
20. Pilgrim (hadji) wearing a six foot long cloth, four and a half feet wide (*ihram*) draped round his body and carrying a rosary (used by Buddhist, Islamic and Christian people).
21. Man of rank from Medina.

1 and 2. Persian woman's slipper (seen from above and below).
3. Woman's slipper, green. Persian and Tartar styles (Caucasus).
4. Woollen knitted travelling shoe for men with hemp sole.
5. Persian women's high boots made of red velvet.
6. Persian man's shoe.
7. Persian woman's shoe.
8. Persian shoe.
9. Woollen sock used as shoe. Persia.
10. Woman's shoe, Samarkand.
11. Woman's shoe, Yarkand (Chinese East Turkestan. The inhabitants are mainly Turkish Tartars).
12. Woman's stilted shoe from Bokhara.
13. Peasant boot from Bokhara.
14. Shoe worn by Turkomans.
15. Women's boots from Yarkand. Leather, embroidered cloth and silk tassels.
16. Boot made of soft leather. Over this a shoe (fig. 20) is worn; when stepping on carpets in the living rooms the over-shoes are taken off. Asia and Turkey. Jewesses also wear them sometimes.
17. Men's boots with heels worn in bad weather. Decorated with silver cords.
18. Ceremonial boots made of velvet and embroidered with gold and silver.
19. Man's shoe from Bokhara.
20. cf. fig. 16.
21. Leather sandal from Ildshi, East Turkestan.
22. Woman's shoe from Madras, India. Red cloth and silver embroidery.
23. Children's shoe.
24. Woman's shoe from India.
25. Mohammedan man's shoe from Madras.
26. Syrian man's shoe.
27. Turkish shoe for men and women.
28. Woman's house shoe, Turkish-Syrian.
29. Gold embroidered lady's slipper.
30. Bedouin boot worn by Syrian Kurds, red or yellow with silk tassel. Iron heel.
31. Man's shoe from Jerusalem, red.
32. Stilted shoe (called *kabkab*) used in the baths and as a protection against the dirt of the streets, comparable to the European wooden under-shoes in the Middle Ages. In the baths they protect the feet from the heat of the floors. Damascus.
33. Bosnian woman's shoe.
34. *Opanke*, shoe or sandal made of hard hide laced with cords that are made of animal's intestines. Herzegovina and other western districts of the Balkan peninsula. The foot is covered by a thick heelless sock.
35. Woman's shoe, Bosnia.
36 and 37. Footwear of a Zanzibar princess of Arabic descent (representing the nobility of the island). Wooden stilted shoe.
38. Woman's boot from Morocco, red. The same in yellow are often worn in Turkey. With it over-shoe of the same colour, called *babouches* (cf. fig. 41).
39 and 40. Soft Moroccan leather boots, fig. 40 with silk embroidery. With them shoes are worn like figs. 32 and 43.
41. Over-shoes cf. 38.
42 and 43. Red and yellow over-shoes (cf. 39 and 40). Similar shoes are worn in the other North African districts.
44. Wooden under-shoe with iron point. The leather parts are embroidered with silk. Morocco.
45-51. Details of shoes worn in Northern India.
45. Man's shoe, Hindustan.

46. Man's shoe worn by a Raja from Kashmir, with iron heel.
47. Woman's shoe from Srinagar.
48. Women's shoes from Kashmir with double sole and iron heel.
49. Woman's shoe from Kabul with velvet-like covering.

50. Afghan woman's shoe with silk tassel from Peshawar.
51. Woman's white leather shoe with silver edging and imitation jewels from Lucknow. (The part over the heel is usually trodden down).

1. Bedouin horseman from the Libyan Desert wrapped in the white woollen *hiram* with rifle *(bundugír)* and box-like stirrups.
2. Horseman belonging to the southern tribes of Algeria. A tuft of ostrich feathers on his camel hair turban.
3. Pure blooded Arab from Maskat (Oman). Met with all along the Asiatic coasts and at princes' courts.
4. Young Tunisian horseman. The horse's harness and saddle consist of leather and velvet embroidered with gold and silver. The saddle cloth made of silk damask.
5. Kabail horseman from Algeria.
6. Dragoon from Syria.
7. Bedouin chieftain, Gaza. Wearing kaftan *(entari)* and mantle *(aba)*. Kerchief *(kofia)* with cord *(ogal)*. Lance *(tromblom)*.

8. Poor Bedouin from Moab. The mantle *(aba)* is draped round the legs. Lance, sword, pistols. The saddles of 6–8 have cloths of dyed lambskin. 1–8 according to photographs. Late 19th century.
9. Egyptian woman with child on a donkey from Cairo.
10. Travelling women under a hood *(palankin)* on a camel. Southern Algeria. The wooden frame is covered by an awning. The women are sitting in baskets on both sides of the camel's hump. A thin piece of cloth can be drawn in front of the *palankin*. This word comes from India and is used there for large travelling sedan chairs *(palki)*.
11. Camel's head decoration in Persian style.
12. Camel lying down. The saddle in the Egyptian style.
13. Kabail horseman in Southern Algeria. The camel has one bridle fixed to the nose ring.

The Inca empire (Peru) was destroyed by Francisco Pizarro in 1533

1–12. The Incas in ancient Peru. The Inca empire with its capital Cuzco (in about 1500 reaching from Quito to Valparaiso) was built up by subjugating many tribes who subsequently adopted a common language and religion and were governed by the Incas. From the old remnants of garments, gold figures and jugs representing figures, the painter Max Tilke has reconstructed a picture of the costume of the Inca culture.

Top Group

1. Man of rank wearing loin-cloth the tassel of which is seen hanging down. Sleeved semi-long coat woven in many colours and large white wrap similar to the Arabian burnous. On his right hip he wears a bag woven of fine vicuña wool (vicuña is a small wild species of the llama). Sandals with white woollen top. In his left hand: a bundle fastened by cords *(quipu)* which by means of colour variations and knots was of arithmetical and mnemotechnical value.
2. Warrior of rank. Helmet decorated with the sickle of the moon, also feather crest and neck protection. Girdled *poncho* with meander-like decoration at the edges. Over it quite a short poncho similar to the European collar cape. Ornamented bag, golden bracelets round the wrists. Painted legs. Wooden weapon to be thrown and copper battle-axe. – Only the ruling Inca tribe and aristocratic men from the subjugated people were trained as soldiers. The wooden peg in the ear was a sign of the warrior of rank.
3. Warrior of rank in a feather coat with decorative silver plates. Helmet made of plant fibres and covered "scale-like", with coloured feathers. Feather tuft. Nape protection and chin band. Golden ear plates. The legs are tattooed. Painted round shield made of hide. Battle-axe.
4. Man of rank in a white woollen garment with multi-coloured woven edge and ornaments sewn on. Turban-like head-dress. Bag with long fringes.

5. Warrior wearing helmet with nape covering, feather tuft, sickle of the moon and animal's head. Bag, shield made of basket work, stone axe. Legs tattooed (as shown on preserved mummies).
6. Man of the lower classes who were called *hatunruna*. Simple brown poncho with edging, woollen cap and bag. Hair plaited. (Behind him a jug in the shape of a figure wrapped in a sort of burnous).

Centre Group

7. Porter. On his back a basket made of agave fibres.
8. Woman with hand spindle. Long under-garment, shorter poncho, scarf, necklace, woollen cap made of cords.
9. Llama driver with a coarse cotton shoulder cape. Reed flute. The llama is carrying sacks made of agave fibres.
10. Warrior with gong or tambourine. Loin-cloth with tassels, feather coat, helmet. Tattooing and painting on arms and legs.
11. Hostile Indian of primitive culture. Loin-cloth, feather tuft. Ear decorations, shield and mace.
12. Sacrificing priest. Face tattooed or painted.

Bottom Group

13–17. Ancient Mexico.
13. Man from the lower classes, porter with loin-cloth.
14. Woman of the Zapotec Indians in more elaborate dress with characteristic hair style. Skirt (or large loin-cloth) and straight, sleeveless outer garment to be pulled over the head. The materials are skilfully woven in many colours.
15. Native business-man in loin-cloth and mantle fastened by knotting on the chest. Shoes covering half the feet, ear pegs made of nephrite, feather fan.
16. Woman of the Huastec Indians (North-eastern Mexico), probably belonging to the aborigines before the invasion of the Aztecs. Skirt or loin-cloth, three-cornered breast

kerchief, sandals, large hair ribbon, silver necklace and hip decoration, bracelets made of balls.

17. Mexican woman (retinue of Cortez) wearing long skirt and large mantle with slits for head and arms.

13–17. (like plate 196, Mexico) according to contemporary paintings done by native Indian artists on linen. Rome, Vatican Library.

194 MEXICO *at the Time of the Discovery and Conquest by Fernando Cortez. 1519–20*

Top Group

1 and 3. Warriors from Mexico with cotton protective garments (similar to 6).

2. Leader of Cortez auxiliary troops. As an emblem he has a bird flying over him.

4–7. Group of Mexican warriors

Centre Group

8. Warrior from Mexico dressed in war doublet made of jaguar skin. The mace is studded with hard and sharp pieces of obsidian (a stone resembling bottle glass). Weapons and utensils in ancient America belong to the Palaeolithic Age.

9–10. Warriors belonging to Cortez' native auxiliary troops, dressed in padded protective garments. The shields painted or decorated with feather mosaics. On their backs symbolic emblems or those denoting their ranks.

11. Leader, *kazike* from Mexico with feather dress and stone mace.

12. Leader from Mexico. The feather dress imitating a bird of prey.

Bottom Group

Priest of the rain god Tlaloc wearing a diadem with fan-like wings and golden ear-pegs. Otherwise he only wears the loin-cloth (here too, as in Ancient Egypt, the scanty clothes of the priests, a custom preserved from ancient times); incense burner and receptacle for alms. (According to the copy of an original old Mexican statuette formerly in the Museum für Völkerkunde, Berlin.)

14. Sacrificing priest. Skin painted. Temples stained with blood, loin-cloth with coloured edging, mantle with black edging, shoes. Golden ear decorations. The right hand holds the curved piece for holding the neck of the animal to be sacrificed, the left holds the obsidian knife.

15. Indian belonging to the Mixteca tribe (civilized Indian tribe). Fillet, mantle knotted on the right shoulder covers the loin-cloth. Shoes.

16. The king (Montezuma?) wearing gold diadem with feather crest. Thick gold and jewelled necklace. Gold bracelets, gold rings below the knees, shoes. Decorated loin-cloth and finely woven mantle knotted in front. Lance with gold point (according to a representation in the manuscript containing the genealogical tree of the Montezuma family in the Archivo general de la nacion Mejicana).

17. Priest castigating himself like the Indian fakirs. Painted dark like 14. On his back emblems of his priesthood. Perhaps he wears a sort of feather mantle. Loin-cloth, long hair. In his hand a pointed bone, the instrument of his religious practice of castigating himself.

195 CENTRAL AMERICA, MEXICO, GUATEMALA AND OTHERS

(Mexico at the Beginning of the 19th Century)

Top Group

1. Hacendado (estate owner). Straw hat, kerchief, neck cloth, short leather jacket, *faja* (sash), leather trousers. Wide boots with spurs, sword; *zarape* (mantle) worn over one shoulder.

2. *Maja* silk dress, silk stockings, satin slippers, short sleeveless jacket, the hair decorated with coloured ribbons.

3. Mexican woman.

4. Water carrier.

5. Creole woman wearing skirt and cape-like sateen cloth. Satin slippers without stockings.

Centre Group

6. Poblano (citizen). The gaily coloured *zarape* (cape) seems an imitation of old Mexican Aztec models.

7. Seminarist.

8. Girl wearing lace mantilla.

9. Creole woman wearing simple mantilla.

10. Rich Mexican wearing felt hat with silver braids. Leather jacket, velvet trousers with silver trimming.

11. Sereno (night watchman).
(1–11 chiefly according to dolls and original costumes from Mexico.)

Bottom Group

12. Indian fisherman.

13. Indian woman from Guatemala.

14. Half caste woman from Guatemala.
(13 and 14 do not wear closed skirts, but these are large woollen cloths draped round the body, a fashion preserved from the old Indian and Mexican costume worn before the Spanish Conquest).

15. Indian from Honduras in an attire adopted from the Spanish settlers.

16. Native chicken vendor.

17. Vaquero, shepherd on horseback wearing the characteristic costume of Mexico and Texas.

196 SOUTH AMERICA. *Modern Times. (Bolivia, Chile, Peru, Colombia)*

Top Group

1. Indian woman from Bolivia with pulled-up poncho over another smaller poncho.

2. Indian worker from Bolivia. Straw hat, poncho and apron cut open in the middle in the Spanish fashion, and tied over European trousers.

3. Indian man-servant, Bolivia. Woollen cap, poncho, loin-cloth, European trousers.

4. Chuncho (wild mountain dweller of Bolivia) with very long bow.
5 and 6. Peruvians in travelling attire for the Cordilleras: felt hat, woollen scarf, poncho made of llama wool (vicuña). Leggings made of leather or thick material, knife worn at the knee, large silver wheel spurs.

Centre Group

7. Araucanian (Indian from Chile) wearing kerchief, poncho, loin-cloth, all in dark colours.
8. Araucanian woman, dressed up. Over the blouse the *chamal (or ciamal)* which is draped from the left over the right shoulder where it is fastened by a safety pin and gathered by a girdle. Over it cape or cloth fastened with a large silver brooch. Silver and glass beads decoration.
9. Peon (Spanish word for low class worker) living in the country in Chile. He wears woollen cap, kerchief, poncho,

leather jacket, fur over-trousers (with the fur inside), large wheel spurs, lasso.
10. Carretero (ox-cart driver) from Chile. Felt hat, kerchief, leather jacket, wide leather breeches over linen ones, sash round the hips, woollen stockings (without the foot part), sandals.
11. Chilean country-man wearing felt hat, poncho, leggings, wheel spurs.

Bottom Group

12. Peruvian woman from the country in festive attire about 1825–30.
13. Woman from Lima, the capital of Peru, dressed for church and walking with the mantilla wrapped round head and shoulders.
14 and 15. Women from Arequipa (Southern Peru).
16. Man from Honda on the Magdalena river, Colombia.

Top Group

1. Warrior of a smaller tribe in dancing attire. The head decorated with feathers. The so-called leggings are two separate pieces (also worn in Europe till about 1400) and are pulled up to the belt, thus necessitating a special cloth drawn from back to front between the legs.
2. Iroquois Indian (living west of the Mississippi). Body painted and tattooed. A feather tuft on the scalp.
3. Man of the Crows with feather of birds of prey on his head.
4. Fox Indian from the central Mississippi. A crest of dyed horse hair on the scalp. Face painted. Bison mantle with the fur inside. It is only due to the trade with the white men that blankets have replaced the old skin and leather clothes.
5. Dyed buck skin attire ornamented with feathers the quills of which are cut open.
6. Great chieftain of the Dakota or Sioux (west of the Mississippi and north of Arkansas). Head and back decorations consist of eagle feathers. The trousers are decorated with the scalps of slain enemies. Buck skin clothes. Belt with wampum ornaments, made of snails, shells and teeth (also necklaces and bracelets of the same kind). A scalping knife in the belt. Necklace made of bears' claws. Lance with scalps. Tobacco pipe. Shoes made of animal skin *(moccasins)* similar to the primitive European shoes or *opanken*.
7. Warrior dressed for the Bison dance. Body painted, his head decorated with horns and skin of a bison and feathers. Hanging down from the back the head and gutted body of a dead raven. Moccasins decorated with wolf tails. Painted leather shield. In his right hand the old-fashioned breaker with stone head (left below: skull breaker made of hard wood, above right: tomahawk with iron blade).

Centre Group

8. Iowa chieftain wearing beaver cap with feather. Bison coat decorated with drawings commemorating his achievements. In his hand a wooden skull breaker.
9. Chieftain of the Sacs from the Mississippi. Doublet embroidered with glass beads. Necklace made of animal claws.

Leather leggings with knee band. Coat made of a woollen coloured blanket.
10. Young Sioux (as appearing once in a show group in Europe). Painted body, loin-cloth fur bandolier decorated with small glass mirrors. Long hair with horse hair and feather decoration (illustrated at his side).
11. Chieftain. Clothes made of woven material bought from the whites. The tomahawk decorated with feathers encased on top. Neck decoration of bears' claws.
12. Chieftain.
13. Chieftain of the Pani. Cotton tunic. Richly embroidered leggings. Ample feather decoration.

Bottom Group

14. Mandan warrior (on the upper Missouri belonging to the Dakota tribes). Hair ornamented with jewellery and fur strips. Roll-like neck band. Bison mantle. Leggings without fringes. Moccasins with wolf tails. Feather sceptre in his hand.
15. Chieftain of the Sacs (district of Chicago). Face painted red with white hands on the cheeks. Cap with fur tufts. Green woollen coat covered by a wolf skin.
16. Warrior of the Sacs. Shorn head with beard (very sparse with the Red Indians). Woollen tunic; leather breeches, knee bands made of skunk skin, turned-up moccasins. Tomahawk decorated with animals' tails.
17. Chieftain of the *Grosventres* on the prairies.
18. Red Indian of the upper Missouri. Bison mantle with the sun painted on it.
19. Chieftain of the Cvih Indians. Body painted with dark stripes. (below):
20. Chieftain of the Chippeway or Ojibway originally living between Lakes Michigan and Huron but who retreated to the district near Lake Superior.
Partly according to Maximilian, Prinz zu Wied: *Reise durch Nordamerika*. 2 vols. 1838–41.

Top Group

1. Woman from Kiowa with a girdle studded with metal.
2. Canadian Red Indian woman wearing leather clothes and with basket for carrying a baby.
3. Woman from Dakota wearing a painted mantle made of hairless painted animal's skin.
4. Child of the Assiniboin Indians with earrings made of glass beads.
5. Woman of the Snake Indians.
6. Woman of the Cvih Indians.

1 and 2. According to Lampert: *Völker der Erde;* 3–6 according to Maximilian, Prinz zu Wied: *Reise durch Nordamerika.* 1838–41).

Centre Group

7. Red Indian from Utah.

8. Man belonging to the Shoshoni tribe.
9. Young Red Indian of a northern tribe in a decorated leather attire with fur cap.
10. Warrior of the Cvih Indians.
11. Red Indian from Kansas.
12. Red Indian from Nebraska.

Bottom Group

13. Red Indian from Colorado belonging to the Yuma tribe; his body decorated with war paint.
14. Chieftain of a tribe of the Apaches from Arizona.
15 and 16. Man and woman belonging to the North American Red Indians.
17. Pueblo Indian from Arizona and New Mexico.
18. Lipan chieftain in dancing attire.

199   NORTH AMERICA. *End of the 18th to the End of the 19th Centuries*

Trappers, Red Indians, Soldiers, Cowboys

Top Group

1–4. Trappers (men setting traps for wild animals, hunters of fur-bearing animals, pathfinders in leather and fur attires.
5. Captain Meriwether Lewis 1805.

Centre Group

6. Light foot soldier.
7. Chief of the Seminole, an Indian tribe which migrated from Georgia to Florida in 1750, fought many battles against the armies of the United States and after the war 1835–42 were for the most part transferred to the Red Indian Territory. Cotton tunic with iron decorations on his chest. Cloth gaiters. Ostrich feather.
8. Marine on leave (gala dress).
9. Sailor.
10. Infantry officer. 1–10 types as described by Cooper in his novels (for instance: *The Pathfinder* in the last decades of the 18th century.

Bottom Group

11. Cowboy in cotton blouse. Leather belt for pistol and cartridges. Leather leggings (unconnected) reaching up to the hips (similar to Red Indian leggings) over other trousers with fringes; pockets sewn on.
12. Cowboy seated with sheepskin outer trousers, large leather gauntlets.
14. Leather doublet, velvet trousers with leather pieces sewn on. High-heeled boots with very large leather spur bands.
15. Cowboy wearing hat with silver embroidered band and rim. Red Indian leather doublet, bead embroidered gauntlets (native work). Leather outer trousers with side fastening. On the wall: harness and lasso, a saddle under the seat.

11–15. According to original drawings and North American representations.

200   ESKIMOS. NORTHERN PEOPLE *(Europe, Asia, America). Modern Times*

Top Group

1–4. Samoyede family.
5. Tunguse on snow shoes.

Centre Group

6. Tunguse shaman (sorcerer-priest) from the Yenissei river in Siberia, Government of Irkutsk. Leather attire with iron ornamentation: little bells, bands, mask and ghost drum.
7 and 8. Voguls-Ostyaks: dealer in furs and mammoth tusks. The Voguls, a tribe belonging to the Ugrians live on the east slope of the northern Ural. Ostyaks in the Siberian government of Tobolsk and Tomsk.
9 and 10. European polar explorers in their Arctic outfit.

Bottom Group

11. Man of the Gilyaks in the Amur district in East Siberia, ethnographically belonging to the Ainos in Japan.

12–14. Young woman, man and old woman of the Greenland Eskimos. The doublet *(timiak)* is pulled over the head, is made of bird or seal skins or reindeer hide, and has a hood and an outer cover mostly made of imported cotton in present times. Seal skin trousers, the bare feet covered by fur-lined leather boots *(kamiks)*. Trimmings of dog's skin. – Women often wear the timiak without hood and they like gay colours in the cotton outer covering. Their trousers decorated with fur strips or leather embroidery are usually shorter than the men's, but the gaily decorated kamiks (boots) reach up to over the knee.
15 and 16. Child and woman of the Chukches living in the northern tundra of Siberia. Tattooing.

INDEX OF PLATES

PLATES

ALTÄGYPTEN
ANCIENT EGYPT
EGYPTE ANCIENNE
ANTICO EGITTO

Altes Reich um 3000 v. Chr.
Old Kingdom about 3000 B. C.
Ancien Empire,
environ 3000 av. J. C.
Antico Impero
circa 3000 a. C.

1 2 3 4 5

Mittleres Reich um 2100 v. Chr.
Middle Kingdom
about 2100 B. C.
Moyen Empire
environ 2100 av. J. C.
Medio Impero
circa 2100 a. C.

6 7 8 9 10

Neues Reich 1600—1100 v. Chr.
New Kingdom 1600—1100 B. C.
Nouvel Empire,
1600—1100 av. J. C.
Nuovo Impero
1600—1100 a. C.

11 12 13 14 15 16

ALTÄGYPTEN
Neues Reich
(Ramessidenzeit
1350—1200 v. Chr.)
ANCIENT EGYPT
New Kingdom
(Time of Rameses I.
to Rameses III.
1350—1200 B. C.)
EGYPTE ANCIENNE
Nouvel Empire
(Epoque des Ramsès,
1350—1200 av. J. C.)
ANTICO EGITTO
Nuovo Impero
(periodo ramessita)
1350—1200 a. C.

Priester, Beamte
Priests, Officials
Prêtres, fonctionnaires
Sacerdoti, dignitari

1 2 3 4 5

Der König und sein Hof
The King and his Court
Le roi et sa cour
Il Re e la sua corte

6 7 8 9 10

Soldaten
Soldiers
Soldats
Soldati

11 12 13 14 15

2

ALTÄGYPTEN
Neues Reich
1600—1100 v. Chr.
ANCIENT EGYPT
New Kingdom 1600—1100 B. C.
EGYPTE ANCIENNE
Nouvel Empire
1600—1100 av. J. C.
ANTICO EGITTO
Nuovo Impero
1600—1100 a. C.

Der König und sein Hof
The King and his Court
Le roi et sa cour
Il Re e la sua corte

1 2 3 4 5

König, Priester
und Göttergestalten
Kings, Priests
and Images of Gods
Roi, prêtre et dieux
Re, sacerdoti, e
immagini di divinità

6 7 8 9 10

Sklavinnen u. a.
Slave Girls
Esclaves et autres personnages
Schiave

11 12 13 14 15

ALTÄGYPTEN
Neues Reich (Spätzeit;
Ramessiden u. Nachf.
14. u. 13. Jahrh. v. Chr.)
ANCIENT EGYPT
New Kingdom
(Late Period: Rameses I. and
Successors, 14th and 13th
Centuries B. C.)
EGYPTE ANCIENNE
Fin du Nouvel Empire
(Epoque des Ramsès
et de leurs successeurs,
XIVᵉ et XIIIᵉ s. av. J. C.)
ANTICO EGITTO
Nuovo Impero (epoca tarda)
Ramessiti e succ.
XIV e XIII sec. a. C.

Könige und Gefolge
Priester, Soldaten, Geräte
Kings and their Retinue
Priests, Soldiers, Implements
Rois et leurs suites
Prêtres, soldats, objets divers
Re e loro seguito
Sacerdoti, soldati, utensili

Priesterinnen, Priester u. a.
Priestesses, priests, etc.
Prêtresses,
prêtres et autres personnages
Sacerdotesse, sacerdoti

8—15

4

ASSYRIEN
und Nachbarvölker
12. bis 7. Jahrhundert v. Chr.
ASSYRIA AND
NEIGHBOURING
PEOPLES
12th–7th Centuries B. C.
ASSYRIE et pays voisins
XIIᵉ à VIIᵉ s. av. J. C.
ASSIRIA
e popoli limitrofi
dal XII al VII sec. a. C.

König und Gefolge
King and Retinue
Le roi et sa suite
Re e seguito

1 2 3 4 5 6 7

Krieger u. a.
Warriors, etc.
Guerriers et autres personnages
Guerrieri, contadini

8 9 10 11 12 13

Tributbringer, Opfergewänder
Tribute-bearers
Sacrificial Garments
Porteur d'offrande,
vêtements de sacrifice
Portatori di tributi,
vesti sacrificali

14 15 16 17 18 19

BABYLON UND
ASSYRIEN
(2800—700 v. Chr.)
BABYLONIA AND ASSYRIA
(2800—700 B. C.)
BABYLONE ET
ASSYRIE
(2800—700 av. J. C.)
BABILONIA
E ASSIRIA
(2800—700 a. C.)

Babylon
Babylonia
Babylone
Babilonia

1 2 3 4 5 6

Assyrien, König und sein Hof
Assyria, King and his Court
Assyrie, le roi et sa cour
Assiria: il Re e la sua corte
(Assiria, Re, sua corte)

7 8 9 10 11 12

Assyrische Krieger
Assyrian Warriors
Guerriers assyriens
Guerrieri assiri

13 14 15

6

ARMENIER, PARTHER,
PHILISTER, SUMERER,
HETTITER, ARABER

ARMENIANS, PARTHIANS
PHILISTINES, SUMERIANS
HITTITES, ARABS

ARMENIENS, PARTHES,
PHILISTINS,
SUMERIENS,
HITTITES, ARABES

ARMENI, PARTI,
FILISTEI, SUMERI,
ITTITI, ARABI

WESTASIEN
IM ALTERTUM
WESTERN ASIA IN ANTIQUITY
ASIE OCCIDENTALE
dans l'Antiquité
L'ASIA OCCIDENTALE
NELL'ANTICHITA'

Kreta, Palästina, Syrien
Crete, Palestine, Syria
Crète, Palestine, Syrie
Creta, Palestina, Siria

1   2   3   4   5

Beduinen, Syrien, Palästina
Bedouins, Syria, Palestine
Bédouins, Syrie, Palestine
Beduini della Palestina

6   7   8   9   10   11

Hebräer
Hebrews
Hébreux
Ebrei

12   13   14   15   16   17

MYKENAE,
KRETA, CYPERN
(Agäische und
phönikische Kultur)
2000—500 v. Chr.)
MYCENAE, CRETE, CYPRU
(Aegean and Phoenician
Cultures)
2000—500 B. C.
MYCENES, CRETE,
CHYPRE (civilisations
du bassin Egéen
et de la Phénicie)
2000—500 av. J. C.
MICENE,
CRETA, CIPRO
(Cultura Egea e Fenicia)
2000—500 a. C.

Mykenae
Mycenae
Mycènes
Micene

1—11

Kreta
Crete
Crète
Creta

12—18

Cypern
Cyprus
Chypre
Cipro

19—25

PERSIEN
Altertum und
frühes Mittelalter
PERSIA
Antiquity and Early Middle Ages
PERSE
Antiquité et
début du Moyen-Age
PERSIA
Evo Antico e primo
Medio Evo

Altpersien
6. bis 5. Jahrhundert v. Chr.
Ancient Persia
6th—5th Centuries B. C.
Perse ancienne
VIe à Ve s. av. J. C.
Antica Persia
dal VI al V secolo a. C.

1 2 3 4 5 6

Altpersien
6. bis 5. Jahrhundert v. Chr.
Ancient Persia
6th—5th Centuries B. C.
Perse ancienne
VIe à Ve s. av. J. C.
Antica Persia
dal VI al V secolo a. C.

7 8 9 10 11 12

Persien
um 600 n. Chr.
Persia about 600 A. D.
Perse, environ 600 après J. C.
Persia
intorno al VI sec. a. C.

13—25

SKYTHEN UND
KLEINASIATEN
8. und 7. Jahrhundert v. Chr.
SCYTHIANS AND INHABITANTS
OF ASIA MINOR
8th and 7th Centuries B. C.
SCYTHES ET PEUPLES
D'ASIE MINEURE
VIIIᵉ et VIIᵉ s. av. J. C.
SCITI E POPOLI
dell'ASIA MINORE
VIII e VII sec. a. C.

Skythen
Scythians
Scythes
Sciti

1 2 3 4 5 6

Phryger
Phrygians
Phrygiens
Frigi

7 8 9 10 11

Andere Kleinasiaten
Other Inhabitants of Asia Minor
Autres peuples d'Asie Mineure
Altri popoli dell'Asia Minore

12 13 14—21

11

GRIECHENLAND
6. und 5. Jahrhundert v. Chr.
GREECE
6th and 5th Centuries B. C.
GRECE
VIᵉ et Vᵉ s. av. J. C.
GRECIA
VI e V secolo a. C.

1. Hälfte des 6. Jahrhunderts
1st Half of 6th Century
Première moitié du VIᵉ s.
I metà del VI sec.

1 2 3 4 5 6

6. und 5. Jahrhundert
6th and 5th Centuries
VIᵉ et Vᵉ siècle
VI e V secolo

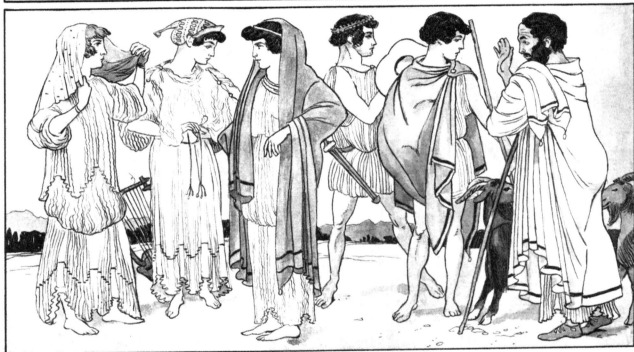

7 8 9 10 11 12

5. Jahrhundert
5th Century
Vᵉ siècle
V secolo

13 14 15 16 17

GRIECHENLAND
4. bis 5. Jahrhundert
GREECE
5th–4th Centuries
GRECE, Ve à IVe siècle
GRECIA
dal IV al V sec.

Himation
Himation
Himation
Imatio

1　2　3　4

Chiton und Peplos
Chiton and Peplos
Chiton et Peplos
Chitone e Peplo

5　6　7　8

Chiton, Chlamys
Chiton, Chlamys
Chiton, Chlamyde
Chitone, Clamida

9　10　11　12

13

GRIECHENLAND
GREECE
GRECE
GRECIA

Waffen, Tafelsitten,
Spiel, Musik
Armour, Banqueting, Games,
Music
Armement, banquets, jeux
et musique
Armi, vasellame
giuochi, musica

GRIECHENLAND
Spätzeit
4. Jahrhundert v. Chr.
GREECE
Late Period
4th Century B. C.
GRECE
période hellénistique,
IVe s. av. J. C.
GRECIA
seconda metà
del IV sec. a. C.

Spätgriechische Stadttrac[h]
Late Greek Town Costum[e]
Costumes de ville de la
période hellénistique
abiti cittadini

Bemalte Tonfiguren
aus Tanagra
in Böotien
Painted Terra-cotta
Figures from
Tanagra, Boeotia
Figurines en terre-cuite
peintes de Tanagra
en Béotie
Statuette di terracotta
da Tanagra
in Beozia

ETRUSKER
um 750 v. Chr.
ETRUSCANS
About 750 B. C.
ETRUSQUES
environ 750 av. J. C.
ETRUSCHI
Intorno al 750 a. C.

Trachten
Costume
Costumes
Costumi

1—18

Krieger
Warriors
Guerriers
Guerrieri

19 20 21 22 23 24

Festmahl, Tanz, Musik
Banquet, Dance, Music
Banquets, danses, musique
Banchetto, danza, musica

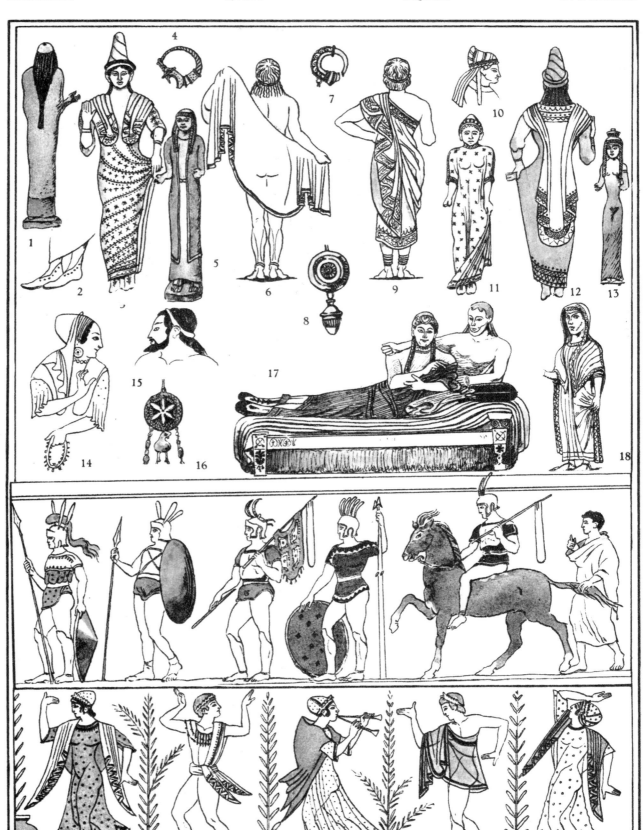

25—35

ROM
Männertrachten
ROME
Men's Costume
ROME
Costumes d'hommes
ROMA
Costumi maschili

Toga, Paludamentum, Sagum
Toge, Paludamentum, Sagum
Toge, Paludamentum, Sagum
Toga, paludamenta, sago

Toga, Toga, Paenula
Toga, Toga, Paenula
Toge, Pénule
Toga, toga, penula

Cucullus u. a.
Cucullus, etc.
Cuculle et autres vêtements
Cucullo ecc.

ROM
Volk, Frauen,
Priesterinnen
ROME
Ordinary People,
Women, Priestesses
ROME
Gens du peuple,
femmes, prêtresses
ROMA
Popolo, donne,
Sacerdotesse

Volk
Ordinary People
Gens du peuple
Popolo

1   2   3   4   5

Frauen, Priesterinnen
Women, Priestesses
Femmes, prêtresses
Donne, sacerdotesse

6—14

Frauen in der Palla
Women dressed in the Palla
Femmes vêtues de la palla
Donne in palla

15   16   17   18   19

GRIECHENLAND
UND ROM
Antike Frisuren
und Kopfbedeckungen
GREECE AND ROME
Ancient Hair styles and
Head-dresses
GRECE ET ROME
Coiffures antiques
GRECIA E ROMA
Pettinature e
copricapi antichi

Griechische Frisuren
Greek Hair Styles
Coiffures grecques
Pettinature greche

1—19

Römische Frisuren
Roman Hair Styles
Coiffures romaines
Pettinature romane

20—28

GRIECHENLAND
UND ROM
Fußbekleidungen
(Griechisch, Römisch,
Koptisch)
GREECE AND ROME
Footwear (Greek, Roman,
Coptic)
GRECE ET ROME
Chaussures grecques,
romaines et coptes
GRECIA E ROMA
Calzari
(greci, romani, copti)

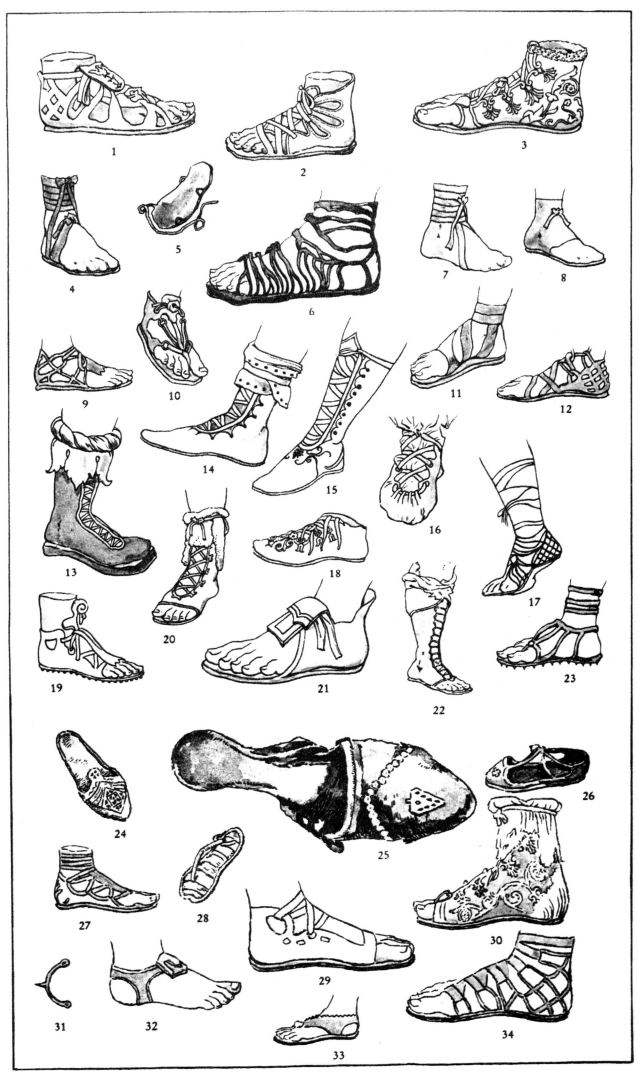

GERMANEN
Vorzeit bis Römerzeit
TEUTONS
Prehistoric to Roman Times
GERMAINS
De la période préhistorique
à la période romaine
GERMANI
EPOCA PREROMANA

Germanen in Jütland
(Bronzezeit 2000—800 v. Chr.)
Teutons in Jutland
(Bronze Age 2000—800 B. C.)
Germains du Jutland
(Age du bronze,
2000—800 av. J. C.)
Germani dello Jutland
(età del bronzo
2000—800 a. C.)

1   2   3   4   5

Germanen in Norddeutschland
(Bronzezeit 2000—800 v. Chr.)
Teutons in North Germany
(Bronze Age 2000—800 B. C.)
Germains d'Allemagne du Nord
(Age du bronze,
2000—800 av. J. C.)
Germani del Nord
(età del bronzo
2000—800 a. C.)

6   7   8   9   10

Ostgermanen
(Römerzeit)
East Teutons (Roman Period)
Ostrogoths (Période romaine)
Germani orientali
(epoca romana)

11   12   13   14   15

GERMANEN
Ältere Zeit und Römerzeit
TEUTONS
Prehistoric
and Roman Times
GERMAINS
Période ancienne
et période romaine
GERMANI
Epoca Preromana
e Romana

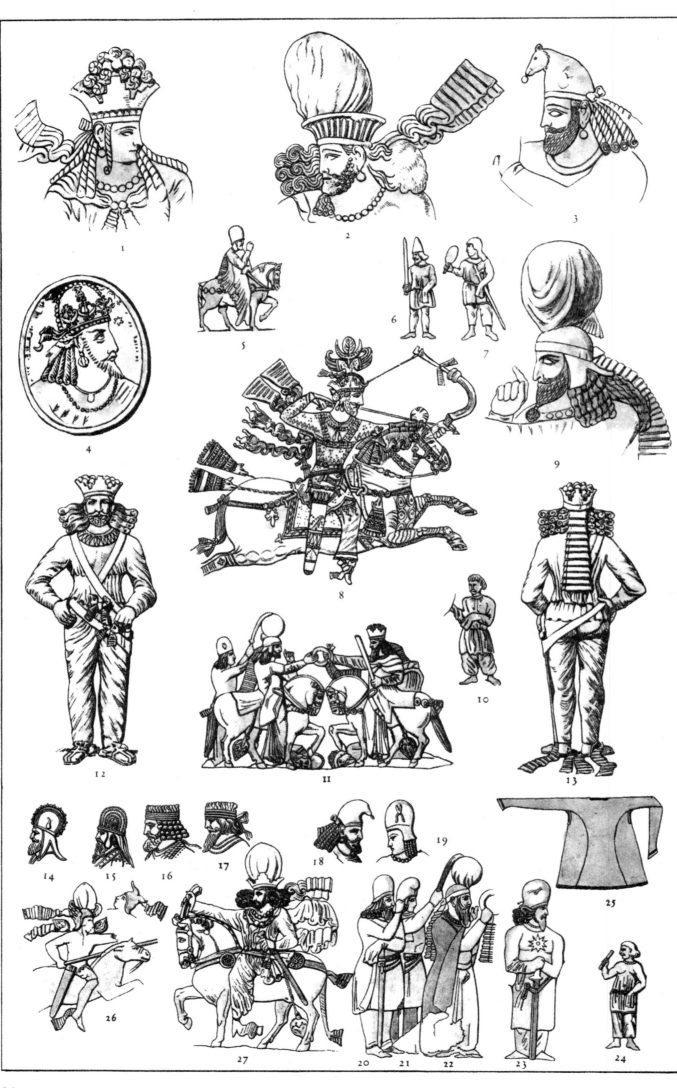

PERSIEN
Sassanidenzeit
227—651 n. Chr.
PERSIA
227—651 A. D.
Sassanian Period
PERSE
Période des Sassanides
227—651 après J. C.
PERSIA
Epoca dei sassanidi
227—651 d. C.

Götter, Könige, Parther
Jagd, Reiter
Gods, Kings, Parthians
Huntsmen, Horsemen
Dieux, rois, Parthes,
chasseurs et cavaliers
Divinità, re, Parti
Caccia, cavalieri

GALLIER, WIKINGER,
ÄLTERE NORMANNEN
GAULS, VIKINGS
AND NORSEMEN
GAULOIS, VIKINGS,
PREMIERS NORMANDS
GALLI,
VICHINGHI,
NORMANNI SETTENTRIONALI

Gallier
Gauls
Gaulois
Galli

1   2   3   4   5

Gallier
Gauls
Gaulois
Galli

6   7   8   9   10

Wikinger und Normannen
Vikings and Norsemen
Vikings et Normands
Vichinghi e Normanni

11   12   13   14   15

ALTERTUM   ANTIQUITY   ANTIQUITE   EVO ANTICO

ROM
Heerwesen, Fechtwesen
ROME
Soldiers, Gladiators
ROME
Armée, jeux du cirque
ROMA
Ufficiali, cavalieri
truppa ausiliaria

Legionäre
Legionaries
Légionnaires
Legionarii

1   2   3   4

Offiziere, Reiter, Hilfsvölker
Officers, Horsemen
Auxiliary Troops
Officiers, cavaliers peuples alliés
Ufficiali, cavalieri,
truppa ausiliaria

5   6   7   8

Fechter
Gladiators
Gladiateurs
Combattenti

9   10   11   12   13

25

FRÜHCHRISTL. ZEIT
300—600 n. Chr.
EARLY CHRISTIAN
PERIOD
300—600 A. D.
DEBUT DU CHRISTIANISME
300—600 après J. C.
PRIMA ERA
CRISTIANA
300—600 a. C.

Dalmatika, Tunika
Dalmatic, Tunic
Dalmatique, tunique
Dalmatica, tunica

1 2 3 4 5

Dalmatika, Tunika
Dalmatic, Tunic
Dalmatique, tunique
Dalmatica, tunica

6 7 8 9 10

Verschiedene Formen
der Tunika und Toga
Various Forms of Tunic and Toga
Formes diverses de la tunique
et de la toge
Diverse forme di
tuniche e toghe

11 12 13 14 15

BYZANZ
4. bis 11. Jahrhundert
BYZANTINE EMPIRE
4th—11th Centuries
BYZANCE, IVᵉ au XIᵉ s.
BISANZIO
dal IV all' XI secolo

Kaiserhof
4. bis 5. Jahrhundert
Emperor's Court
4th—5th Centuries
Cour Impériale
IVᵉ au Vᵉ s.
Corte imperiale
(IV V) secolo

1 2 3 4 5 6

Kaiserhof
6. Jahrhundert
Emperor's Court 6th Century
Cour Impériale
VIᵉ s.
Corte imperiale
VI secolo

7 8 9 10 11 12

Kaiserhof
10. bis 11. Jahrhundert
Emperor's Court
10th—11th Centuries
Cour Impériale
Xᵉ au XIᵉ s.
Corte imperiale
X XI secolo

13 14 15 16 17

27

MÖNCHSORDEN
und geistliche Ritterorden
MONASTIC ORDERS
AND ORDERS OF
KNIGHTS
ORDRES MONASTIQUES
ET ORDRES
DE CHEVALERIE
ORDINI MONASTICI
e Ordini Religiosi
Cavallereschi

Geistliche Ritterorden
Orders of Knights
Ordres de Chevalerie
Ordini Religiosi
Cavallereschi

1   2   3   4   5

Mönchsorden
Monastic Orders
Ordres Monastiques
Ordini Monastici

6   7   8   9   10   11

Mönche und Nonnen
Monks and Nuns
Moines de religieuses
Monaci e suore

12   13   14   15   16

GEISTLICHE TRACHT
und geistliche Ritterorden
ECCLESIASTICAL
GARMENTS AND
ORDERS OF KNIGHTS
COSTUMES
ECCLESIASTIQUES ET ORDRES
DE CHEVALERIE
COSTUME
ECCLESIASTICO
e Ordini Religiosi Cavallereschi

Priester, Bischöfe, Päpste
Priests, Bishops, Popes
Prêtres, évêques, papes
Sacerdoti, Vescovi, Papi

1 2 3 4 5
Bischöfe, Päpste
Bishops, Popes
Evêques, papes
Vescovi, Papi

6 7 8 9 10
Geistliche Ordenstrachten
15. bis 18. Jahrhundert
Costumes of Orders of Knights
15th—18th Centuries
Costumes d'ordres religieux
XVe au XVIIIe s.
Costumi di Ordini Religiosi
dal XV al XVIII sec.

11 12 13 14 15

DEUTSCHLAND
500—1200 n. Chr.
GERMANY
500—1200 A. D.
ALLEMAGNE
500—1200 après J. C.
GERMANIA
500—1200 d. C.

Franken
(Merowinger- und
Karolingerzeit)
7. bis 9. Jahrhundert
Frankish Kingdom
(Merovingian and Carlovingian
Periods)
7th—9th Centuries
Francs (Périods mérovingienne
et carolingienne)
VIIe au IXe s.
Franchi
(Merovingi e Carolingi)
dal VII al IX sec.

1   2   3   4   5   6

Fränkische Männer und Frauen
(9. bis 11. Jahrhundert)
Frankish Men and Women
(9th—11th Centuries)
Hommes et femmes francs
(IXe au XIe s.)
Uomini e donne franchi
dal IX all' XI sec.

7   8   9   10   11   12   13

Männer und Frauen
(11. bis 12. Jahrhundert)
Men and Women
(11th—12th Centuries)
Hommes et femmes
(XIe au XIIe s.)
Uomini e donne
(XI—XII sec.)

14   15   16   17   18   19

ÄLTERES
MITTELALTER
und Byzanz
(300—1000 n. Chr.)
EARLY MIDDLE AGES AND
BYZANTINE EMPIRE
(300—1000 A. D.)
COMMENCEMENT
DU MOYEN-AGE ET BYZANCE
(300—1000 après J. C.)
ALTO MEDIOEVO
A BISANZIO
(300—1000 d. C.)

Männer, Krieger
Men, Warriors
Hommes, guerriers
Uomini e guerrieri

1   2   3   4   5

Vornehme, Kaiser, Krieger
Persons of Rank,
Emperor, Warriors
Gens de qualité, empereur,
guerrier
Nobili, Imperatore
Guerrieri

6   7   8   9   10

Geistliche u. a.
Ecclesiastics, etc.
Gens d'Eglise et autres
personnages
Ecclesiastici ecc.

11   12   13   14   15

31

DEUTSCHLAND
Minnesängerzeit
und Kreuzzüge
12. bis 13. Jahrhundert
GERMANY
Time of the Minnesingers
and Crusades
12th—13th Centuries
ALLEMAGNE
Période féodale et Croisades.
XIIe au XIIIe s.
GERMANIA
Epoca dei Trovatori e delle Crociate
XII—XIII sec.

Hohe und niedere Stände
People of High and Low Ranks
Seigneurs et gens du peuple
Alti e bassi ceti

1　2　3　4　5　6

Minnesänger und höfische Kreise
Minnesingers and Courtiers
Ménestrels et gens de cour
Trovatori e cortigiani

7　8　9　10　11　12

Sänger und Spielleute
Singers and Minstrels
Chanteurs et musiciens
Trovatori e musici

13　14　15　16　17　18　19

FRANKREICH
FRANCE
FRANCE
FRANCIA

900—1400

Krieger
Warriors
Guerriers
Guerrieri

1 2 3 4 5 6

Ritter und Knappen
Knights and Squires
Chevaliers et écuyers
Cavalieri e scudieri

7 8 9 10

Herren und Damen
Men and Women
Seigneurs et dames
Gentiluomini e dame

11 12 13 14 15

NORMANNEN
UND ANGELSACHSEN
11 bis 14. Jahrhundert
NORMANS AND
ANGLO-SAXONS
11th—14th Centuries
NORMANDS ET
ANGLO-SAXONS
XIe au XIVe s.
NORMANNI
E ANGLOSASSONI
dall' XI al XIV sec.

Krieger
Warriors
Guerriers
Guerrieri

1 2 3 4

Krieger
Warriors
Guerriers
Guerrieri

5 6 7 8 9

Landleute und Reisende
Peasants and Travellers
Paysans et voyageurs
Campagnoli e viaggiatori

10 11 12 13 14 15

RITTERTRACHTEN
ARMOURED KNIGHTS
COSTUMES DE CHEVALIERS
COSTUMI
DI CAVALIERI

800—1300

Ritter
Knights
Chevaliers
Cavalieri

1 2 3 4 5

Kreuzritter zu Pferde
Crusaders on Horseback
Croisés à cheval
Cavalieri crociati a cavallo

6 7

Ritter in verschiedenen
Rüstungen
Knights in various types
of Armour
Chevaliers vêtus
d'armures diverses
Cavalieri in armature diverse

8 9 10 11 12

35

RITTERTRACHTEN
14. bis 15. Jahrhundert
ARMOURED KNIGHTS
14th—15th Centuries
COSTUMES DE CHEVALIERS
XIVe au XVe s.
COSTUMI
DI CAVALIERI
XIV—XV secolo

Burgundisch,
englisch, französisch
Burgundy, England, France
Bourgogne, Angleterre, France
Borgognoni, Inglesi,
Francesi

1   2   3   4   5

Burgundisch,
polnisch, französisch
Burgundy, Poland, France
Bourgogne, Pologne, France
Borgognoni,
Polacchi, Francesi

6   7   8   9   10

Italienisch
Italy
Italie
Italiani

11   12   13   14   15   16   17

ENGLAND
10. bis 15. Jahrhundert
ENGLAND
10th—15th Centuries
ANGLETERRE
Xᵉ au XVᵉ s.
INGHILTERRA
dal X al XV secolo

10. bis 13. Jahrhundert
10th—13th Centuries
Xᵉ au XIIIᵉ s.
Dal X al XIII sec.

1 2 3 4 5 6

14. Jahrhundert
14th Century
XIVᵉ s.
XIV secolo

7 8 9 10 11 12 13

15. Jahrhundert
15th Century
XVᵉ s.
XV secolo

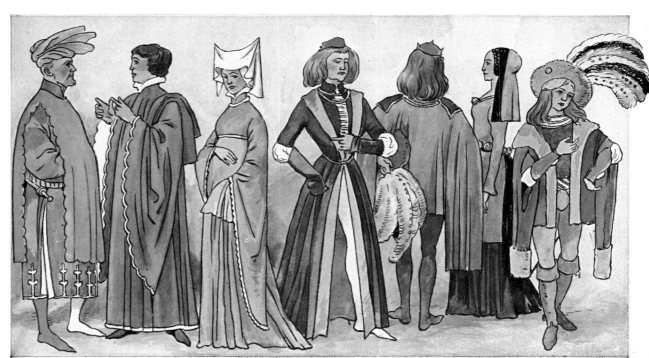

14 15 16 17 18 19 20

RITTERTRACHTEN
Frankreich und Deutschland
15. Jahrhundert
ARMOURED KNIGHTS
France and Germany
15th Century
COSTUMES DE CHEVALIER
Chevaliers français
France et Allemagne XVe s.
COSTUMI DI CAVALIERI
Francia e Germania
XV secolo

Französische Ritter
French Knights
Chevaliers français
Cavalieri francesi

1 2 3 4 5

Deutsche Ritter
German Knights
Chevaliers allemands
Cavalieri tedeschi

6 7 8 9 10

Deutsche Ritter
German Knights
Chevaliers allemands
Cavalieri tedeschi

11 12 13 14 15

RITTERTRACHTEN
Italien
13. bis 15. Jahrhundert
ARMOURED KNIGHTS
Italy 13th—15th Centuries
COSTUMES DE CHEVALIERS
Italie XIIIᵉ au XVᵉ s.
COSTUMI DI CAVALIERI
ITALIA   XIII—XV sec.

Verona
Florenz
Genua
Verona
Florence
Genoa
Vérone
Florence
Gênes
Verona
Firenze
Genova

DEUTSCHLAND
Naumburg, Straßburg, Bamberg
GERMANY
Naumburg, Strasburg, Bamberg
ALLEMAGNE
Naumbourg, Strasbourg, Bamberg
GERMANIA
Naumburg, Strasburgo, Bamberga

Tracht vornehmer Stände
13. Jahrhundert
Costume of People of Rank
13th Century
Costumes seigneuriaux
XIIIe s.
Costumi dell'alto ceto
XIII secolo

RITTERTRACHTEN
Deutschland und Burgund
14. Jahrhundert
ARMOURED KNIGHTS
Germany and Burgundy
14th Century
COSTUMES DE CHEVALIERS
Allemagne et Bourgogne
COSTUMI DI CAVALIERI
Germania e Borgogna
XIV secolo

Deutsche Ritter
German Knights
Chevaliers allemands
Cavalieri tedeschi

1   2   3   4

Deutsche Ritter
German Knights
Chevaliers allemands
Cavalieri tedeschi

5   6   7   8

Burgundische Ritter
Burgundian Knights
Chevaliers bourguignons
Cavalieri borgognoni

9   10   11   12

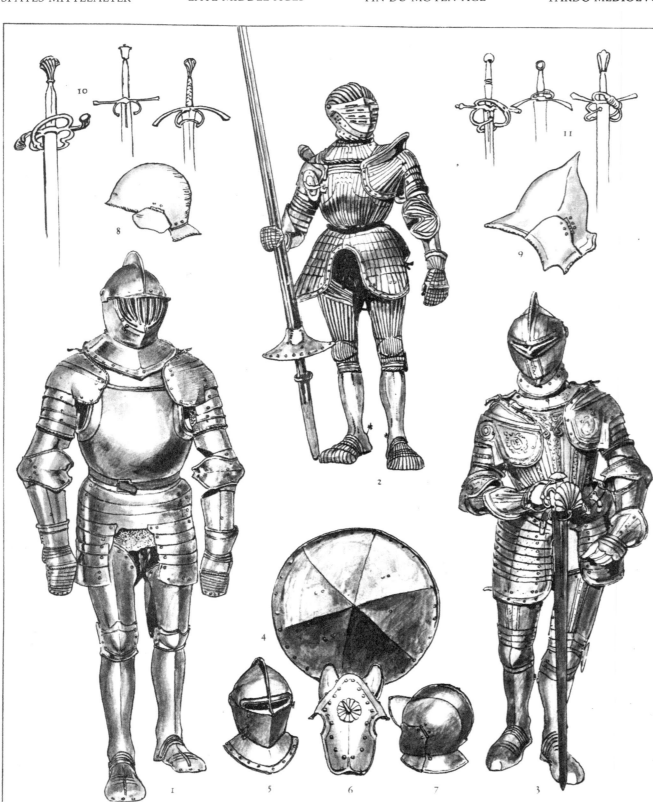

RITTERTRACHTEN
Rüstungen, Helme, Waffen
KNIGHTS' ARMOUR
Armour, Helmets, Weapon
COSTUMES
DE CHEVALIERS
Armures, casques, armes
COSTUMI
DI CAVALIERI
Armature, elmi, armi

1—11

Turnier
Tournament
Joute
Torneo

HELME
UND WAFFEN
HELMETS AND
WEAPONS
CASQUES ET ARMES
ELMI
ED ARMI

1000—1500

FRANKREICH
14. Jahrhundert
FRANCE
14th Century
FRANCE XIVe s.
FRANCIA
XIV secolo

Höfische Trachten
Court dress
Costumes de cour
Costumi di corte

1 2 3 4 5 6 7

8 9 10 11 12

13 14 15 16 17 18

BURGUND
15. Jahrhundert
BURGUNDY
15th Century
BOURGOGNE XVᵉ s.
BORGOGNA
XV secolo

Festmahl
Banquet
Banquet
Banchetto

Krönungsfeier
Coronation Ceremony
Couronnement
Incoronazione

BURGUND
Kopftrachten
15. Jahrhundert
BURGUNDY
Head-dress and Hair Styles
15th Century
BOURGOGNE
Coiffures. XVᵉ s.
BORGOGNA
Acconciature
XV secolo

Frauenhauben
Männerhüte
Männerfrisuren
Women's Head-gear
Men's Hats
Men's Hair Styles
Coiffes de femmes
Chapeaux d'hommes
Coiffures d'hommes
Cuffie femminili
Copricapi maschili
Pettinature maschili

EUROPA
Schuhmoden
14. und 15. Jahrhundert
EUROPE
Footwear
14th and 15th Centuries
EUROPE
Chaussures
du XIX͏ᵉ et du XV͏ᵉ s.
EUROPA
Foggie di scarpe
XIV e XV secolo

nabelschuhe und hölzerne
Unterschuhe (Trippen)
Pointed shoes and wooden
Sandals
ulaines et semelles de bois
surhaussées
Scarpe colle punte
rivoltate e zoccoli

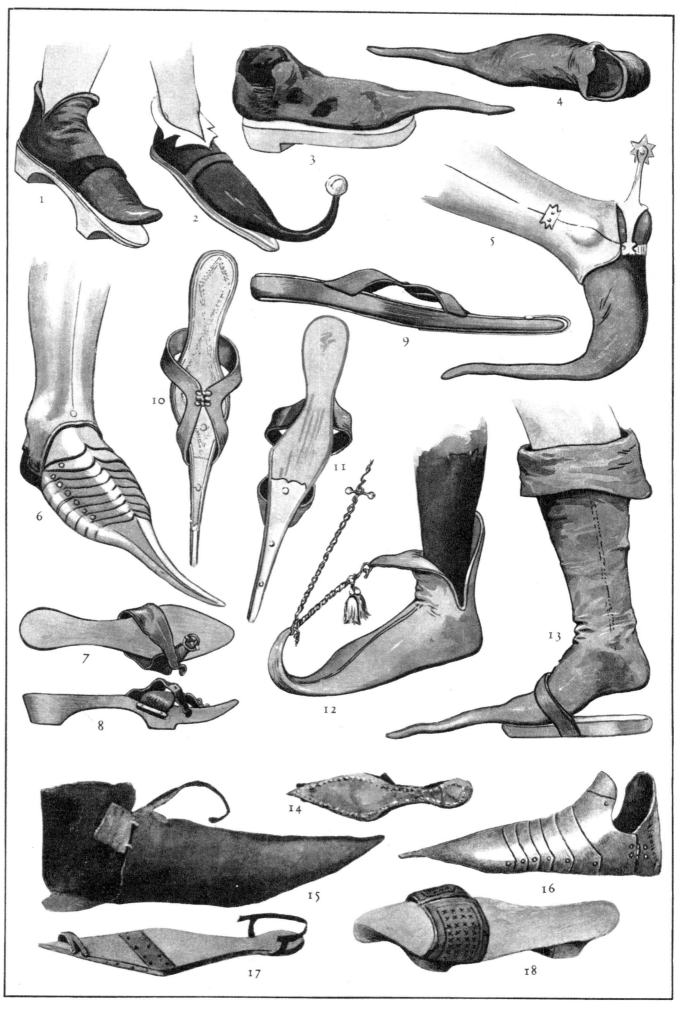

ITALIEN
ITALY
ITALIE
ITALIA

1480—1490

Florentiner Bürgerleben
Florentine Middle Class Life
Scènes de la vie bourgeoise
de Florence
Vita borghese di Firenze

RITTERTRACHTEN
Deutsche Turniertrachten
1500—1515
KNIGTHS' APPAREL
German
Tournament Apparel
1500—1515
COSTUMES DE CHEVALIERS
Tenues allemandes
de tournoi 1500—1515
COSTUMI DI CAVALIERI
Costumi tedeschi da torneo
1500—1515

Deutsches Feldgestech
um 1500
German Jousters about 1500
Tournoi allemand
aux environs de 1500
Lancia da campo tedesca
circa 1500

Deutsches Scharfrennen
um 1515
German Knights jousting
about 1515
Joute allemande
aux environs de 1515
Corsa e carica tedesca
circa 1515

FRANKREICH
15. Jahrhundert
FRANCE
15th Century
FRANCE
Première moitié du XVᵉ s.
FRANCIA
XV secolo

Vornehme Jünglinge
Young Men of Rank
Jeunes nobles
Giovani nobili

1   2   3   4   5   6

Vornehme Gesellschaft
People of Rank
Personnages de la noblesse
Nobile società

7   8   9   10   11   12

Hofdamen
Ladies in Waiting
Dames de la cour
Dame di corte

13   14   15   16   17

FRANKREICH
FRANCE
FRANCE
FRANCIA

1485—1510

Hoftrachten
Court Dress
Costumes de cour
Costumi di corte

1 2 3 4 5

6 7 8 9 10

11 12 13 14 15

BURGUND
BURGUNDY
MODE DU
BOURGOGNE
BORGOGNA

1425—1490

Hoftrachten
Court Dress
Costumes de cour
Costumi di corte

1 2 3 4 5

6 7 8 9 10

11 12 13 14 15

ITALIEN
14. Jahrhundert
ITALY
14th Century
ITALIE XIVᵉ s.
ITALIA
XIV secolo

1310—1350

1 2 3 4 5 6

1325—1350

7 8 9 10 11 12 13

1340—1360

14 15 16 17 18 19 20 21

ITALIEN
ITALY
ITALIE
ITALIA

1425—1480

Herolde, König
King, Heralds
Hérauts, roi
Araldi, re

1 2 3 4 5 6 7 8

Falkenträger, Kriegsleute u. a.
Man with a Falcon, Warriors
Fauconnier,
guerriers et autres personnages
Falconiere, armigeri ed altri

9 10 11 12 13 14 15

Vornehme Männertrachten
Costume of Men of Rank
Costumes de gens de qualité
Costumi signorili da uomo

16 17 18 19 20 21

ITALIEN
15. Jahrhundert
ITALY
15th Century
ITALIE XVᵉ s.
ITALIA
XV secolo

Oberitalien
Northern Italy
Italie du Nord
Italia Settentrionale

1435—1440

1 2 3 4 5

Oberitalien
Northern Italy
Italie du Nord
Italia Settentrionale

1450

6 7 8 9 10 11

Venedig um 1485
Venice about 1485
Venise
aux environs de 1485
Venezia intorno al 1485

12 13 14 15 16

ITALIEN
ITALY
ITALIE
ITALIA

1350—1500

14. Jahrhundert
14th Century
XIVe s.
XIV secolo

1 2 3 4 5

1400—1450

6 7 8 9

1480—1495

10 11 12 13 14

56

ITALIEN
Kopftrachten 1470—1500
ITALY
Head-dresses
and Hair Styles 1470—1500
ITALIE
Coiffures 1470—1500
ITALIA
Acconciature 1470—1500

DEUTSCHLAND
Ende 15. Jahrhundert
GERMANY
End of 15th Century
ALLEMAGNE
Fin du XVᵉ s.
GERMANIA
Fine del XV secolo

Handwerker und Bürger
Craftsmen and Burghers
Artisans et bourgeois
Operai e borghesi

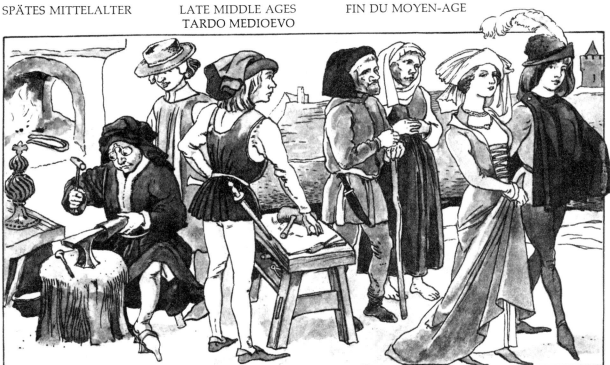

1 2 3 4 5 6 7

Tanzkostüme u. a.
Dancing Costume, etc.
Costumes de bal et autres
Costumi da danza ed altri

8 9 10 11 12 13

Bauern, Söldner, Jude
Peasants, Mercenaries, Jew
Paysans, mercenaire, juif
Contadini, mercenari, ebreo

14 15 16 17 18

SPANIEN
13. bis 15. Jahrhundert
SPAIN
13th—15th Century
ESPAGNE, XIIIe au XVe s.
SPAGNA
XII—XV sec.

Bürger und Ritter
Burghers and Knights
Bourgeois et chevaliers
Borghesi e cavalieri

1 2 3 4 5 6

Hoftrachten
Court Dress
Costumes de cour
Costumi di corte

7 8 9 10 11 12

Berühmte Persönlichkeiten
Famous People
Personnalités célèbres
Personalità celebri

13 14 15 16 17 18

DEUTSCHLAND
GERMANY
ALLEMAGNE
GERMANIA

1500—1525

Bürger und Bauern
Citizens and Peasants
Bourgeois et paysans
Borghesi e contadini

1   2   3   4   5   6   7

Bauern
Peasants
Paysans
Contadini

8   9   10   11   12   13

Fahrendes Volk
Vagrants
Gens du peuple
oyageant à la suite de l'armée
Popolo errante

14   15   16   17   18   19

HOCHRENAISSANCE
ITALIEN

RENAISSANCE
ITALY

HAUTE-EPOQUE DE LA RENAISSANCE
ITALIE

TARDO RINASCIMENTO
ITALIA

Patrizier 1520—1530   Patricians 1520—1530   Patriciens 1520—1530   Patrizi 1520—1530

DEUTSCHLAND
Kopftrachten
1500—1550
GERMANY
Head-dress
1500—1550
ALLEMAGNE
Coiffures 1500—1550
GERMANIA
Foggie di copricapi
e acconciature
1500—1550

Barett und langes Haar
at Bonnet and Long Hair
arrettes et cheveux longs
Berretta e capelli lunghi

Barett und
Gelehrtenhaube
Flat Bonnet
and Scholar's Cap
rettes et bonnet de lettré
Berretta e cuffia
da scienziato

Frauenbarett
und Netzhaube
Women's Bonnets
and Net-hood
Barrettes féminines et
coiffe à filet
Berretta da donna e
cuffia a rete

REFORMATIONSZEIT
ENGLAND

REFORMATION PERIOD
ENGLAND

PERIODE DE LA REFORME
ANGLETERRE

TEMPO DELLA RIFORMA
INGHILTERRA

Zeit Heinrichs VIII.   Time of Henry VIII.   Epoque de Henri VIII   Periodo di Enrico VIII

SPANIEN
SPAIN
ESPAGNE
SPAGNA

Zeit Philipps II. 1556—1598
Time of Philip II. 1556—1598
Epoque de Philippe II. 1556—1598
Periodo di Filippo II 1556—1598

DEUTSCHLAND
GERMANY
ALLEMAGNE
GERMANIA

1510—1550

Deutsche Bürger aller Stände
German Citizens of all Ranks
Bourgeois allemands
de toutes conditions
Borghesi tedeschi
di tutti i ceti

ITALIEN
Kopftrachten
1500—1550
ITALY
Head-dress
and Hair Styles
1500—1550
ITALIE
Coiffures 1500—1550
ITALIA
Foggie di copricapi
e acconciature
1500—1550

ITALIEN
ITALY
ITALIE
ITALIA

1460—1500

Ferrara 1460—1470
Ferrarra 1460—1470
Ferrare, 1460—1470
Ferrara 1460—1470

1   2   3   4   5   6   7   8

Venedig 1495
Venice 1495
Venise, 1495
Venezia 1495

9   10   11   12   13

Ferrara 1470
Florenz 1490

Ferrarra 1470
Florence 1490

Ferrare, 1470
Florence, 1490

Ferrara 1470
Firenze 1490

14   15   16   17

ITALIEN
um 1500
ITALY
about 1500
ITALIE
aux environs de 1500
ITALIA
circa 1500

Venedig
Doge und sein Gefolge
Venice
Doge and his Retinue
Venise
Doge et sa suite
Venezia
Doge e il suo seguito

1 2 3 4 5 6 7 8

Oberitalien
Northern Italy
Italie du Nord
Italia Settentrionale
1505—1508

9 10 11 12 13

14 15 16 17 18 19

DEUTSCHLAND
15. Jahrhundert
GERMANY
15th Century
ALLEMAGNE XV e s.
GERMANIA
XV secolo

1410—1460

1   2   3   4   5   6

1410—1460

7   8   9   10   11   12

1450—1470

13   14   15   16   17   18

KRIEGSTRACHTEN   MILITARY COSTUME   TENUES DE GUERRE   COSTUMI GUERRESCHI

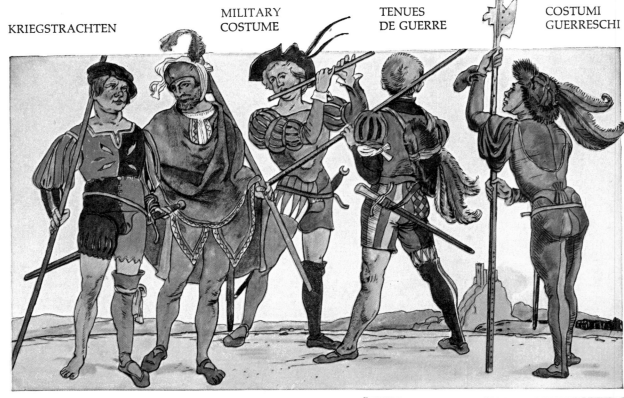

DEUTSCHLAND
16. Jahrhundert
Landsknechte

GERMANY
16th Century
Mercenaries

ALLEMAGNE XVIᵉ s.
Lansquenets

GERMANIA
XVI secolo
Lanzichenecchi

1500—1520

1 2 3 4 5

1520—1540

6 7 8 9

10 11 12 13

DEUTSCHLAND
16. Jahrhundert
Landsknechte

GERMANY
16th Century
Mercenaries

ALLEMAGNE XVIe s.
Lansquenets

GERMANIA
XVI secolo
Lanzichenecchi

1540—1550

1 2 3 4 5

1550

6 7 8 9 10

1560

11 12 13 14 15

DEUTSCHLAND
GERMANY
ALLEMAGNE
GERMANIA

1500—1530

Nürnberger Bürgerinnen
Nuremberg Middle Class Women
Bourgeoises de Nuremberg
Borghesi di Norimberga

1 2 3 4

Basler Bürgerinnen
Basle Middle Class Women
Bourgeoises de Bâle
Borghesi de Basilea

5 6 7 8

die Männerschaube,
der Faltrock
Men's Furlined Mantle,
Pleated Coat
La houppelande,
la tunique plissée
Pelliccia da uomo
gonnellino a pieghe

9 10 11 12 13

DEUTSCHLAND
GERMANY
ALLEMAGNE
GERMANIA

1550—1600

Spanische Mode in Deutschland
Spanish Fashion in Germany
Mode espagnole en Allemagne
La moda spagnola
in Germania

1590—1595

1   2   3

Verlobungsfeier 1585
Betrothal Ceremony 1585
Fiançailles en 1585
Festa fidanzamento 1585

4   5   6   7   8

Herzog Albrecht V. v. Bayern
und Standespersonen
Duke Albrecht V. of Bavaria
and People of Rank
Le Duc Albert V de
avière et personnages de qualité
Duca Alberto V di Baviera
e persone di rango

9   10   11   12   13

73

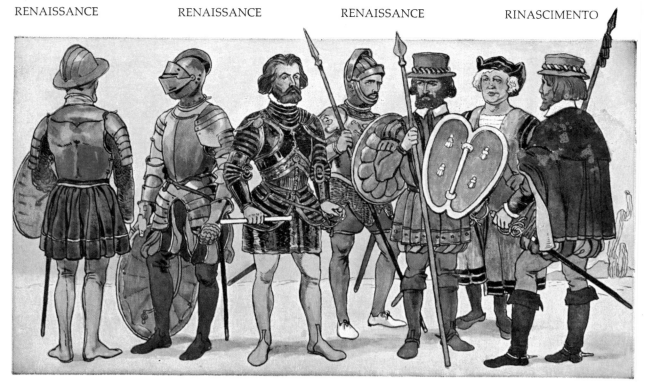

SPANIEN UND
PORTUGAL
SPAIN
AND PORTUGAL
ESPAGNE
ET PORTUGAL
SPAGNA
E PORTOGALLO

1500—1540

Spanische Fürsten
und Entdecker
Spanish Princes and Discoverers
Princes espagnols et navigateurs
Principi spagnoli e scopritori

1 2 3 4 5 6 7

Portugiesische Entdecker
Portuguese Discoverers
Navigateurs portugais
Scopritori portoghesi

8 9 10 11

Spanische Mauren
15. Jahrhundert
Spanish Moors, 15th Century
Maures espagnols
XVᵉ s.
Mauri spagnoli
XV secolo

12 13 14 15 16 17 18

FRANKREICH
FRANCE
FRANCE
FRANCIA

1500—1575

Franz I. und sein Hof
Francis I. and his Court
François Ier et sa cour
Francesco I e la sua corte

1515—1550

1 2 3 4 5

Franz I. und sein Hof
um 1540—1560
Francis I. and his Court
about 1540—1560
François Ier et sa cour
vers 1540—1560
Francesco I e la sua corte
intorno al 1540—1560

6 7 8 9 10

„Spanische Mode"
am französischen Hofe
Spanish Fashion
at the French Court
«Mode espagnole»
à la Cour de France
«Moda spagnola»
alla corte francese

11 12 13 14 15

FRANKREICH
Spanische Mode
FRANCE
Spanish Fashion
FRANCE
Mode espagnole
FRANCIA
Moda spagnola

1560–1590

Karl IX. und sein Hof
Charles IX. and his Court
Charles IX et sa cour
Carlo IX e la sua corte

1560—1574

1 2 3 4 5

Soldaten und Bürger
Soldiers and Citizens
Soldats et bourgeois
Soldati e borghesi

1560—1580

6 7 8 9 10 11

Bürger und Bauern
Citizens and Peasants
Bourgeois et paysans
Borghesi e contadini

1580—1590

12 13 14 15 16 17

FRANKREICH
Spanische Mode
FRANCE
Spanish Fashion
FRANCE
Mode espagnole
FRANCIA
Moda spagnola

1575—1590

Heinrich III. und sein Hof
Hugenotten
Henry III. and his Court
Huguenots
Henri III et sa cour
Huguenots
Enrico III e la sua corte
Ugonotti

1   2   3   4   5

Edeldamen, Pagen u. a.
Noble Women, Pages
Dames de la noblesse,
pages et autres personnages
Nobildonne, paggi ecc.

6   7   8   9   10   11

Höflinge, Leibwache
Courtiers, Bodyguard
Courtisans, hommes de garde
Cortigiani, guardia del corpo

12   13   14   15   16

77

SPÄTRENAISSANCE   LATE RENAISSANCE   FIN DE LA RENAISSANCE   TARDO RINASCIMENTO

ITALIEN
ITALY
ITALIE
ITALIA

1590—1610

Ehrbare Frauen und Kurtisanen
Respectable Women and Courte-
sans
Femmes honorables et courtisanes
Dama di riguardo e
cortigiana

1 2 3 4 5

Venedig und Ferrara
Venice and Ferrara
Venise et Ferrare
Venezia e Ferrara

1590—1610

6 7 8 9 10

Mailand
1604
Milan 1604
Milan 1604
Milano 1604

11 12 13 14 15

FRANKREICH
FRANCE
FRANCE
FRANCIA

1600—1640

Heinrich IV. und sein Hof
Henry IV. and his Court
Henri IV et sa cour
Enrico IV e la sua corte

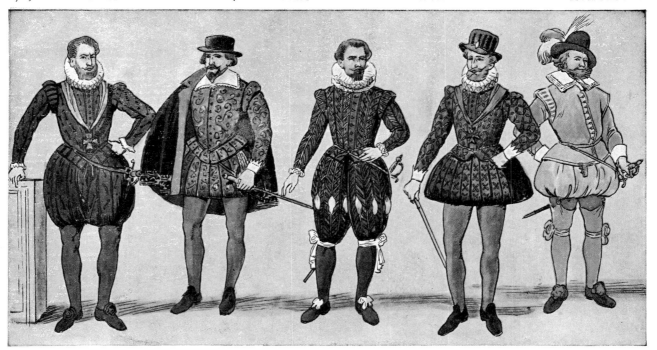

1 2 3 4 5

Heinrich IV. und Ludwig XIII.
Henry IV. and Louis XIII.
Henri IV et Louis XIII
Enrico IV e Luigi XIII

6 7 8 9 10

«Messieurs à la mode»
«Messieurs à la mode»
Dame et seigneurs
«Messieurs à la mode»

1630—1640

11 12 13 14 15 16

SPANIEN
16. und 17. Jahrhundert
SPAIN
16th and 17th Centuries
ESPAGNE
XVIe et XVIIe s.
SPAGNA
XVI e XVII secolo

1 2 3 4 5

6 7 8 9 10

11 12 13 14 15

RUSSLAND
RUSSIA
RUSSIE
RUSSIA

Bojarenfrauen, Krieger
Boyard Women, Warriors
Femmes de boyards, guerriers
Donne boiarde, guerrieri

1 2 3 4 5

Bojaren
Boyards
Boyards
Boiardi

6 7 8 9 10

Zar und Bojaren
Tsar and Boyards
Tsar et boyards
Zar e boiardi

11 12 13 14 15

POLEN, UNGARN,
UKRAINE
POLAND, HUNGARY,
UKRAINE
POLOGNE, HONGRIE,
UKRAINE
POLONIA, UNGHERIA
UCRAINA

Polen
Poland
Pologne
Polacchi

1 2 3 4 5 6

Polen
Poland
Pologne
Polacchi

7 8 9 10 11 12

Ungarn und Ukraine
Hungary and Ukraine
Hongrie et Ukraine
Ungheresi e Ucraini

13 14 15 16 17

Reformation und spanische Mode
1514—1564
Reformation and Spanish
Fashion 1514—1564
Réforme et mode espagnole 1514—1564
Riforma e moda spagnola 1514—1564

Trachten am sächsischen Hofe
Costume worn at the Court of Saxony
Costumes de la Cour de Saxe
Costumi alla corte di Sassonia

DEUTSCHLAND
um 1560—1580
(Spanische Mode)
GERMANY
about 1560—1580
(Spanish Fashion)
ALLEMAGNE
aux environs de 1560—1580
(mode espagnole)
GERMANIA
circa 1560—1580
(moda spagnola)

Bürger- und Handwerkerfrauen
in Danzig, Köln und Lübeck
Citizens' and Craftmen's Wives
from Dantzig, Cologne and Lübeck
Bourgeoises et femmes d'artisans
de Dantzig, Cologne et Lubeck
Spose di borghesi ed operai
a Danzica, Colonia e Lubecca

1 2 3 4 5

Bürger- und Handwerkerfrauen
in Nürnberg und Augsburg
Citizens' and Craftmen's Wives
from Nuremberg and Augsburg
Bourgeoises de femmes d'artisans
de Nuremberg et d'Augsbourg
Spose di borghesi ed operai a
Norimberga e Augusta

6 7 8 9 10

Männertrachten
Men's Costume
Costumes d'hommes
Costumi maschili

11 12 13 14 15

EUROPA
EUROPE
EUROPE
EUROPA

1550—1590

Spanisches Militär
1555 und 1590
Spanish Soldiers
1555 and 1590
Costumes militaires espagnols
1555 et 1590
Militari spagnoli
1555—1590

1   2   3   4   5

Spanisches Militär in den
Niederlanden 1585
Spanish Soldiers
in the Netherlands 1585
Costumes militaires espagnols
aux Pays-Bas
1585
Militari spagnoli
nei Paesi Bassi
1585

6   7   8   9

Französisches Militär um 1581
French Soldiers about 1581
Costumes militaires français
aux environs de 1581
Militari francesi
intorno al 1581

10   11   12   13

DEUTSCHLAND
Kopftrachten
1550—1595
(Spanische Mode)
GERMANY
Head-dress 1550—1595
(Spanish Fashion)
ALLEMAGNE
Coiffures. 1550—1595
(Mode espagnole)
GERMANIA
Foggie di copricapi
1550—1595
(moda spagnola)

Kurzes Barett (Toque)
Small Cap (Toque)
Toque
Berretta breve (tocco)

Kleine spanische Hüte
Small Spanish Hats
Petits chapeaux espagno
Piccolo capelli spagnoli

Steife Halskrausen
Stiff Ruffs
Fraises
Collaretti rigidi

DEUTSCHLAND
UND FRANKREICH
Dreißigjähriger Krieg
GERMANY
AND FRANCE
Thirty Years' War
LLEMAGNE ET FRANCE
(Guerre de Trente Ans)
GERMANIA
E FRANCIA
Guerra dei Trent'anni

Alla modo-Trachten 1629
lla modo'' Costume 1629
Costumes d'élégants et
d'élégantes 1629
stumi «Alla modo» 1629

Kavalier, Frauen
Courtier, Women
Chevalier, femmes
Cavaliere, dame

Alla modo-Trachten
''Alla modo'' Costume
Costumes d'élégants
et d'élégantes
Costumi «Alla modo»

ENGLAND
Zeit der Elisabeth
und der Maria Stuart
ENGLAND
Time of Elizabeth and
Mary Queen of Scots
ANGLETERRE
Epoque d'Elisabeth
et de Marie Stuart
INGHILTERRA
Epoca di Elisabetta
e Maria Stuarda

1550—1605

SPANIEN
Zeit Philipps IV.
SPAIN
Time of Philip IV.
ESPAGNE
Epoque de Philippe IV
SPAGNA
Epoca di Filippo IV

1630—1660

89

TÜRKEI
TURKEY
TURQUIE
TURCHIA

Türkei um 1575
Turkey about 1575
Turquie, aux environs de 1575
Turchia intorno al 1575

1 2 3 4 5

Türkei um 1575
Turkey about 1575
Turquie, aux environs de 1575
Turchia intorno al 1575

6 7 8 9 10

Frauen im Serail, Derwisch u. a.
Women of the Seraglio,
Dervish, etc.
Femmes au sérail, derviche
et autres personnages
Donne del «serail»
Derviscio ecc.

11 12 13 14 15

TÜRKEI
TURKEY
TURQUIE
TURCHIA

Amtspersonen u. a.
Officials, etc.
Fonctionnaires
et autres personnages
Notabili e altri

1   2   3   4   5

Offiziere und Soldaten
Officers and Soldiers
Officiers et soldats
Ufficiali e soldati

6   7   8   9   10

Gefolge des Sultans
Sultan's Retinue
Suite du Sultan
Seguito del sultano

11   12   13   14   15

EUROPA
Kriegstrachten des Dreißig-
jährigen Krieges 1600—1650
EUROPE
Military Costume during
the Thirty Years' War
1600—1650
EUROPE
Tenues de la Guerre de Trente ans.
1600—1650
EUROPA
Costumi guerreschi
della guerra dei Trenta
anni 1600—1650

Musketiere und Pikeniere
Musketeers and Pikemen
Mousquetaires et piquiers
Moschettieri e picconieri

1600—1615

1 2 3 4 5

Heerführer
um 1630—1635
Commanders
about 1630—1635
Chefs militaires
aux environs de 1630—1635
Condottiere dell' esercito
1630—1635

6 7 8 9 10

Soldaten und Offiziere
Soldiers and Officers
Soldats et officiers
Soldati e ufficiali

1635—1650

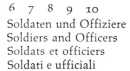

11 12 13 14 15

FRANKREICH
1650—1700 (Ludwig XIV.)
FRANCE
1650—1700 (Louis XIV.)
FRANCE
1650—1700 (Louis XIV)
FRANCIA
1650—1700 (Luigi XIV)

Offiziere und
vornehme Gesellschaft
Officers
and People of Rank
Officiers et personnes de qualité
Ufficiali
e alta società

1 2 3 4 5 6

Ludwig XIV.
und Standespersonen
Louis XIV.
and People of Rank
Louis XIV et nobles
Luigi XIV
e persone di rango

7 8 9 10 11

12 13 14 15 16

FRANKREICH
Theater und Tanz
FRANCE
Theatre and Dancers
FRANCE
Théâtre et danse
FRANCIA
Teatro e danza

Italienische Komödie um 1715
Italian Comedy about 1715
Comédie italienne
aux environs de 1715

Commedia Italiana
intorno al 1715

1   2   3   4   5   6

Tanz um 1725
Dancers about 1725
Danse aux environs de 1725
Danza intorno al 1725

7   8   9   10   11

Tanz um 1730
Dancers about 1730
Danse aux environs de 1730
Danza intorno al 1730

12   13   14   15   16   17

DEUTSCHLAND
Bürgertrachten
GERMANY
Citizen's Costume
ALLEMAGNE
Costumes bourgeois
GERMANIA
Costumi borghesi

1625—1675

Nürnberg, Augsburg, Köln
Nuremberg, Augsburg, Cologne
Nuremberg, Augsburg, Cologne
Norimberga, Augusta, Colonia

1   2   3   4   5

Die Rheingrafenhose
in Deutschland u. a.
The "Rhinegrave"
Breeches in Germany, etc.
La rhingrave en Allemagne
et autres costumes
Calzoni dei conti renani
in Germania ecc.

6   7   8   9   10

Augsburger und Straßburger
Frauentrachten um 1640
Augsburg and Strasburg
Women's Costume about 1640
Costumes féminins
d'Augsbourg et de Strasbourg
aux environs de 1640
Costumi femminili di
Augusta e Strasburgo
intorno al 1640

11   12   13   14   15   16

NIEDERLANDE
NETHERLANDS
PAYS-BAS
PAESI BASSI

1650—1680

Holländische Bürgertrachten
Dutch Citizens' Costume
Costumes de bourgeois
hollandais
Costumi borghesi
dell'Ollanda

1 2 3 4 5

6 7 8 9

10 11 12 13

NIEDERLANDE
Kopf- und Halstrachten
NETHERLANDS
Head-dresses,
Hair Styles;
Collars and Ruffs
PAYS-BAS
Coiffures et collerettes
PAESI BASSI
Foggie di copricapi
e acconciature

ENGLAND
um 1640
ENGLAND
about 1640
ANGLETERRE
aux environs de 1640
INGHILTERRA
intorno al 1640

Vornehme Damen
Noble Ladies
Dames de qualité
Nobili dame

1   2   3   4

Bürgerinnen und
Handwerkerfrauen
Citizens' and Craftmen's Wive
Bourgeoises et femmes d'artisa
Donne borghesi e di
ceto operaio

5 6 7 8 9

Vornehme Damen
Noble Ladies
Dames de qualité
Nobili dame

10 11 12 13 14

Zeit Ludwigs XIV. um 1700
(Hoftrachten zu Versailles)

Time of Louis XIV. about 1700
(Court Dress at Versailles)

Epoque de Louis XIV aux environs
de 1700
(costumes de la Cour de Versailles)

Epoca di Luigi XIV,
intorno al 1700
(Costumi di corte a Versailles)

FRANKREICH
FRANCE
FRANCE
FRANCIA

1695—1700

Pariser Bürgertrachte
Paris Citizens' Costu
Costumes de bourge
parisiens
Costumi borghesi di

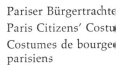

FRANKREICH
FRANCE
FRANCE
FRANCIA

1715–1720

Pariser Bürger
Paris Citizens
rgeois parisiens
stumi borghesi
di Parigi

ITALIENISCHE
KOMÖDIE
ITALIAN COMEDY
COMEDIE ITALIENNE
COMMEDIA
ITALIANA

1680—1730

103

HOLLAND
UND ENGLAND
HOLLAND AND
ENGLAND
HOLLANDE ET ANGLETERRE
OLANDA
E INGHILTERRA

1740—1750

FRANKREICH UND   FRANCE AND GERMANY   FRANCE ET ALLEMAGNE   FRANCIA E GERMANIA
DEUTSCHLAND 1730—1760   1730—1760   1730—1760   1730—1760

ITALIEN. Venedig um 1750　　　ITALY. Venice about 1750　　　ITALIE. Venise, aux environs de 1750　　　ITALIA: Venezia intorno al 1750

FRANKREICH
um 1740
Pariser Straßenleben
FRANCE
about 1740
Paris Street Life
FRANCE
aux environs de 1740
Peuple de Paris
FRANCIA
intorno al 1740
Vita cittadina di Parigi

Ausrufer und Händler
Street-criers and Tradesmen
Marchands à la criée et
marchands ambulants
Strilloni e venditori ambulanti

1 2 3 4 5

Händler und Hausierer
Tradesmen and Hawkers
Marchands ambulants
et colporteurs
Strilloni ambulanti
e rivenditori

6 7 8 9 10

Musikanten und Ausrufer
Itinerant Musicians
and Street-criers
Musiciens et marchands
à la criée
Musici e imbonitori

11 12 13 14

WIEN UND VENEDIG
Straßentypen 1770—1790
VIENNA AND VENICE
Street Life 1770—1790
VIENNE ET VENISE
Peuple 1770—1790
VIENNA E VENEZIA
Gente di strada 1770—1790

Wiener Ausrufer 1775
Viennese Street-criers 1775
Marchands à la criée
Vienne 1775
Strilloni viennesi 1775

1   2   3   4   5   6   7

Wiener Ausrufer 1775
Viennese Street-criers 1775
Marchands à la criée
Vienne 1775
Strilloni viennesi 1775

8   9   10   11   12

Venezianer Ausrufer 1785
Venetian Street-criers 1785
Marchands à la criée
Venise 1785
Strilloni veneziani 1785

13   14   15   16   17

SPÄTES ROKOKO
FRANKREICH 1770—1780

LATE ROCOCO
FRANCE 1770—1780

FIN DU ROCOCO
FRANCE 1770—1780

TARDO ROCOCO
FRANCIA 1770—1780

Pariser Gesellschaft   Parisian Society   Société parisienne   Società parigina

ENGLAND
ENGLAND
ANGLETERRE
INGHILTERRA

1770—1800

Damen des Adels 1770—1785
Noble Women 1770—1785
Dames de la noblesse 1770—1785
Dame della nobiltà 1770—1785

1 2 3 4

Englische Moden 1770—1795
English Fashions 1770—1795
Mode anglaise 1770—1795
Moda inglese 1770—1795

5 6 7 8 9 10

Englische Moden 1795—1800
English Fashions 1795—1800
Mode anglaise 1795—1800
Moda inglese 1795—1800

11 12 13 14 15

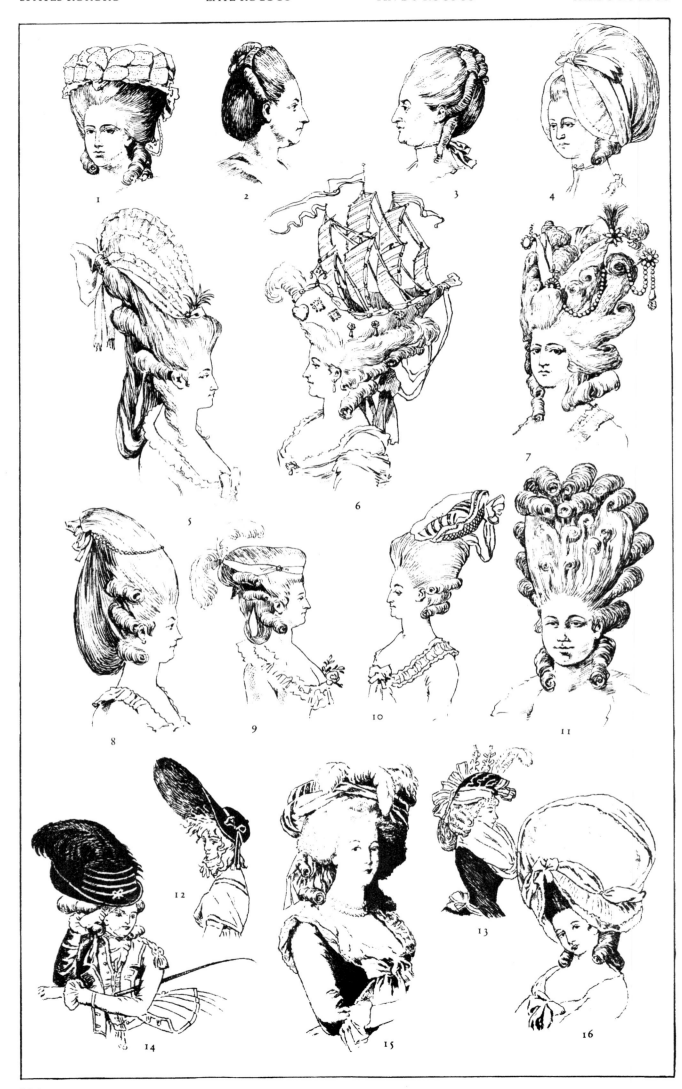

EUROPA
Rokokofrisuren
EUROPE
Rococo Hair Styles
EUROPE
Coiffures Rococo
EUROPA
Pettinature rococò

1770—1790

DEUTSCHLAND
UND ÖSTERREICH
Trachten nach Porzellanfiguren
GERMANY AND AUSTRIA
Costume in China Figures
ALLEMAGNE ET AUTRICHE
Costumes d'après des
statuettes de porcelaine
GERMANIA E AUSTRIA
Costumi da figure di porcellana

1750—1775

Höchst und Frankenthal
Höchst and Frankenthal
Hoechst et Frankenthal
Höchst e Frankenthal

1760

1   2   3

Wien und Nymphenburg
Vienna and Nymphenburg
Vienne et Nymphenbourg
Vienna e Nymphenburg

1750—1765

4   5   6

Meißen u. a.
Meissen and others
Meissen et autres manufactures
Meissen ecc.

1750

7   8   9

FRANKREICH
FRANCE
FRANCE
FRANCIA

1730—1770

1730—1745

1 2 3
1755

4 5 6 7 8
1760—1770

9 10 11 12 13

113

FRANKREICH
Ludwig XVI.
FRANCE
Louis XVI.
FRANCE
Louis XVI
FRANCIA
Luigi XVI

1775—1785

1 2 3 4 5

6 7 8 9 10

11 12 13

SPÄTES ROKOKO UND
REVOLUTION

LATE ROCOCO AND PERIOD
OF THE FRENCH REVOLUTION

FIN DU ROCOCO
ET REVOLUTION

TARDO ROCOCO
E RIVOLUZIONE

FRANKREICH
FRANCE
FRANCE
FRANCIA

1780—1789

1780

1 2 3 4

1780

5 6 7 8 9

1789

115

10 11 12 13 14

REVOLUTION UND
DIRECTOIRE

FRENCH REVOLUTION
AND DIRECTORY

REVOLUTION
ET DIRECTOIRE

RIVOLUZIONE
E DIRETTORIO

FRANKREICH
FRANCE
FRANCE
FRANCIA

1790—1795

Revolution 1790
Revolution 1790
Révolution 1790
Rivoluzione 1790

1 2 3 4 5 6

Revolution 1790
Revolution 1790
Révolution 1790
Rivoluzione 1790

7 8 9 10 11 12

Directoire 1795
Directory 1795
Directoire 1795
Direttorio 1795

13 14 15 16 17 18

116

WENDE
18. UND 19. JAHRHUNDERT

TURN OF 18th
AND 19th CENTURIES

FIN DU XVIIIᵉ
ET DEBUT DU XIXᵉ s.

SCORCIO TRA IL XVIII
E IL XIX SECOLO

FRANKREICH
Revolution, Directoire,
Konsulat
FRANCE
Revolution, Directory,
Consulate
FRANCE
Révolution, Directoire,
Consulat
FRANCIA
Rivoluzione, Direttorio,
Consolato

Revolutionstrachten
Costumes of the Revolution
Costumes révolutionnaires
Costumi rivoluzionari

1792—1795

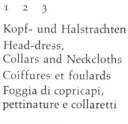

1 2 3

Kopf- und Halstrachten
Head-dress,
Collars and Neckcloths
Coiffures et foulards
Foggia di copricapi,
pettinature e collaretti

1790—1795

4 5 6 7 8 9 10

«Incroyables et Merveilleuses»
«Incroyables et Merveilleuses»
Merveilleuses et Incroyables
«Incroyables et merveilleuses»

1795—1803

11 12 13 14 15 16

DEUTSCHLAND
UND FRANKREICH
GERMANY AND FRANCE
ALLEMAGNE ET FRANCE
GERMANIA E FRANCIA

1680—1790

Deutsche Uniformen
German Uniforms
Uniformes allemands
Divise tedesche

1680—1690

1 2 3 4 5

Französische Uniformen
French Uniforms
Uniformes français
Divise francesi

1725—1757

6 7 8

Französische Uniformen
French Uniforms
Uniformes français
Divise francesi

1757—1790

9 10 11 12 13

118

ENGLAND UND
FRANKREICH
ENGLAND AND FRANCE
ANGLETERRE ET FRANCE
INGHILTERRA E FRANCIA

1800—1830

England um 1800
England about 1800
Angleterre, aux environs de 180
Inghilterra intorno al 1800

1 2 3 4 5 6

Frankreich 1815
France 1815
France 1815
Francia 1815

7 8 9 10 11 12

Frankreich um 1825—1830
France about 1825—1830
France, aux environs de
1825—1830
Francia intorno al 1825—1830

13 14 15 16 17 18

DEUTSCHLAND
Biedermeiermode
GERMANY
"Biedermeier" Fashion
ALLEMAGNE
Mode à la Biedermeier
GERMANIA
«Biedermeier»

1815—1835

Mode 1815—1819
Fashion 1815—1819
Mode 1815—1819
Moda 1815—1819

1 2 3 4 5 6

Mode 1820—1832
Fashion 1820—1832
Mode 1820—1832
Moda 1820—1832

7 8 9 10 11 12

Mode 1834—1835
Fashion 1834—1835
Mode 1834—1835
Moda 1834—1835

13 14 15 16 17

120

EUROPA,
Uniformen
EUROPE,
Uniforms
EUROPE,
Uniformes
EUROPA
Divise

1795—1813

Preußen 1806—1813
Prussia 1806—1813
Prusse 1806—1813
Prussia 1806—1813

1   2   3   4   5   6   7

Rußland u. a.
Russia and others
Russie et autres pays
Russia ecc.

1800—1815

8   9   10   11   12   13   14

Frankreich
France
France
Francia

1795—1813

15   16   17   18   19   20   21

DEUTSCHLAND
Uniformen unter
Friedrich dem Großen

GERMANY
Uniforms
during the Reign of
Frederick the Great

ALLEMAGNE
Uniformes sous
Frédéric le Grand

GERMANIA
Divise sotto
Federico il Grande

1740—1786

DEUTSCHLAND
Modenalmanache
GERMANY
Fashions Almanacs
ALLEMAGNE
Almanachs des Modes
GERMANIA
Almanacchi di mode

1786—1788

Pariser Moden 1830—1835   Paris Fashions 1830—1835   Mode parisienne 1830—1835   Mode parigine 1830—1835

FRANKREICH UND DEUTSCHLAND
19. JAHRHUNDERT

FRANCE AND GERMANY
19th CENTURY

FRANCE ET ALLEMAGNE
XIXᵉ s.

FRANCIA E GERMANIA
XIX SECOLO

Pariser und Berliner Moden
(Krinoline) 1850—1860

Paris and Berlin Fashions
(Crinoline) 1850—1860

Mode parisienne et berlinoise
(crinolines) 1850—1860

Mode parigine e berlinesi
(crinoline) 1850—1860

FRANKREICH
und
DEUTSCHLAND
(Cul de Paris)
RANCE AND GERMANY
(Cul de Paris)
FRANCE ET
ALLEMAGNE
(cul de Paris)
FRANCIA E GERMANIA
(«Cul de Paris»)

1870—1875

1   2   3   4   5

6   7   8   9   10   11

12   13   14   15   16

SPANIEN
SPAIN
ESPAGNE
SPAGNA

1810—1830

Kastilien, Segovia
Castile, Segovia
Castille, Ségovie
Castiglia, Segovia

1 2 3 4 5

Katalonien, Valencia
Catalonia, Valencia
Catalogne, Province de Valence
Catalogna, Valenzia

6 7 8 9 10 11

Kastilien, Aragonien,
Santander, Asturien
Castile, Aragon,
Santander, Asturias
Castille, Aragon,
Province de Santander, Asturies
Castiglia, Aragona,
Santander, Asturie

12 13 14 15 16 17

SPANIEN
Mitte des 19. Jahrhunderts
SPAIN
Middle of 19 th Century
ESPAGNE
milieu du XIXᵉ s.
SPAGNA
metà del XIX secolo

Malaga, Sierra Morena
und Andalusien
Malaga, Sierra Morena and
Andalusia
Province de Malaga,
Sierra, Modena, Andalousie
Malaga, Sierra Morena
e Andalusia

1 2 3 4 5

Andalusien, Granada
Andalusia, Granada
Andalousie,
Province de Grenade
Andalusia, Granada

6 7 8 9 10

Zigeuner u. a.
Gipsies, etc.
Tziganes et autres personnages
Zingari ecc.

11 12 13 14

SPANIEN
Stiergefecht (Neuzeit)
SPAIN
Bull-fighting (Modern)
ESPAGNE
Corrida (Période actuelle)
SPAGNA
Corrida (età moderna)

1 2 3 4 5 6

7 8 9 10

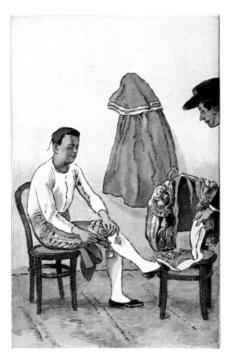

11 12 13 14 15 16

VOLKSTRACHTEN   NATIONAL COSTUME   COSTUMES NATIONAUX ET REGIONAUX
COSTUMI POPOLARI

PORTUGAL
PORTUGAL
PORTUGAL
PORTOGALLO

1 2 3 4 5 6

7 8 9 10 11

12 13 14 15 16

ITALIEN
19. Jahrhundert
ITALY
19 th Century
ITALIE XIXᵉ s.
ITALIA
XIX secolo

Genua
und Umgebung um 1810
Genoa and District about 1810
Gênes et régions voisines
aux environs de 1810
Genova e dintorni
intorno al 1810

1 2 3 4 5

Kirchenstaat um 1830
Papal States about 1830
Etats de l'Eglise aux
environs de 1830
Stato Pontificio
intorno al 1830

6 7 8 9 10

Sizilien um 1830
Sicily about 1830
Sicile aux environs de 1830
Sicilia nel 1830

11 12 13 14 15 16

132

ITALIEN
ITALY
ITALIE
ITALIA

1800—1830

Oberitalien, Toskana
Northern Italy, Tuscany
Italie du Nord, Toscane
Italia Settentrionale, Toscana

1 2 3 4 5 6

Unteritalien
Southern Italy
Italie du Sud
Italia Meridionale

7 8 9 10 11

Sardinien
Sardinia
Sardaigne
Sardegna

12 13 14 15 16

ITALIEN
um 1850—1890
ITALY
about 1850—1890
ITALIE
aux environs de 1850—1890
ITALIA
nel 1850—1890

Venedig, Friaul, Campagna
Venice, Friuli, Campagna, etc.
Venise, Frioul,
Campanie et autres régions
Venezia, Friuli, Campania

1 2 3 4 5 6

Campagna, Calabrien, Abruzzen
Campagna, Calabria, Abruzzi
Campagne romaine, Calabre,
Abruzzes
Campania, Calabria, Abruzzi

7 8 9 10 11

Calabrien, Sardinien
Calabria, Sardinia
Calabre, Sardaigne
Calabria, Sardegna

12 13 14 15 16 17

ALBANIEN
ALBANIA
ALBANIE
ALBANIA

1 2 3 4 5

Malissoren
Inhabitants of Malis
Malissores
Malissori

6 7 8 9 10 11

12 13 14 15 16

SÜDSLAWIEN
SOUTHERN SLAVONIA
YOUGOSLAVIE
JUGOSLAVIA

Herzegowina,
Dalmatien
Herzegovina,
Dalmatia
Herzégovine,
Dalmatie
Erzegovina
Dalmazia

1 2 3 4 5 6

Dalmatien,
Bosnien,
Montenegro
Dalmatia,
Bosnia,
Montenegro
Dalmatie,
Bosnie,
Monténégro
Dalmazia
Bosnia
Montenegro

7 8 9 10 11

Bosnien,
Serbien,
Montenegro
Bosnia,
Serbia,
Montenegro
Bosnie,
Serbie,
Monténégro
Bosnia
Serbia
Montenegro

12 13 14 15 16 17

136

VOLKSTRACHTEN   NATIONAL COSTUME   COSTUMES NATIONAUX ET REGIONAUX
COSTUMI POPOLARI

UNGARN
HUNGARY
HONGRIE
UNGHERIA

1 2 3 4 5 6

7 8 9 10 11 12

13 14 15 16 17 18

RUMÄNIEN
UND SIEBENBÜRGEN
RUMANIA AND
TRANSYLVANIA
ROUMANIE,
TRANSYLVANIE
ROMANIA
E TRANSILVANIA

Siebenbürgen
Transylvania
Transylvanie
Transilvania

1 2 3 4 5 6

Rumänien
Marmaros
„Banat" u. a.
Rumania
Marmaros
Banat, etc.
Roumanie,
Marmaros,
Banat et autres régions
Romania
«Marmaros»
«Banat» ecc.

7 8 9 10 11 12

Walachei
Bukowina
Wallachia
Bukowina
Valachie
et Bukovine
Valacchia
Bucovina

14 15 16 17 18 19

GRIECHENLAND
Neuzeit 1800—1880
GREECE
Modern Times 1800—1880
GRECE
Epoque moderne 1800—1880
GRECIA
età moderna 1800—1880

Albanien, Inselgriechen
um 1800
Albania, Greek Islands
about 1800
Albanie, Grèce insulaire
aux environs de 1800
Albania, Greci isolani nel 1800

1 2 3 4 5

Athen, Nauplia, Arkadien
Athens, Nauplia, Arcadia
Athènes, Nauplie, Arcadie
Atene, Nauplia, Arcadia

1825—1830

6 7 8 9

Hirten, Deputierter u. a.
Shepherds, Deputy, etc.
Bergers, notables et autres
personnages
Pastori, deputati ecc.

1879

10 11 12 13 14

BELGIEN
19. Jahrhundert
BELGIUM
19th Century
BELGIQUE XIXᵉ s.
BELGIO
XIX secolo

Brabant
Brabant
Brabant
Brabante

1   2   3   4   5   6

Flandern
Flanders
Flandre
Fiandra

7   8   9   10   11

Flandern u. a.
Flanders, etc.
Flandre et autres régions
Fiandra ecc.

12   13   14   15   16

FRANKREICH
FRANCE
FRANCE
FRANCIA

Burgund, Bresse,
Hoch-Savoyen
Burgundy, Bresse,
Savoy
Bourgogne, Bresse,
Haute-Savoie
Borgogna, La Bresse,
Alta Savoia

1 2 3 4 5

Elsaß-Lothringen
Alsace-Lorraine
Alsace et Lorraine
Alsazia-Lorena

6 7 8 9 10

Elsaß
Alsace
Alsace
Alsazia

11 12 13 14 15

FRANKREICH
FRANCE
FRANCE
FRANCIA

Bretagne
Burgund
Auvergne

Brittany
Burgundy
Auvergne

Bretagne
Bourgogne
Auvergne

Bretagna
Borgogna
Alvernia

1 2 3 4 5

Auvergne
Auvergne
Auvergne
Alvernia

6 7 8 9 10

Auvergne
Burgund

Auvergne
Burgundy

Auvergne
Bourgogne

Alvernia
Borgogna

12 13 14 15

FRANKREICH
FRANCE
FRANCE
FRANCIA

Bretagne
Brittany
Bretagne
Bretagna

1 2 3 4 5

6 7 8 9 10

11 12 13 14 15 16

FRANKREICH
FRANCE
FRANCE
FRANCIA

Normandie
Normandy
Normandie
Normandia

1   2   3   4   5

Guyenne
Dauphiné
Auvergne
Guyenne
Dauphiné
Auvergne
Guyenne
Dauphiné
Auvergne
Guienna
Delfinato
Alvernia

6   7   8   9   10   11

Provence
Marche u. a.
Provence
Marche, etc.
Provence
Marche et autres régions
Provenza
Marche ecc.

12   13   14   15   16   17

NIEDERLANDE
19. Jahrhundert
NETHERLANDS
19th Century
PAY-BAS XIXᵉ s.
PAESI BASSI
XIX secolo

Insel Walcheren
Island of Walcheren
Ile de Walcheren
Isola Walcheren

1 2 3 4 5

Insel Marken
Island of Marken
Ile de Marken
Isola Marken

6 7 8 9 10 11

Volendam
Volendam
Volendam
Volendam

12 13 14 15 16

SCHOTTLAND
SCOTLAND
ECOSSE
SCOZIA

15.—17. Jahrhundert
15th—17th Centuries
XVᵉ au XVIIᵉ s.
XV—XVII secolo

1 2 3 4 5

17.—18. Jahrhundert
17th—18th Centuries
XVIIᵉ au XVIIIᵉ s.
XVII—XVIII secolo

6 7 8 9

19. Jahrhundert
19th Century
XIXᵉ s.
XIX secolo

10 11 12 13 14

SCHWEIZ
Anfang 19. Jahrhundert
SWITZERLAND
Beginning of 19th Century
SUISSE
début du XIXᵉ s.
SVIZZERA
Inizio del XIX secolo

1   2   3   4   5

6   7   8   9   10   11

12   13   14   15   16

SCHWEIZ
Mitte 19. Jahrhundert
SWITZERLAND
Middle of 19th Century
SUISSE
milieu du XIXe s.
SVIZZERA
Metà del XIX secolo

1 2 3 4 5

6 7 8 9 10

11 12 13 14 15

DEUTSCHLAND
Nordfriesische Inseln
und Holstein
18. bis 19. Jahrhundert
GERMANY
North Frisian Islands and
Holstein 18th—19th Centuries
ALLEMAGNE
Iles Frisonnes et Holstein
XVIIIe à XIXe s.
GERMANIA
Isole Frisoene Settentrionali
e Holstein
XVIII—XIX secolo

Insel Sylt und Föhr
Islands of Sylt and Föhr
Iles de Sylt et Foehr
Isole Sylt e Föhr

1 2 3 4 5

Halligen, Helgoland
The Halligen, Heligoland
Halligen, Heligoland
Halligen, Helgoland

6 7 8 9 10 11

Holstein
Holstein
Holstein
Holstein

12 13 14 15 16

DEUTSCHLAND
GERMANY
ALLEMAGNE
GERMANIA

Vorpommern
Western Pomerania
Poméranie maritime
Pomerania tedesca

1 2 3 4 5 6

Hinterpommern
Eastern Pomerania
Poméranie intérieure
Pomerania polacca

7 8 9 10 11 12

Mecklenburg
Brandenburg
Mecklenburg
Brandenburg
Mecklembourg
Brandebourg
Meclemburgo
Brandeburgo

13 14 15 16 17

150

DEUTSCHLAND
GERMANY
ALLEMAGNE
GERMANIA

Hannover
Hanover
Hanovre
Hannover

1 2 3 4 5 6 7

Hannover
Hamburg
Hanover
Hamburg
Hanovre
Hambourg
Hannover
Amburgo

8 9 10 11 12 13

Braunschweig
Brunswick
Brunswick
Brunswick

14 15 16 17 18 19

DEUTSCHLAND
Westfalen und
Schaumburg-Lippe
GERMANY
Westphalia and
Schaumburg-Lippe
ALLEMAGNE
Westphalie et
Schaumbourg-Lippe
GERMANIA
Vestfalia
e Schaumburg Lippe

Westfalen
Westphalia
Westphalie
Vestfalia

1   2   3   4   5   6

Westfalen und Waldeck
Westphalia and Waldeck
Westphalie et Waldeck
Vestfalia e Valdecca

7   8   9   10   11   12

Schaumburg-Lippe
Schaumburg-Lippe
Schaumbourg-Lippe
Schaumburg Lippe

13   14   15   16   17   18   19

DEUTSCHLAND
GERMANY
ALLEMAGNE
GERMANIA

Hessen
Hesse
Hesse
Assia

1 2 3 4 5 6 7 8

Hessen
Hesse
Hesse
Assia

9 10 11 12 13 14 15

Braunschweig (Harz)
Brunswick (Harz)
Brunswick (Harz)
Brunswick (Ercinia)

Thüringen
Thuringia
Thuringe
Turingia

16 17 18 19 20

DEUTSCHLAND
GERMANY
ALLEMAGNE
GERMANIA

Die alte Lausitz und
Schlesien
Old Lusatia and Silesia
Ancienne Lusace et Silésie
L'antica Lusazia e la Slesia

Spreewald
Spreewald
Région de la Sprée
Selva Spreana

1 2 3 4

Schlesien
Silesia
Silésie
Slesia

5 6 7 8 9

Oberschlesien
Upper Silesia
Haute-Silésie
Alta-Slesia

10 11 12 13 14

154

DEUTSCHLAND
GERMANY
ALLEMAGNE
GERMANIA

Bayern
Franken

Bavaria
Franconia

Bavière
Franconie

Baviera
Franconia

1   2   3   4   5

Oberbayern
Upper Bavaria
Haute-Bavière
Alta Baviera

6   7   8   9   10

11   12   13   14   15   16   17

DEUTSCHLAND
Baden
GERMANY
Baden
ALLEMAGNE
Bade
GERMANIA
Baden

Schwarzwald
Black Forest
Forêt-Noire
Selva Nera

1   2   3   4   5   6

Rheinebene
Rhine Valley
Plaine du Rhin
Renania

7   8   9   10   11

Schwarzwald u. a.
Black Forest, etc.
Forêt-Noire et autres régions
Selva Nera

12   13   14   15   16

DEUTSCHLAND
GERMANY
ALLEMAGNE
GERMANIA

Württemberg
Würtemberg
Wurtemberg
Wurttemberg

1 2 3 4 5 6

7 8 9 10 11

12 13 14 15 16

ÖSTERREICH
Kärnten, Oberösterreich,
Salzburg
AUSTRIA
Carinthia, Upper Austria
Salzburg
AUTRICHE
Carinthie, Haute-Autriche,
Salzbourg
AUSTRIA
Carinzia, Alta-Austria,
Salisburgo

1 2 3 4 5

Steiermark, Niederösterreich,
Salzburg
Styria, Lower Austria
Salzburg
Styrie, Basse-Autriche,
Salzbourg
Stiria, Bassa Austria
Salisburgo

6 7 8 9 10

Vorarlberg, Lechtal, Ötztal
Vorarlberg, Lech Valley,
Ötztal
Vorarlberg, Lechtal, Oetztal
Vorarlberg, Valle del Lech,
Valle dell'Otz

11 12 13 14 15 16

ÖSTERREICH
UND ITALIEN
(Tirol 1800—1850)
AUSTRIA AND ITALY
(Tyrol 1800—1850)
AUTRICHE ET ITALIE
(Tirol 1800—1850)
AUSTRIA E ITALIA
(Tirolo 1800—1850)

Pustertal, Zillertal,
Bregenzer Wald
Pustertal, Zillertal,
Bregenz Forest
Pustertal, Zillertal,
région de Bregenz
Val Pusteria
Valle dello Ziller
Selva di Bregenz

1 2 3 4 5 6 7

Pustertal, Ötztal,
Brennerpaß
Pustertal, Ötztal,
Brenner Pass
Pustertal, Oetztal,
Brenner
Val Pusteria
Valle dell'Otz
Passo del Brennero

8 9 10 11 12

Grödnertal, Bozen
Grödnertal, Bolzano
Val Gardena, Bolzano
Val Gardena
Bolzano

13 14 15 16 17

DÄNEMARK
um 1800
DENMARK
about 1800
DANEMARK
aux environs de 1800
DANIMARCA
intorni al 1800

Seeland und Amager
Zealand and Amager
Seeland et Amager
Zelanda e Amager

1 2 3 4 5

Amager
Amager
Amager
Amager

6 7 8 9 10 11

Amager
Amager
Amager
Amager

12 13 14 15 16

160

DÄNEMARK
DENMARK
DANEMARK
DANIMARCA

Neuzeit
Modern Times
Epoque actuelle
Età moderna

1   2   3   4   5

6   7   8   8   9   10   11

12   13   14   15   16

SCHWEDEN
SWEDEN
SUEDE
SVEZIA

Schwedische Lappen
Swedish Lapps
Lappons suédois
Lapponi Svedesi

1   2   3   4   5

Schonen u. a.
Skane, etc.
Suède méridionale
et autres régions
Sconia ecc.

6   7   8   9   10

11   12   13   14   15

NORWEGEN
NORWAY
NORVEGE
NORVEGIA

Lappen im Norden
Northern Lapps
Lappons
Lapponi del Nord

1 2 3 4 5 6

Westnorwegen
Western Norway
Norvège occidentale
Norvegia Occidentale

7 8 9 10 11

Südnorwegen
Southern Norway
Norvège méridionale
Norvegia Meridionale

12 13 14 15 16

BÖHMEN, MÄHREN,
SLOWAKEI
BOHEMIA, MORAVIA,
SLOVAKIA
BOHEME, MORAVIE,
SLOVAQUIE
BOEMIA, MORAVIA,
SLOVACCHIA

Böhmen
Bohemia
Bohème
Boemia

1 2 3 4 5 6

Mähren
Moravia
Moravie
Moravia

7 8 9 10 11

Slowakei
Slovakia
Slovaquie
Slovacchia

12 13 14 15 16

POLEN
POLAND
POLOGNE
POLONIA

1800—1900

Galizien
Galicia
Galicie
Galizia

1 2 3 4 5 6 7

Lowicz u. a.
Lowicz, etc.
Lowicz et autres régions
Lowicz ecc.

8 9 10 11 12

Lubelskj, Warschau, Radom
Lubelskj, Warsaw, Radom
Lubeskj, Varsovie, Radom
Lubelskj, Varsavia, Radom

13 14 15 16 17

RUSSLAND
19. Jahrhundert
RUSSIA
19th Century
RUSSIE, XIXe s.
RUSSIA
Secolo XIX

Leningrad und Moskau
Leningrad and Moscow
Leningrad et Moscou
Leningrado e Mosca

1   2   3   4   5

Großrussen und Kalmücken
Great Russians and Kalmucks
Grands-Russiens et Kalmouks
Russi, Calmucchi

6   7   8   9   10

Wolga-Finnen
Volga Finns
Finnois de la Volga
Finlandesi del Volga

11   12   13   14   15

Großrussen, Weißrussen
Great Russians, White Russians
Grands-Russiens,
Blancs-Russiens
Grandi Russi,
Russi bianchi

1   2   3   4   5

Kleinrussen (Ukrainer)
Little Russians (Ukrainians)
Petits-Russiens (Ukrainiens)
Piccoli Russi (Ucraini)

6   7   8   9   10

Kleinrussen, Don-Kosaken
Little Russians, Don Cossacks
Petits-Russiens, Cosaques du Don
Piccoli Russi, Cosacchi del Don

11   12   13   14   15   16

BALTISCHE LÄNDER
UND FINNLAND
BALTIC PROVINCES
AND FINLAND
PAYS BALTES
ET FINLANDE
PAESI BALTICI
E FINLANDIA

Lettland, Estland
Latvia, Estonia
Lettonie, Esthonie
Lettonia, Estonia

1 2 3 4 5 6

Finnland
Finland
Finlande
Finlandia

7 8 9 10

Finnland, Estland
Finland, Estonia
Finlande, Esthonie
Finlandia, Estonia

11 12 13 14 15

TURBANFORMEN
Indien bis
Nordwestafrika

TURBAN STYLES
India to Northwest
Africa

LE TURBAN
ET SES DIVERSES FORMES
de l'Inde au nord-ouest de l'Afrique

FOGGIE DI TURBANTI
Dall' India fino all'
Africa Nord-Occidentale

TÜRKEI
TURKEY
TURQUIE
TURCHIA

1800—1825

Janitscharen u. a.
Janizaries, etc.
Janissaires et autres personnages
Giannizzeri e altri

1   2   3   4   5   6

Soldaten und Frauen
Soldiers and Women
Soldats et femmes
Soldati e donne

7   8   9   10   11   12

Würdenträger, Serail
Dignitaries, Seraglio
Dignitaires, Sérail
Dignitari, abito per il
«serail»

13   14   15   16   17   18

TÜRKEI
19. Jahrhundert
TURKEY
19th Century.
TURQUIE, XIXᵉ s.
TURCHIA
Secolo XIX

Albanien
Makedonien
Konstantinopel

Albania,
Macedonia,
Constantinople

Albanie, Macédoine,
Constantinople

Albania
Macedonia
Constantinopoli

1   2   3   4   5   6

Konstantinopel
Constantinople
Constantinople
Constantinopoli

7   8   9   10   11   1

Ankara
Konstantinopel

Ankara,
Constantinople

Angora, Constantinople

Ankara
Constantinopoli

13   14   15   16   17

RUSSLAND
Kaukasus
19. Jahrhundert
RUSSIA
Caucasus
19 th Century
RUSSIE
Caucase, XIXᵉ s.
RUSSIA
Caucaso
Secolo XIX

Tscherkessen u. a.
Tcherkesses, etc.
herkesses et autres peuples
Circassi ed altri

1   2   3   4   5   6

Georgier,
Armenier u. a.
Georgians, Armenians, etc.
Géorgiens,
rméniens et autres peuples
Georgiani, Armeni ed altri

7   8   9   10   11

Kurden
Tataren u. a.
Kurds, Tartars, etc.
Kurdes,
Tartares et autres peuples
Curdi, Tartari ed altri

12   13   14   15   16

172

SÜDWESTLICHER
KAUKASUS
SOUTH-WESTERN CAUCASUS
SUD-OUEST
DU CAUCASE
CAUCASO
SUDOCCIDENTALE

Jmeritiner, Adjharen, Lazen
Imeritians, Adighe, Laze
Imérèthes, Adjariens, Lazes
Jmereti, Adjari, Lazi

1 2 3 4 5 6 7 8

Armenier, Griechen
Armenians, Greeks
Arméniens, Grecs
Armeni, Greci

9 10 11 12 13

Armenier, Türken, Kurden
Armenians, Turks, Kurds
Arméniens, Turcs, Kurdes
Armeni, Turchi, Curdi

14 15 16 17 18

SÜDÖSTLICHER
KAUKASUS
UND ARMENIEN
SOUTH-EASTERN
CAUCASUS AND ARMENIA
SUD-EST DU CAUCASE
ET ARMENIE
CAUCASO
SUDORIENTALE
E ARMENIA

Tscherkessen u. a.
Tcherkesses, etc.
Tcherkesses et autres peuples
Circassi ed altri

1 2 3 4 5

Grusier (Georgier)
Kabardiner, Armenier
Grusians, (Georgians),
Kabardians, Armenians
Géorgiens, Karbades, Arméniens
Grusi (Georgiani)
Cabardi, Armeni

6 7 8 9 10 11

Kurden, Tartaren, Daghestan
Kurds, Tartars, Daghestan
Kurdes, Tartares,
habitants du Daghestan
Curdi, Tartari, Daghestani

12 13 14 15 16 17

174

TURKESTAN UND
IRAN (Persien)
TURKESTAN AND
IRAN (Persia)
ET REGIONAUX
TURKESTAN ET IRAN
(Perse)
TURCHESTAN
E IRAN (Persia)

Westturkestan und Bochara
West-Turkestan and Bokhara
Turkestan occidental et Bokhara
Turchestan Occidentale
e Buchara

1 2 3 4 5 6

Iran
Iran
Iran
Iran

7 8 9 10 11 12

Iran
Iran
Iran
Iran

13 14 15 16 17 18

WESTTURKESTAN
UND ASIATISCHES
RUSSLAND
WEST TURKESTAN
AND ASIATIC
RUSSIA
TURKESTAN OCCIDENTAL
ET RUSSIE D'ASIE
TURCHESTAN
OCCIDENTALE
E RUSSIA ASIATICA

Turkestan und Bochara
Turkestan and Bokhara
Turkestan et Bokhara
Turchestan e Buchara

1 2 3 4 5 6

Baschkiren, Kirgisen
Bashkirs, Kirghiz
Baskirs, Kirghizs
Bachiri, Kirghisi

7 8 9 10 11 12

Tartaren, Kalmücken
Tartars, Kalmucks
Tartares, Kalmouks
Tartari, Calmucchi

13 14 15 16 17

BELUTSCHISTAN, AFGHANISTAN
MONGOLEI UND TIBET

BALUCHISTAN, AFGHANISTAN,
MONGOLIA AND TIBET

BELOUTCHISTAN, AFGHANISTAN
MONGOLIE ET THIBET

BELUCISTAN, AFGANISTAN,
MONGOLIA E TIBET

Belutschistan, Afghanistan
Baluchistan, Afghanistan
Béloutchistan, Afghanistan
Belucistan, Afganistan

1 2 3 4 5 6

Tibet, Tungusen
Tibet, Tunguses
Thibétains, Toungouzes
Tibet, Tungusi

7 8 9 10 11 12

Chinesisch Ostturkestan,
Burjäten, Dunganen

Chinese East-Turkestan,
Buriats, Dunganians

Turkestan chinois
Turchestan Orientale Cinese
Buriati, Dungani

13 14 15 16 17 18 19

AFGHANISTAN
UND INDIEN
AFGHANISTAN AND INDIA
AFGHANISTAN ET INDE
AFGANISTAN E INDIA

Afghanistan
Afghanistan
Afghanistan
Afganistan

1 2 3 4 5

Indien
India
Inde
India

6 7 8 9 10 11

Indien
India
Inde
India

12 13 14 15 16 17

INDIEN
Mohammedanische Fürsten
INDIA
Mohammedan Princes
INDE
Princes mahométans
INDIA
Principi maomettani

1600—1800

16. und 17. Jahrhundert
16th and 17th Centuries
XVIe et XVIIe s.
secolo XVI e XVII

1 2 3

16. und 17. Jahrhundert
16th and 17th Centuries
XVIe et XVIIe s.
secolo XVI e XVII

4 5 6 7 8

18. Jahrhundert
18th Century
XVIIIe s.
secolo XVIII

9 10 11 12

INDIEN
Neuzeit
INDIA
Modern Times
INDE
Epoque moderne
INDIA
età moderna

Bombay, Madras
Bombay, Madras
Bombay, Madras
Bombay, Madras

1   2   3   4   5   6

7   8   9   10   11   12

Ceylon und Südindien
Ceylon and South India
ylan et Inde méridionale
ylon e India Meridionale

14   15   16   17   18

180

VOLKS- UND
STANDESTRACHTEN

NATIONAL COSTUME
AND DIGNITARIES' COSTUME

VETEMENTS POPULAIRES
ET COSTUMES DE CASTES

COSTUMI POPOLARI
E DI RANGO

CHINA
19. Jahrhundert
CHINA
19th Century
CHINE, XIXe s.
CINA
secolo XIX

Volkstrachten
National Costume
Vêtements populaires
Costumi popolari

1 2 3 4 5 6

Standestrachten
Dignitaries' Costume
Costumes de castes
Persone di rango

7 8 9 10 11 12

Frauentrachten
Women's Costume
Costumes féminins
Costumi femminili

13 14 15 16 17

CHINA
19. Jahrhundert
CHINA
19 th Century
CHINE, XIXᵉ s.
CINA
secolo XIX

Standestrachten
Dignitaries' Costume
Costumes de castes
Persone di rango

1 2 3 4 5

Frauentrachten
Women's Costume
Costumes féminins
Costumi femminili

6 7 8 9 10

11 12 13 14 15 16

JAPAN
JAPAN
JAPON
GIAPPONE

Offiziere, Damen
Officers, Ladies
Officiers, Dames
Ufficiali, dame

1 2 3 4 5 6 7

Schauspieler
Actors
Acteurs
Attori

8 9 10 11

Mönche, Musiker u. a.
Monks, Musicians, etc.
Moines, musiciens et autres
personnages
Monaci, musici ecc.

12 13 14 15 16 17 18

JAPAN
JAPAN
JAPON
GIAPPONE

Priester, Pilger u. a.
Priests, Pilgrims etc.
Prêtre,
pélerins et autres personnages
Sacerdoti, pellegrini ed altri

1 2 3 4 5

Sänftenträger u. a.
Sedan-chair bearers, etc.
Porteurs de palanquin
et autres personnages
Portatori di lettighe ed altri

6 7 8 9 10

Samurai u. a.
Samurai, etc.
Samouraïs
Samurai ed altri

11 12 13 14 15

BIRMA, SIAM, JAVA
BURMA, SIAM, JAVA
BIRMANIE,
SIAM, JAVA
BIRMANIA
SIAM, GIAVA

Birma, Siam
Burma, Siam
Birmanie, Siam
Birmania, Siam

1   2   3   4   5   6

Java
Java
Java
Giava

7   8   9   10   11

Java
Java
Java
Giava

12   13   14   15   16

MAROKKO
UND ALGIER
MOROCCO AND ALGERIA
MAROC ET ALGERIE
MAROCCO
E ALGERI

Marokko
Morocco
Maroc
Marocco

1 2 3 4 5 6

Marokko
Morocco
Maroc
Marocco

7 8 9 10 11

Algier
Algeria
Algérie
Algeri

12 13 14 15 16 17

WESTAFRIKA UND
OSTAFRIKA
WEST AND EAST AFRICA
AFRIQUE
OCCIDENTALE ET ORIENTALE
AFRICA OCCIDENTALE
E ORIENTALE

Senegal
Senegal
Sénégal
Senegal

1   2   3   4   5

Nubien, Abessinien,
Somaliland, Suaheli,
Sansibar
Nubia, Abyssinia, Somaliland,
Swahili, Zanzibar
Nubie, Abyssinie,
Côte des Somalis,
Tanganyika, Zanzibar
Nubia, Abissinia, Somalia,
Suaheli, Zanzibar

6   7   8   9   10   11   12

Somali, Abessinien u. a.
Somali, Abyssinia, etc.
Côte de Somalis,
Abyssinie et autres régions
Somalia, Abissinia ecc.

13   14   15   16   17   18

ALGIER UND TUNIS
ALGERIA AND TUNIS
ALGERIE ET TUNISIE
ALGERI E TUNISI

Algier
Algeria
Algérie
Algeri

1 · 2   3   4   5

Tunis
Tunis
Tunisie
Tunisi

6   7   8   9   10   11

Tunis
Tunis
Tunisie
Tunisi

12   13   14   15   16   17

ÄGYPTEN UND
OSTAFRIKA
EGYPT AND EAST AFRICA
EGYPTE ET AFRIQUE
ORIENTALE
EGITTO E AFRICA
ORIENTALE

Ägypten
Egypt
Egypte
Egitto

1 2 3 4 5

Ägypten
Egypt
Egypte
Egitto

6 7 8 9 10 11

Ostafrika
East Africa
Afrique orientale
Africa Orientale

12 13 14 15 16 17

SYRIEN UND
PALÄSTINA,
ARABIEN
SYRIA AND PALESTINE,
ARABIA
SYRIE ET
PALESTINE,
ARABIE
SIRIA
E PALESTINA
ARABIA

Syrien
Syria
Syrie
Siria

1 2 3 4 5 6 7

Palästina und Syrien
Palestine and Syria
Palestine et Syrie
Palestina e Siria

8 9 10 11 12 13 14

Arabien
Arabia
Arabie
Arabia

15 16 17 18 19 20 21

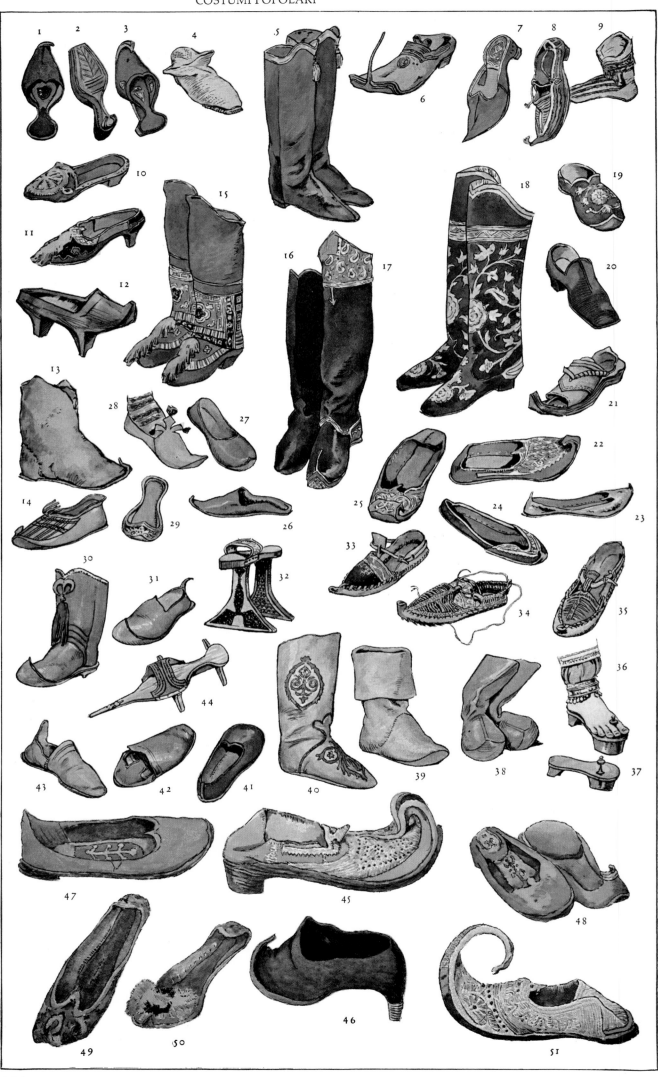

ORIENTALISCHES
SCHUHWERK
ORIENTAL FOOTWEAR
CHAUSSURES
ORIENTALES
CALZARI ORIENTALI

ARABISCHE REITER
ARABIAN HORSEMEN
CAVALIERS ARABES
CAVALIERI ARABI

Pferde- und Kamelgeschirr
Horse and Camel Harness
Harnachements de chevaux
et de chameaux
Bardature da
cavallo e cammello

SÜD- UND
MITTELAMERIKA
SOUTH AND
CENTRAL AMERICA
AMERIQUE DU
SUD ET AMERIQUE CENTRALE
AMERICA
MERIDIONALE
E CENTRALE

15. und 16. Jahrhundert
15th and 16th Centuries
XVᵉ et XVIᵉ s.
secolo XV e XVI

Die Inka in Peru
Incas in Peru
Incas du Pérou
Gli Incas nel Perù

1   2   3   4   5   6

Die Inka in Peru
Incas in Peru
Incas du Pérou
Gli Incas nel Perù

7   8   9   10   11   12

Alt-Mexiko
Ancient Mexico
Vieux Mexique
Messico antico

13   14   15   16   17

193

ALTMEXIKO
um 1519—1520
ANCIENT MEXICO
about 1519—1520
VIEUX MEXIQUE,
aux environs de 1519—1520
MESSICO ANTICO
intorno al 1519—1520

Krieger
Warriors
Guerriers
Guerrieri

1 2 3 4 5 6 7

Krieger
Warriors
Guerriers
Guerrieri

8 9 10 11 12

Priester, König u. a.
Priest, King, etc.
Prêtres, roi
et autres personnages
Sacerdoti, re ecc.

13 14 15 16 17

MITTELAMERIKA
Neuzeit
CENTRAL AMERICA
Modern Times
AMERIQUE CENTRALE
Epoque moderne
AMERICA CENTRALE
età moderna

Mexiko
Mexico
Mexique
Messico

1   2   3   4   5

Mexiko
Mexico
Mexique
Messico

6   7   8   9   10   11

Guatemala, Honduras u. a.
Guatemala, Honduras, etc.
Guatémala, Honduras
et autres pays
Guatemala, Honduras ecc.

12   13   14   15   16   17

SÜDAMERIKA
Neuzeit
SOUTH AMERICA
Modern Times
AMERIQUE DU SUD
Epoque moderne
AMERICA
MERIDIONALE
Età moderna

Bolivien, Peru
Bolivia, Peru
Bolivie, Pérou
Bolivia, Perù

1 2 3 4 5 6

Chile
Chile
Chili
Cile

7 8 9 10 11

Peru, Kolumbien
Peru, Colombia
Pérou, Colombie
Perù, Colombia

12 13 14 15 16

196

NORDAMERIKA
Indianer
NORTH AMERICA
Red Indians
AMERIQUE DU NORD
Indiens
AMERICA DEL NORD
Indiani

Irokesen, Krähen-Indianer,
Fuchs-Indianer, Dakota-Sioux
Iroquois, Crows, Foxes,
Dakota Sioux
Iroquois, Tribu des Corbeaux,
Tribu des Renards, Sioux du
Dakota
Irochesi, «Indiani-cornacchia»
«Indiani-volpe», Dakota-Sioux

1 2 3 4 5 6 7

Jova, Saki, Sioux, Pani
Iowa, Sacs, Sioux, Pani
Iowa, Saki, Sioux, Pani
Iowa, Saki, Sioux, Pani

8 9 10 11 12 13

Mandan, Saki,
Dickbäuche, Cvih u. a.
Mandan, Sacs, Grosventres,
Cvih, etc.
Mandan, Saki, Ventrus,
Crihs et autres
Mandani, Saki,
Cvih ed altri
«Ventri-enfiati»

14 15 16 17 18 19 20

NORDAMERIKA
Indianer
NORTH AMERICA
Red Indians
AMERIQUE DU NORD
Indiens
AMERICA DEL NORD
Indiani

Kiawa, Kanada, Dakota,
Assiniboin, Cvih
Kiowa, Canada, Dakota,
Assiniboin, Cvih
Kiaway, Canada, Dakota,
Assiniboin, Crih
Kiawa, Canadà, Dakota,
Assiniboini, Cvih

1 2 3 4 5 6

Utah, Schoschonen,
Kansas, Nebraska
Utah, Shoshoni, Kansas,
Nebraska
Utah, Chochones, Kansas,
Nebraska
Utah, Shoshoni
Kansas, Nebraska

7 8 9 10 11 12

Colorado, Apatschen,
Pueblo, Lipan u. a.
Colorado, Apaches, Pueplos,
Lipan etc.
Colorado, Apaches, Pueblo,
Lipan et autres
Colorado, Apaches
Pueblos, Lipani ecc.

13 14 15 16 17 18

NORDAMERIKA
NORTH AMERICA
AMERIQUE DU NORD
AMERICA DEL NORD

Volkstypen
(Cowboys und Soldaten)
Cowboys and Soldiers
Types du populaires
(Cowboys et soldats)
Gente del popolo
(Cowboys e soldati)

ESKIMOS
ESKIMOS
ESQUIMAUX
ESCHIMESI

Sibirien
Siberia
Sibérie
Siberiani

1 2 3 4 5

Sibirien, Polarforscher
Siberia, Polar-Explorers
bérie, explorateurs polaires
Siberiani, esploratori polari

6 7 8 9 10

Grönland u. a.
Greenland
Groenland et autres pays
Groenlandia ecc.

11 12 13 14 15 16